PYTHAGORAS AND EARLY PYTHAGOREANISM

PHOENIX

SUPPLEMENTARY VOLUMES

PYTHAGORAS
AND EARLY
PYTHAGOREANISM

J. A. PHILIP

PHOENIX

JOURNAL OF THE CLASSICAL

ASSOCIATION OF CANADA

SUPPLEMENTARY VOLUME VII

UNIVERSITY OF TORONTO PRESS

© University of Toronto Press 1966

Reprinted 1968

Printed in U.S.A.

SBN 8020 5175 8

PREFACE

I EMBARKED on an inquiry into Pythagoreanism in order to discover what was the nature and extent of Pythagorean influence on Plato, an influence to which all commentators allude. I found that the pre-Platonic evidence was slight, and that it was greatly inflated by a literature of interpretation and conjecture in which both early and late sources were used. Instead of attempting once more to solve all the problems I decided for the more modest but I hope more useful task of surveying all the evidence up to and including Aristotle, using Aristotle as a principal basis for reconstruction.

The difficult problem of presentation I have attempted to solve by a distinction between exposition and controversy, controversial discussion being relegated to notes at the ends of chapters. This distinction involves some repetition both in the text and the notes, in order to render them independently intelligible. Its aim is to render the exposition clearer and the thesis more perspicuous. It is my hope that the notes may prove useful to the specialist reader, even if he does not accept the general thesis.

My manuscript was complete before K. von Fritz's article "Pythagoras" in the *Paulys-Real Encyclopedie der Classischen Altertumswissenschaft* became available to me; but as that article does not modify his earlier position substantially I have confined myself to referring to it.

I wish to thank the Editorial Committee of *Phoenix*, under whose auspices this volume is published, and in particular the late Professor William P. Wallace, who was the first and most critical reader. I am also greatly indebted to the present Editor of *Phoenix*, Professor A. Dalzell, to the former Editor, Professor Mary E. White, and to the Editors of the University of Toronto Press. My errors are doubtless more numerous because in some of them I have persisted.

This work has been published with the help of grants from the Humanities Research Council, using funds provided by the Canada Council, and from the Publications Fund of the University of Toronto Press.

J.A.P.

CONTENTS

ABBREVIATIONS

A. PERIODICALS

AJP   *American Journal of Philology*
Ann.Math.   *Annals of Mathematics*
Arch.Ges.Phil.   *Archiv für Geschichte der Philosophie*
ANS notes   *American Numismatic Society Notes*
CQ   *Classical Quarterly*
Class.etMed.   *Classica et Mediaevalia*
Harv.Stud.   *Harvard Studies in Classical Philology*
JHS   *Journal of Hellenic Studies*
LSJ   Liddell-Scott-Jones, *A Greek-English Lexicon*, Ninth edition, 1940.
Num.Chron.   *Numismatic Chronicle*
Math.Ann.   *Mathematische Annalen*
Proc.Arist.Soc.   *Proceedings of the Aristotelian Society*
REG   *Revue des Études Grecques*
Rh Mus.   *Rheinisches Museum*
Sitzber.Pr.Ak.   *Sitzungsberichte der Preussischen Akademie der Wissenschaften, Berlin*
Sitzber.Heid.Ak.   *Sitzungsberichte der Heidelberger Akademie der Wissenschaften*
Sitzber.Bay.Ak.   *Sitzungsberichte der Bayerischen Akademie der Wissenschaften, München*
TAPA   *Transactions of the American Philological Association*

B. GENERAL WORKS

Dox.Gr.   Diels, H., *Doxographi Graeci*. Berlin 1879.
FPG   F. W. A. Mullach, *Fragmenta Philosophorum Graecorum*. Paris 1860–1881.
FGrH   Jacoby, F. *Die Fragmente der griechischen Historiker*. Berlin, 1923–.
KR   Kirk, G. S. and J. E. Raven, *The Presocratic Philosophers*. Cambridge 1957.

RE Wissowa, G., Kroll, W., Witte, K., Mittelhaus, K., and Zeigler, K. *Paulys Real-Encyclopädie der classischen Altertumswissenschaft.* Stuttgart 1894–.

Heath *Maths* Heath, Sir Thos. *A History of Greek Mathematics.* Vol. 1 (Oxford 1921).

Heath *Aristarch.* Heath, Sir Thos. *Aristarchus of Samos.* Oxford 1913.

Heath, *Euclid* Heath, Sir Thos., *The Thirteen Books of Euclid's Elements.* Cambridge 1926.

Heath, *Aristotle* Heath, Sir Thos., *Mathematics in Aristotle.* Oxford 1949.

Vors. Diels, H. and Kranz, W., *Die Fragmente der Vorsokratiker.* 6th ed., Berlin 1951–52.

Wehrli Wehrli, F., *Die Schule des Aristoteles.* 10 Hefte, Basel 1944–1959. Referred to by name of Peripatetic.

ZN Zeller, E. and W. Nestle, *Die Philosophie der Griechen.* Leipzig Vol. 1, pt. 1, 7th ed. 1923; pt. 2, 6th ed. 1920.

ZM Zeller, E. and R. Mondolfo, *La Filosofia dei Greci.* Florence. 1.1 3rd ed. 1951; 1.2 2nd ed. 1950.

C. Texts Frequently Cited*

Metaph. Ross, W. D., *Aristotle's Metaphysics.* 2 vols., Oxford 1924. Usually referred to by page and line of Berlin edition, omitting *Metaph.*

Phys. Ross, W. D., *Aristotle's Physics.* Oxford 1936.

De An. Ross, W. D., *Aristotle De Anima.* Oxford 1961.

Anal. Ross, W. D., *Aristotle's Prior and Posterior Analytics.* Oxford 1949.

Fr.Sel. Ross, W. D., *Aristotelis Fragmenta Selecta.* Oxford 1955. Referred to by page number.

E.N. ed. Bywater, I., *Aristotelis Ethica Nicomachea.* Oxford 1913.

D.L. ed. Long, H. S., *Diogenis Laertius Vitae Philosophorum.* 2 vols., Oxford 1964.

Études Delatte, A., *Études sur la littérature pythagoricienne.* Paris 1915.

Vie Delatte, A., *La Vie de Pythagore de Diogene Laërce.* Brussels 1922.

Iambl. *VP* Deubner, L., *Iamblichi De Vita Pythagorica.* Leipzig 1937.

Iambl. *Pr.* Pistelli H., *Iamblichus Protrepticus.* Leipzig 1888.

Iambl. *c.m.sc.* Festa, N. *Iamblichus de communi mathematica scientia.* Leipzig 1891.

Porph. *V.P.* Nauck, A. *Porphyrii Opuscula Selecta.* 2nd ed. Leipzig 1886.

*See also Bibliography, p. 209.

Porph. *V. Plot.*   Henry P. and Schweitzer, H. R., *Plotini Opera*. Vol. 1, Oxford 1964.

Theol. Ar.   De Falco, V., *Iamblichi Theologoumena Arithmetica*. Leipzig 1922.

Commentaria in Aristotelem Graeca. Berlin 1882–1909. The Aristotelian Commentators are cited by name, treatise and page and line of the Prussian Academy edition.

PYTHAGORAS AND EARLY PYTHAGOREANISM

I

THE PROBLEM

PYTHAGORAS casts a long shadow in the history of Greek thought, but when we attempt to discern the person casting that shadow, when we look for a figure of history and a body of doctrine, then Pythagoras eludes us. Ancient sources provide us material ampler than that for any other Greek thinker, but it is only as they become more distant in time from Pythagoras that the accounts grow more precise and more detailed; after a millenium they tell us the composition of the cakes that were his principal sustenance. On these ancient elaborations supervene the constructions of modern scholars, who have used the Pythagoras legend to bridge gaps in the history of early Greek thought, and especially to explain origins in mathematics, astronomy, and music. So there emerges a multifarious Pythagoras who can be depicted, and has indeed been depicted, as anything from a Greek shaman to the first mathematical physicist, and whose doctrines become anything from elaborate para-mathematical system to religious mumbo-jumbo.

All the sources are familiar to us. They have been used, with infinite critical ingenuity, by three generations of scholars. The result of their inquiry has been much controversy but little or no agreement that can be said to form a *communis opinio*. If the problem were not a central one we could agree to designate as Pythagorean an area of uncertain geography somewhere at the frontiers of Greek thought. But in fact how we conceive the origins of philosophy depends in large measure on how we conceive the origins of Pythagoreanism, and our picture of the early development of thought largely depends on the role we assign to Pythagoras and early Pythagoreans.

Our problem in understanding early Greek thought is not so much how to assess the individual thinker, difficult as that may be with the paucity of contemporary evidence. It is rather a problem of understanding the period as a whole: how speculation about our world began, how its linguistic and logical tools were forged, and especially how dialogue between thinkers developed, how they reacted to one another's theories and attempted, when they did attempt, to deal with common problems. We cannot be satisfied with an account that presents us thinkers in isolation, and allows for neither interaction nor attempt at synthesis before Plato. If the period is to be understandable at all we must somehow determine the relations—independent, tributary, or hostile—obtaining among the principal thinkers. This we can achieve only by the construction, on the basis of our tenuous evidence, of reasonable hypotheses.

It is here that the inquirer enlists the aid of Pythagoras and Pythagoreanism. If he can impute to a "school" doctrines that provide answers to his problems of interdependence and reaction, and can find some evidence for so doing, that "school" can be assigned the mediating role in his hypothesis. The questions he asks are vague and general ones, such as: How did the speculations about *physis* of the earliest natural philosophers move from the physical towards the conceptual? Who first saw physical problems quantitatively, and put physical thought on the road to quantitative abstraction? How did the notions of identity and contrariety, of unity and plurality, acquire their role? And above all how and why does philosophy become a way of life as well as a mode of inquiry? Pythagoras is the *deus ex machina* who provides us with the answers to these questions. He not only formulates the problems; with the aid of a Pythagorean "brotherhood" he develops his answers, and defends them against attack, until they can be delivered safely into the hands of Plato.

If such speculations were simply a hypothetical structure of modern times they would be easier to attack and easier to defend. But from the time the ancient world began to be aware of its intellectual past—that is, from the time of Plato and the Early Academy—thinkers began to speculate about origins, and to erect hypotheses that would make the history of thought continuous rather than episodic. Here Plato was a forerunner. He not only interpreted the past in doxographical hints, in myths like the myth of Theuth, and in some puzzling digressions, such as Socrates' account of his own philosophical development in the *Phaedo* or the "Battle of the Giants" in the *Sophistes*, he also gave a new character to philosophical thought, a character described by the Early Academy as Pythagorean. This pythagorizing tendency produced its mature fruits in Neopythagoreanism and Neoplatonism. So we have, especially from the later period of antiquity, ample warrant for a Pythagoras who was the first philosopher, mathematician, and astronomer, and was also author of an ethical discipline of intellectualist character; and we are told of a "brotherhood" that, orally and in anonymity, carried on his tradition.

These ancient sources merit our scrutiny, and especially those nearest in time to Pythagoras. Do they reflect fact or legend? Is the approach factual or tendentious? Are the authors probing a past largely unknown to them? Are some of them seeking to annex provinces of thought for a Pythagorean empire? On our answers to these and similar questions will depend what use we make of our sources, whether and in how far we judge them to be an adequate foundation for further hypotheses.

It is for these reasons that an examination of the evidence for Pythagoras and early Pythagoreanism is worth undertaking. It is regularly undertaken, on a larger or a smaller scale, by historians of philosophy. We may distinguish three principal methods by which they attack the problem. The first of these might be called intuitive. On the basis of a knowledge of the history and literature of the period, and of the philosophical and religious background, an attempt is made to select, among the data of our tradition, elements that will yield a credible and plausible reconstruction. In the best of hands this method has given us important insights. In other hands it amounts to little more than picking flowers in the meadows of our evidence.

The second method is that of source criticism. The attempt is made to trace our evidence back through the centuries to its original source, and then to evaluate that original source. In the Pythagorean tradition we are obliged to follow statements through intermediaries, often two or three in number, of whose tendencies and trustworthiness we know little and whose writings are lost to us, to some author whose text we possess in the best case in fragments, these often being negligible. This method has led to the most disparate conclusions both in questions of detail and in general lines of reconstruction.

The third method, and the one which I propose to follow, is to base our inquiry on the evidence of Aristotle in the treatises and in the fragments that remain of his monograph, *On the Pythagoreans* (the two parts of which were originally separate monographs). It is our earliest evidence of any philosophical importance. It is not the product of borrowings but is based on painstaking inquiry. It is of sufficient extent to justify the assumption that it presents the main features of Pythagorean doctrine. And it comes to us with the authority of Aristotle who, whatever his defects as a historian of philosophy, remains our most acute, impartial, and important witness.

The primary importance of Aristotle's evidence is generally conceded. Attempts to exploit it as a principal basis of reconstruction have been made in the past. It was used by A. Rothenbücher in an able but all too brief study the object of which was to attack Boeckh's defence of the fragments of Philolaus. It was used again by O. Gilbert in a penetrating study of the doctrines, which is, however, vitiated by the assumption that the Aristotelian analysis of matter-form-privation is applicable to the Pythagoreans, and that the numbers are paradigmatic. A further attempt to formulate the Aristotelian account was made by Jenny Bollinger. It was made under the shadow of Erich Frank and is confined to simple statement.

Ideally it might seem desirable to study the whole tradition, rather than confine oneself to Aristotle. In practice it seems to me preferable to limit myself to the more modest task of stating, and examining critically, what Aristotle says of Pythagorean doctrine in the treatises and what he tells us of the Pythagorean legend and teachings in the fragments. I have sought to establish elsewhere[1]* that he had adequate sources of information, that he is a principal source for subsequent writers, and that there is no esoteric tradition deriving from a Pythagorean "brotherhood" and subsequently debouching in the Neo-pythagorean writings. In my next chapter I shall sketch the general characteristics and the evolution of the Pythagorean tradition. Without such an outline the cardinal importance of Aristotle's testimony is not apparent. But I have used the material of this tradition only when it throws light on the Aristotelian account. What little testimony we have that is earlier than Aristotle I have of course considered, except for hints and allusions in the Platonic dialogues. Before we attempt to determine the nature and extent of Pythagorean influence in Plato we must have some knowledge of the Pythagoreanism of the generations preceding him.

It may be argued that Aristotle is not always a reliable witness, and that Cherniss has shown him to be in some respects a biased one. Cherniss' conclusions, however, and in particular the conclusions that other scholars drew on the basis of his strictures, have been modified as a result of subsequent discussion.[2] We appreciate that it is part of Aristotle's method to use other philosophers as foils in the dialectical elaboration of his own thesis and that this method entails some falsification of perspective for which we must allow. But he does not

---

*All numbered references are to the notes at the end of each chapter. The bibliography (p. 209) gives details of works referred to either by author's name alone or by name and short title.

willingly distort or fabricate fact. He is attempting to lead us rather than to mislead us. Usually, even in discussions of Platonism where his passions are engaged, the whole tenor and context of the discussion shows how we should evaluate facts or opinions he reports. His testimony—as that of even the most reliable of witnesses—must remain subject to question. But the testimony of a witness of Aristotle's intelligence, discussing doctrines he has been at pains to ascertain, is of infinitely more value than the protreptical writings of Porphyry and Iamblichus. I have sought first of all to state what he says and only then to evaluate.

I have not attempted to give a full and complete account of early Pythagoreanism—and by that I mean Pythagoreanism of the fifth century down to the time of Archytas—in the fields of mathematics, astronomy and music. Detailed studies in these fields are properly the preserve of the specialist and beyond the scope of the present inquiry. I have had to consider them, however, in so far as they impinge on the general problem.

I shall refer to the works that form part of the Aristotelian corpus as "the treatises" and to the fragments collected under the title *On the Pythagoreans* as "the monograph." In this monograph Aristotle gives us detail of the legend but no biographical data. The legend must be held to reflect, in however indirect and distorted a fashion, the person. It demands interpretation. It cannot however be transformed into a Life by the addition of dates and a historical framework, as was done by the biographers of the fourth and subsequent centuries. Their accounts are discussed in an appendix, as is the problem of chronology.

Pythagoras and Pythagoreanism have provided matter for controversy for many centuries now. Even by restricting myself to Aristotle's testimony I cannot hope to command general assent. I hope, however, to establish the importance of his testimony for the understanding of Pythagoras and early Pythagoreanism, and their role in the development of Greek thought.

NOTES

[1]"Pythagoras—The Biographical Tradition," *TAPA* 90 (1959) 185–194; *Phoenix* (1964) 251–265. The tradition is outlined in chap. II.

[2]S. Mansion, in A. Mansion, ed., *Aristote et les problèmes de méthode* Louvain 1961.

2

THE TRADITION

IF we are to appreciate the authority of Aristotle's evidence we must see it against the background of the whole Pythagorean tradition. By tradition I do not mean (as is meant in the case of the Platonic or the Aristotelian tradition) a scholarly tradition in which Platonists or Aristotelians seek to interpret the thought of Plato or Aristotle as expressed in their works. I mean rather a tradition that arises in teachings at first orally transmitted, that creates a legend around the person of the teacher, and that through ensuing centuries exhibits a dynamic of its own such that it provokes rebirths or revivals. Each succeeding revival has a contemporary colouring, and the persons then calling themselves Pythagoreans feel themselves licensed to great latitude in interpreting the thought of Pythagoras, so long as they preserve in their interpretation something of the religious aura surrounding the person and something of the arithmological character of the doctrines. Such revivals occurred repeatedly in antiquity, and have since occurred. Even in our own times, in the year 1955, a World Congress of Pythagorean Societies, having the characteristic of a revival, was held in Athens. In 1962 a German mathematician, and in 1963 a professor of the University of Athens,[1] produced highly intelligent but entirely uncritical biographies, representing Pythagoras as the prototype and paradigm of the mathematical physicists, and his teachings as a comforting gospel for an atom-troubled world.

The tradition I propose to discuss is that of antiquity. It takes written form in the fourth century B.C. and continues to evolve until the fifth century A.D. It is dominated by the person of Pythagoras, but in that person we observe changes to suit the taste and temper of the times. Such changes need not surprise us. We observe them occurring in the typical Greek hero-figure, Heracles, in the Platonic, Cynic, Stoic, and Christian portrait of Socrates, and in Christian iconography. The developments of Pythagorean doctrine are not as radical as those we observe in the early Church.[2]

This tradition spans a millenium. Its documents may be divided roughly into three classes: those of Presocratic period, during which the tradition was largely oral; those of early written formulation, chiefly in the Academy and the Peripatos; and those of the full-fledged legend, the *Lives* of Diogenes Laertius, Porphyry, and Iamblichus, and the *Bibliotheca* of Photius. These classes are merely a convenience of exposition, corresponding to epochs of Pythagoreanism but not constituting a total description of it. We now possess only remnants. There are lacunae of centuries during which the tradition continued to evolve, but of the course of its evolution there remain mere hints and fragments. It is only in the context of the whole tradition that any one part can be fully understood.

Already in the earliest period, while the tradition was still oral, fact began to be coloured by legend and to be distorted by polemical intent. Xenophanes, a contemporary and a fellow Ionian who, like Pythagoras, migrated from Ionia to the West, ridiculed his doctrine of transmigration (*D.L.* 8.36 = *Vors.* 21 B 7) in the spirit in which Heraclitus, likewise an Ionian and almost contemporary, questioned his spurious learning (*D.L.* 9.1 = *Vors.* 22 B 40, 129). Both of them were exponents of the Ionian enlightenment and could not but repudiate his departure from that tradition. In the same spirit of protest Herodotus, writing half a century later, tells us the tale of Salmoxis (*Hdt.* 4, 95) and though he himself migrated to Magna Graecia and knew of the Pythagoreans there (*Hdt.* 2, 123) he chose to pass over their history in silence. He tells us nothing of the role of Pythagoras and the Pythagoreans in Magna Graecia.[3] We have one further reference, probably hostile, made by Ion of Chios[4] and the famous passage of Empedocles (Porph. *V.P.* 30 = *Vors.* 31 B 129). This is the sum of the references made to him during the fifth century, the century during which the legend grew. It is significant that they may all be seen as in some fashion reflecting that legend.

It need not surprise us that we cannot observe the legend in the making. Legends are a popular growth. In the Christian dispensation we see something of the manner of their elaboration in the Lives of the Saints. As soon as the heroic merits of a saint begin to be popularly recognized there is a stock of attributes, actions, miracles from which the popular imagination draws to construct the life; and the less there is known about the events and circumstances of the actual life the more closely the legendary life conforms to the traditional morphology. What saints have in common is their sainthood, and sainthood is a notion clearly defined not only theologically but also in the imagination of those among whom the legend grows.

The same process occurred in the early—and not only in the early—

age of Greece. The myths of the heroes are in many respects particular-
ized, especially in their literary elaboration, but there are certain
heroic virtues that they share and certain aspects of their cult that are
common. When in later times historical persons began to be accorded
heroic or something similar to heroic status the same process of legend-
building occurred. Where the legend grew in an oral tradition we may
assume that it was more vigorous and was conceded greater licence.
The "pro-Pythagorean" oral tradition is reflected only once in the early
fragments, in a passage in which Empedocles (*Vors.* 31 B 129) makes
reference to Pythagoras, though not by name, with a respect bordering
on reverence, and in which it is plain that if Pythagoras is not already
invested in the whole heroic panoply he enjoys a more than mortal
status.

At the beginning of the fourth century the oral tradition ends and
we have the first written expositions and discussions of Pythagoreanism. The written tradition begins at a time critical not only for
Greek but for all philosophy. In Plato's youth there were professing
Pythagoreans in mainland Greece whose views were known, but the
younger Plato appears to have been little influenced by them. The
only plausible explanation of the radical change in his thought that
later produced the *Timaeus* and the *Philebus* is his encounter with
Archytas in Tarentum. Even then his writings do not reveal the extent
of that influence. He refers to Pythagoras once, and to the Pythagoreans once. What we believe to be the distinguishing mark of
Pythagoreanism, a doctrine of the mathematical structure of reality
and of the soul that comprehends reality, is explicit only in the *agrapha
dogmata*, or "unwritten doctrines."

The Plato taught, or held, or was concerned with some such theory
is to be seen from the fact that it was an immediate and primary concern of the first generation of the Academy with one exception,
Heraclides Ponticus.[5] Aristotle differs from the other members of the
Academy in that he combats these theories. He held that Plato's
doctrine was similar to that of the Pythagoreans, in that Plato believed
the One to be a substance and not that there was some other substance
of which unity was an attribute; and further, like the Pythagoreans,
that numbers were for other things the cause of their substantial
nature (*Metaph.* 987b 23–25).

The attitude of Speusippus and Xenocrates is more complex. As
Platonists they seek to defend the substance of the Theory of Ideas,
but in the face of criticism they feel themselves obliged to modify it.
They do so in a Pythagorean sense. In one principal respect, however,
Plato, Speusippus, and Xenocrates differ from the Pythagoreans. For

the Pythagoreans, as Aristotle repeatedly insists, "things are numbers," and there can be no derivation of sensibles from mathematicals or ideas of mathematicals. Things which *are* numbers need not be derived from numbers. For Plato the ideal numbers are generated from the One and the indefinite dyad. If and how Plato's world of sensibles is derived from these numbers is a matter of dispute. But it is beyond doubt that Speusippus (who recognized mathematical numbers but not ideas) and Xenocrates (who equated ideal numbers and mathematical numbers) both derived sensibles from these numbers. Xenocrates (fr. 39 Heinze) may not have equated the One with the point—for Plato the first generated number was two—but in his treatise on Pythagorean numbers (*Theol. Ar.* 82–85 = Speus. fr. 4 Lang = *Vors.* 44 A 13) Speusippus equated point and one, line and two, plane surface and three, solid and four.[6]

This account of the derivation of sensibles from mathematicals which Speusippus presents as Pythagorean is in direct contradiction to what Aristotle considers to be Pythagorean. If for the Pythagoreans "things are numbers," there can be no point as monad having position, but only an atomic unit as primary magnitude.

It is not surprising that at the time of the Early Academy Pythagorean doctrine should be in a state of flux. It is surprising indeed to find that Speusippus' account becomes the accepted one. Subsequent tradition accepts as Pythagorean the derivation of sensibles from mathematicals, and this becomes a cornerstone of Pythagorean physical doctrine.[7]

The platonizing of Pythagorean theory is not to be ascribed to the error or ignorance of a later time. It occurred within the Academy and was accepted by the Peripatos. We should expect that Theophrastus, Aristotle's successor and the primary source of the doxography, would cite Aristotle's report. Instead he can write of the Pythagoreans (*Metaph.* 11a 27–b7): "For Plato and the Pythagoreans there is a great distance separating good and evil."[8] He goes on to explain that evil arises from the opposition of the One and the indefinite dyad, without which there would be no universe. Now Aristotle clearly tells us that the pair One-indefinite dyad is characteristically Platonic, and that the Pythagoreans derive their numbers which are things from the One. So Theophrastus is here conflating what Aristotle distinguishes.

In the absence of any criterion of orthodoxy it is of course possible that Speusippus and Xenocrates are right, and that Aristotle is wrong. But it seems highly improbable, and for two reasons. First, the derivation point–line–surface–solid is a geometrical one, and we have grounds for believing that early Pythagorean thought was not phrased in geometrical terms. Second, according to all our accounts the dyad is typically Platonic. We can only conclude that the pythagorizing of the Early Academy was so thoroughgoing as to persuade even a Theophrastus that doctrines characteristic of Plato's thought were not Platonic but Pythagorean. In the following century, however, as Burkert (82–84) has shown, by another swing of the pendulum the Middle Academy, now sceptical, repudiated the platonizing Pythagoras on behalf of a sceptical Plato, abandoning to others the elaboration of the Pythagoras scheme with all its Platonic contaminations. So the post-Aristotelian tradition differs in important respects from the Aristotelian report, and does so because Speusippus, Xenocrates, and in a measure Plato himself pythagorized.

The reinterpretation of the Early Academy was devised to explain rather than to distort. It was an attempt to formulate what Pythagoras "must have meant." The reinterpretation offered by the first generation of the Peripatos, by Dicaearchus, and Aristoxenus, is without any real pretence at good faith, historical documentation being no part of their purpose. The tradition subsequent to Theophrastus derives from the following principal sources: the Presocratic references;[9] the reinterpretation of life and doctrine in the Early Academy; the treatises and monographs of Aristotle; and the *Physical Opinions* of Theophrastus. The immediate contribution of other sources would appear to be negligible.[10]

In the third phase of the tradition there are two main streams, the biographical[11] and the doxographical.[12] The doxographical tradition has its origin in the *Physical Opinions* of Theophrastus, the fragments of which are collected in Diels' *Doxographi Graeci*. Theophrastus adopted Aristotle's method of prefacing his discussion of major problems by a survey and critique of the views of his predecessors. He organized his book not according to thinkers or schools of thinkers but according to principal doctrines, the first book, for example, dealing with first principles and the last—the only part of the work we possess intact—dealing with sense perception.[13] This vast systematic survey was epitomized in the first century B.C., probably in the school of Posidonius, and at the same time was extended to cover subsequent thought and thinkers. The epitome, called by Diels the *Vetusta Placita*, was again epitomized by the otherwise unknown Aëtius in the first century of our era. Both *Vetusta Placita* and Aëtius are lost to us, but Aëtius is the source of our two surviving summaries, that of pseudo-Plutarch and that of Stobaeus which, together with other doxographical fragments, appear in the *Doxographi Graeci*. We must not think of this doxography, however, as simply a dilution of the treatise of Theophrastus. Material deriving from the biographical tradition has been incorporated into it, some of it coming from Aristoxenus and subsequent writers of *Bioi* (*Dox. Gr.* 150–152). For this reason the doxography, especially in respect of Pythagoras and the Pythagoreans, can mislead us as to the status and authority of its evidence, and so oblige us to seek the source of its statements and opinions.

The doxographical tradition is an academic one. The biographical tradition is literary. As regards Pythagoras it was shaped and given new impulse by Heraclides Ponticus (Wehrli, *Her. Pont.*, and Heft 10.101–102, 111–115). Some ten years older than Aristotle and for thirty years a member of the Academy, Heraclides played an important role in the Platonic circle. He was a man of noble birth, wealthy, and of great personal dignity. The consideration he enjoyed is shown by the fact that Plato left him as the acting head of the Academy during his third voyage to Sicily, and that he was a candidate for the headship on Speusippus' death. He enjoyed a great reputation as a stylist, and Plutarch (*de aud. poet.* 1.14E = Wehrli, *Her. Pont.* fr. 73) tells us that the youth of his time still delighted in his writings.

As a philosopher Heraclides displayed remarkable insights and made some inspired conjectures, especially in the field of astronomy. But his principal interest was the life of the soul, the supernatural, the miraculous, the occult—an interest that appears to derive rather from the intellectual's reaction against excessive rationalism than from any recrudescence of superstition or reversion to traditional faith. The legend of Pythagoras was as if made for his purpose. He fastened on it and reshaped it. His Pythagoras emerged as a sage possessed of occult wisdom, capable of performing miracles, aware of his soul's past; as the author of an ethical rule or discipline for an austere Pythagorean way of life. His friend Speusippus sought to adapt and give expression to the more scientific aspects of Pythagoreanism. Heraclides sought to revive the Pythagorean way of life. His writings gave new life to a legend that was destined to have great influence in later antiquity and the early Christian centuries.

Heraclides left Athens on the death of Speusippus, in 347 B.C. Aristoxenus was a candidate for the succession to Aristotle on his death in 322 B.C., and so must have been a mature man at that time. But as he was born in Tarentum and had his early musical education in Mantinea it is unlikely that he came under the direct influence of Heraclides (Wehrli, *Aristoxenus* fr. 1–7). He, however, contributed to the reshaping of the Pythagoras legend even more than did Heraclides. He appears to have been an aggressive and disgruntled man, hostile to the philosophical and intellectual tendencies of his time and in particular to the contemporary Academy. In his published *Lives*—he was immensely prolific—he attacked the memory of Socrates, recounting scandalous tales of his matrimonial misadventures. He attacked Plato for plagiarizing the *Republic* from Protagoras. As he maintained contacts with the Pythagorean group in Phlius (Wehrli, fr. 19) he may be the source for the suggestion of Timon of Phlius (Gell. 3.17.4 = *Vors.* 1, 399) that Plato plagiarized an early Pythagorean source also in his *Timaeus*. Disappointed that he did not succeed Aristotle in the headship of the school he insulted his memory (Wehrli, fr. 1). His attitude must be attributed in part to pique, but it is largely due to a basic tendency to deplore his contemporary world and hark back to a better past.

The ancient world recognized him as a great musical theorist—Aristoxenus Musicus. His theory was based on the intervals of perceived sound, and not on intervals expressed in mathematical relations and observable for instance in the length of strings. Pythagorean musical theory was mathematical, but Aristoxenus passed it over in silence. Instead he attacked Plato and the Academy for a philosophical-mathematical corrupting of musical theory. This conservative reaction was part of a total repudiation of the way Pythagoreanism was interpreted in the Academy and the Peripatos. He did not confine himself to protest but went on to write three books on Pythagoreanism, the first a life of Pythagoras, the second a description of the Pythagorean way of life or discipline, the third on Pythagorean maxims. In these books he reinterpreted both the legend and the scientific tradition. The Pythagoras of legend was divested of many of his backward traits, such as abstinence from meat and beans, and became an enlightened sage who had taught all the doctrines Aristoxenus chose to attribute to him. The Pythagorean way of life became a discipline acceptable to the fourth-century intellectual—emphatically not the way practised by the poor, dirty, unshodden, vegetarian "Pythagorists" of his time. The notion may be implicit here of a division of Pythagoreans into a superior scientific class of *mathematici* and a subordinate class of *acusmatici*, instructed by precept only, but these terms are given currency only by Iamblichus (*VP* 80–83; *ZM* 1.2, 405, n. 2).

Some of the material used by Aristoxenus in refashioning the Pythagorean tradition derived from Aristotle and others, some was of his own invention. It is difficult, if not impossible, to disentangle fact and fiction in his composite picture. Perhaps because the truer account of Aristotle, with which his conflicted in many respects, was still present to the minds of his generation, Aristoxenus' picture remained without immediate influence. But it found its way into the doxography, and it was seized on by the Neopythagoreans and especially by Porphyry and Iamblichus, for whom Aristoxenus was a principal source.

During the third and second centuries B.C. the tradition was epitomized and systematized as to successions and schools. The biographical tradition, with the resources of the libraries of Alexandria and Pergamum at its disposal, became a playground of erudition. But this scholarly activity was marginal to the philosophical interests of the period. For the third century saw a revolution in Greek thought, a revolution that was not the product of its own internal tensions and controversies but was induced by external events. Alexander's conquests in Asia and in Africa had opened up a new world of experience in that they made the Greek a citizen of a state or empire the boundaries of which were practically conterminous with those of his world, and had extended Greek culture to all that world. At the same time they had put an end to the day in which a Greek could be an active citizen in a polis-state exercising real sovereignty, and when the non-Greek world could be dismissed as barbarian. One might have expected the resilient Greek to adapt himself at once to the new (but not entirely new) situation, and hasten to take on the commercial and administrative burdens of empire. Many Greeks did so. But the imagination of many balked at the idea of a diluted citizenship in a world state under Macedonian rule. Even Aristotle showed no signs of reconciling himself to that notion, or of contemplating the possibility that the good life could be achieved in a context other than that of the polis.

When Athens grasped that a fundamental and permanent change had occurred the philosophical reaction was significant. At the turn of the century both Academy and Peripatos were tending to specialization or to literary rather than philosophical effort. They reacted to a changed world by becoming "academic" and for the time being lost their influence. Two new schools arose, the Stoic with its doctrine of total commitment and the Epicurean with its doctrine of total detachment. Stoicism was well adapted to become a religion of empire, Epicureanism to dispel the fears and anxieties of those for whom the world had become too wide, too complex, too foreign.

The two schools achieved dominance in the next two centuries, overshadowing both Academy and Peripatos. The efforts of Aristoxenus to revive Pythagoreanism were for the time being forgotten. The sources, even for the major contemporary schools, are so fragmentary that reconstruction of philosophical thought in the period is fraught with difficulties and uncertainties. But we know that in Magna Graecia scientific writings subsequent to Archytas were collected into a Pythagorean Corpus during the second century b.c. (Thesleff, *An Introduction*, 120). In Alexandria pseudepigrapha of the same period indicate an interest in the legend rather than the science. The Pythagorean treatise excerpted by Alexander Polyhistor (*D.L.* 8, 24–36) about the first century b.c. testifies to the fact that during the period of Stoic influence someone chose to write a treatise on Pythagoreanism in sympathetic vein. But these are straws in the wind. Pythagoreanism if not extinct was clearly dormant.

In the first century b.c. there occurred a revival of Pythagoreanism at Rome and in Alexandria that was to be of the greatest consequence for thought in the ancient world. The origins of the revival have long been disputed (see Thesleff [1961] 46–71 for a summary). Scholars have asked whether it is to be imputed to a tradition continuing underground, or to some external and non-Greek source, such as Zeller's Essenes, or simply to a contemporary initiative of scholars. They have asked whether the revival originated at Rome with Nigidius Figulus, as asserted by Cicero (*Tim.* 1), or in Alexandria with Eudorus and Arius Didymus. The questions that interest us here are rather—Why did the revival, occurring at the time it did, encounter such immediate success? And what changes did it provoke in the tradition?

In the first century a.d. Stoicism and Epicureanism were still the dominant philosophical creeds, as yet without serious challengers. But the Hellenistic world was no longer content to be told either to conform to and live consonantly with nature and the universe, or to withdraw. Antiochus of Ascalon, head of the Academy in the first century b.c., had suggested an escape from this antinomy in his eclectic reconciliation of the teachings of the differing schools. Greece had always been tolerant in matters of belief. From the time of Antiochus, the Hellenistic world became increasingly eclectic and increasingly tolerant in questions of philosophical doctrine. The differences between stoicizing Platonists and platonizing Stoics were negligible. The Neopythagoreans felt no compunction in adopting or adapting any doctrine that seemed to fit into their general scheme of thought.

The first stirrings of Neopythagoreanism were followed, probably in the second half of the first century a.d., by an attempt to state the teaching of Pythagoras. Moderatus of Gades interpreted the earlier number theory in a metaphysical sense and symbolically. His writings, very influential at the time, are lost to us, but we have a substantial part of the writings of Nicomachus of Gerasa (*fl. ca.* 100 A.D.)—his *Introduction to Arithmetic, Manual of Harmony,* and *Inquiry into the Divine Nature of Number.* They are a sober restatement of Pythagorean number theory and number mysticism. Neither Moderatus nor Nicomachus by the character of their writings prepare us for their somewhat older and much more colourful contemporary, Apollonius of Tyana. He was a philosopher of some pretensions, an itinerant preacher and teacher, celibate, ascetic, a miracle-worker. He laid claim to semi-divine status and after his death was the object of a cult.

Though the revival of Pythagoreanism may have been the work of scholars we see in Apollonius of Tyana that in practice it produced the salvationist doctrines characteristic of the times. Apollonius claimed to be a reincarnation of Pythagoras, and he wrote a *Life* of Pythagoras in which the legend was presented in conformity with his own ideals. Modern scholarship suggests that this *Life* was the source for the more extravagant tales in Iamblichus, but Apollonius may have been less extreme than we imagine. We are perhaps misled by Philostratus' extravagant, novellistic "biography" of him, and by the damning parallel of Lucian's Alexander of Abonuteichus. Certainly Moderatus and Nicomachus are moderate in theory and in presentation. We must further remember that Neopythagoreanism was not a popular philosophy with a tincture of religion. It was rigidly intellectual, scientific in form, and accessible only to the few with higher philosophical education.

The further history of Neopythagoreanism and of its eventual fusion with Neoplatonism through Numenius (H. Dörrie, "Ammonios der Lehrer Plotins," *Hermes* 83 [1955] 444. n. 3), the predecessors of Plotinus, and Plotinus himself, is a part of the general history of philosophy of the period and a natural development. It is only at the end of this development that we find the life and doctrines of Pythagoras treated again. Porphyry, in his *Life of Pythagoras,* a part of his *History of Philosophy,* treats his theme in a manner surprising to us. That he was capable of sober and factual biography is shown by his *Life of Plotinus.* In dealing with Pythagoras he lacks a guiding principle that, in default of a criterion of evidence, would give his work unity. Instead he picks and chooses in the tradition, sometimes because what he finds seems to him credible, sometimes because it seems consonant with his own picture of the philosopher. What makes his *Life* of great value to us is the fact that he makes a practice of citing his sources.

Iamblichus, his successor, makes a very different use of the tradition.

He sets out to write an encyclopaedia of Pythagorean philosophy and we possess a considerable part of his work. In it he uses his sources indiscriminately and without regard to conflicts. He chooses facts and, if there are none, invents them to suit his thesis. He makes no attempt at critical judgment. But the obvious defects and exaggerations in his works must not lead us to underestimate Iamblichus. His purpose was to produce, in the person of Pythagoras, an ideal portrait of the Sage. Writing in the fourth century after Christ he projects into the sixth century before Christ the methods of contemporary schools and the doctrines of Neoplatonism (Festugière, *La révélation*, 2, 33–47). Like others before him, and like others since, he used the Pythagorean tradition simply as a quarry. His *Life* is a document of the utmost importance for the study of Neoplatonism; its use as a source for Pythagoras is fraught with difficulties.

Let us then attempt to summarize the tradition, observing the division into three phases or periods with which we began. In the lifetime of Pythagoras and in the century following his death (570–400 B.C.) there developed about his person a legend that produced political reactions between followers and opponents, probably once towards the end of his life, certainly again about the middle of the fifth century, possibly at the beginning of the fourth when there occurred a migration of "Pythagorists" from Magna Graecia. The legend was an oral and so a developing one. It represented Pythagoras as semi-divine saint and sage. It is probable that its early, ranker growth ended with the establishment of a stable, pro-Pythagorean regime in Tarentum.

The second phase began with Plato's encounter with Pythagoreanism or, more precisely, with a Pythagoreanism having a mathematical colouring. There ensued a pythagorizing period within the Academy during which, if Platonic doctrines took on a Pythagorean cast, Pythagorean doctrines in their turn took on a Platonic cast. Aristotle appears to have been the sole dissentient. He undertook systematic inquiries into the nature of Pythagoreanism and produced two monographs that served as a basis for the discussion of Pythagoreanism in the treatises.

In the third phase there are two traditions, at the outset largely independent of one another, the doxographical and the biographical. The doxography begins with Theophrastus' academic statement of doctrine in the *Physical Opinions*. Throughout the ensuing centuries the doxographical treatment of philosophers' teachings, and so of Pythagoreanism, remained academic. But schematism became more rigid and treatment became shallower in the epitomes and compendiums of the scholars of Hellenistic times. It was only with a revival of

Pythagoreanism as a way of life or salvation in the last century of the era that there occurred a rethinking of Pythagorean doctrines. The refurbished doctrines however continued to be attributed to Pythagoras himself and in part found their way into the doxography.

Of the biographical tradition we may regard Heraclides Ponticus as the first exponent. His imaginative presentation of the miraculous and occult aspects of the legend, though it does not pretend to be biography, yet had a great influence on the biographical tradition. Aristoxenus, the first learned biographer, largely reshaped the legend to conform to his own Pythagorean ideal, and subsequent biographers continued to retouch. As a result, when the biographical tradition debouched in Neopythagoreanism, Pythagoras had become the Neopythagorean sage—half mystic, half mathematician.

In the first of the three phases of the Pythagorean tradition the elements are too meagre to permit of any real reconstruction. The second phase is suspect of rationalization. The third phase is palpably evangelistic. How then are we to distinguish between fact and fiction, between the excrescences of contemporary fabulation and the legend that reflects the person? This is the problem that confronts us when we attempt to use the lives of Diogenes Laertius, Porphyry, Iamblichus, and Photius.[14]

In the present study I have taken as a basis for reconstruction the testimony of Aristotle.[15] He is the principal "watershed" in our tradition, and he is almost alone in having no Pythagorean axe to grind. I am not suggesting that the tradition subsequent to Aristotle is to be rejected holus-bolus. It clamours for interpretation as one of our principal documents for the evolution from Platonism to Neoplatonism. Once so interpreted it should better reveal the earlier Pythagoreanism that was its point of departure. Occasionally it corroborates or throws light on the testimony of Aristotle. Its independent value, as our outline of the tradition has sought to show, is always subject to question.

NOTES

[1]Ernst Bindel, *Pythagoras* (Stuttgart 1962); G. T. Sakellariou, *Pythagoras— Didaskalos tôn Aiôniôn* (Athens 1963).

[2]I. Lévy, (see bibliography) suggests that the legend served as a model for Christianity.

[3]Herodotus' silence may be explained by the hypothesis that he wrote the early part of his history, with its references to Magna Graecia, before he went to Thurii, and that he never thereafter revised. His arrival, however, is to be dated (F. Jacoby, in *RE* Supp. 1913, Heft 2.247) between the founding of the colony in 444–43 B.C. and his death, after 430 B.C. So he arrived after the *débâcle* of the Pythagoreans about the middle of the century, and must have known what there was to be known about it. It may be that the *débâcle* was of less political importance than we imagine. Certainly the Pythagorean exiles in mainland Greece were few and their impact small until the "Pythagorists" began to arrive about the end of the century.

Herodotus' silence, however, may also be explained by the supposition that "in the West he gave up ethnographic and geographical research" (Jacoby, *ibid.* 380) because his interest was now focused on the Persian War and the conflict between Athens and Sparta.

[4]*Vors.* 36 B 4. For the traditional interpretation A. von Blumenthal, *Ion von Chios* (Stuttgart-Berlin 1939) Fr. 30. For an amended text and new interpretation F. H. Sandbach, *Proceedings of the Cambridge Philological Society* n.s. 5 (1958–59) 36.

[5]Wehrli, *Her. Pont.* fr. 118–123. There is no indication that he was a *number* atomist. Democritus too is said to have been influenced by Pythagoreanism. Q. Cataudella, *Rend. Acad. Lincei. C.*13 (1937) 182–210.

[6]Speusippus is said (*Theol. Ar.* 82) to have devoted the first half of his treatise to linear, plane, and solid numbers. This division assumes some similar derivation. He is also said to have based his treatise on verbal expositions of Pythagoreanism and on a book by Philolaus. Philolaus is discussed below, 112–117. His role is so uncertain and his fragments so questionable that we cannot assess his influence on the tradition, but it was probably not great.

[7]No such reinterpretation occurred in connection with theories of the soul. Speusippus (fr. 40 Lang) defines the soul spatially, as "idea of the everywhere extended," Xenocrates (Arist. *de An.* 404b 27–30, Plut. *de An. Proc.* 1012D) as self-moving number. Both of these definitions are understandable against the background of the *Timaeus*, but there is no Pythagorean doctrine known to us to which we can refer them. The treatise of Iamblichus in Stobaeus (Festugière, *La révélation*, 3, 177–264) suggests that a canonical teaching never developed, probably because the transmigration doctrine referred it to a religious rather than a physical context. Guthrie (307–311) suggests that the soul–harmonia equation is early Pythagorean; but, as he himself notes, this is not generally conceded (Cherniss 323, n. 1; Bluck, *Plato's Phaedo* [London 1955] 197–198). The evolution from Platonism to Neoplatonism is discussed by P. Merlan, in his book *From Platonism to Neoplatonism*, an important contribution to our knowledge of post-Aristotelian development. Merlan considers only incidentally the part played therein by a reinterpretation of Pythagoreanism. See also Burkert 74–85.

[8]This is the sense of Theophr. *Metaph.* 11a 27–b 7. The text, as Usener saw, is corrupt, and the solution offered by W. D. Ross and F. H. Fobes, *ad. loc.*, is not

a possible one. Theophrastus is discussing not "the distance between the real and the things of nature" but between good and evil. If we understand ἐπιμιμεῖσθαι as repeated after καίτοι (b2), ποιοῦσιν as a dative (b3) and read ὅλως δε (b5) with the MSS we get the following sense (1 paraphrase): "For Plato and the Pythagoreans there is a great distance separating good and evil, and everything tends to conform. This conforming implies a sort of opposition between the one and the indefinite dyad in which is implicit the unlimited, lack of order and, one might say, all absence of form *per se*. However there can be no universe without dyad. It must be present in equal part or even predominate over the other principle. As a consequence the first principles, one and indefinite dyad are (shown to be) opposites." Here Theophrastus, whatever the meaning of this obscure passage, is misinterpreting Plato for whom in the *Timaeus* evil, disorder, lack of shape is a consequence of the fact that the Ideas are reflected in the Receptacle. He is misinterpreting the Pythagoreans in attributing to them the dyad as partner of the One in producing the physical world.

Merlan (115) does not seem to me to cast light on this difficult passage. It is not clear what he proposes to read, nor whether it would make the fundamental change in sense he requires.

[9]*Vors.* 14 cites the early fragments in an introductory paragraph and prints Plato and Herodotus. Much of the remaining material should be relegated to 58B. The most judicious and illuminating discussion of the early sources is still Zeller's *Sitzber. Pr. Ak.* (1889) 985–996.

[10]The pseudepigrapha from the fourth century on seem to have contributed rather to the Neopythagorean revival of the first century. Diodorus Siculus 10.3–12 derives from Aristoxenus and later sources. Justinus 20.4 is said to reflect Timaeus, who is alleged to have assembled independent evidence in Magna Graecia, but the reconstructions are problematical.

[11]Wehrli Heft 10.115–121 considers biographical tendencies in the period. Individual members of the school and their biographical practices are discussed in Wehrli's preceding Hefte (*Aristoxenos, Dikaiarchos, Klearchos*). The best general study of the biographical tradition is still F. Leo, *Die griechische-römische Biographie nach ihrer literarischen Form* (Leipzig 1913). A. Dihle, *Studien zur griechische Biographie* (Göttingen 1956), considers philosophical aspects. R. Hirzel, *Plutarchus* (Leipzig 1912) discusses Greek biography under the aspect of its major exponent. I. Düring, *Herodicus the Cratetean* 132–172, discusses aspects of the biographical tradition and (136, 153–155) evaluates Aristoxenus and his influence. (For the *Bioi* of the third century Wilamowitz, *Antigonos von Karystos.* For the cynic diatribe and its relation to the biographical tradition, O. Hense, *Teletis Reliquiae* (Tübingen 1909).) E. Rohde, *Der griechische Roman* 4th ed. (Hildesheim 1960), illustrates the novellistic development of legend. A. Brelich, *Gli Eroi greci* (Rome 1958), studies the morphology of heroic myth after which, at least in a measure, legend is patterned.

Some reference to this literature is necessary. If we do not understand what "Greek biography" professes to be and seeks to do (and if we do not clearly understand the difference from modern biographical method) we cannot judge how evidence gained from it is to be evaluated.

[12]The sources and bibliography are discussed *ZM* 1.1, 25–33; Praechter 10–21; Burnet 33–38; *KR* 1–7. In *Phoenix* 10 (1956) 116–123 I have attempted to summarize. J. B. McDiarmid, "Theophrastus on the Presocratic Causes," *Harv. Stud.* 61 (1953) 85–156, discusses Theophrastus' relations to Aristotle. For a more balanced judgment of the doxography see Kahn, *Anaximander and the Origins of Greek Cosmology* 11–24.

[13]Burnet 28–30 suggests that in the *Physical Opinions* Theophrastus represented early thinkers "as standing to one another in the relation of master to scholar, and as members of regular societies." According to Diels (*Dox. Gr.* 104), "he took some account of successions . . . and appears to have followed in turn the various families—Ionians, Eleatics, atomists—down to the time of Plato; nor did he shrink from connecting Diogenes of Apollonia and Archelaus with the physical philosophers, despite difference of epoch." This is the practice of Aristotle in, for example, *Metaphysics A*, and of Theophrastus. But though they occasionally imply a relation of master and scholar, as of Xenophanes and Parmenides (*Metaph.* 986b 22) or speak of "the circle of Anaxagoras and Heraclitus" (Theophr. *De Sens.* 1.3 = *Dox. Gr.* 499) this does not imply formal successions and schools, a schematic pattern imposed on the history of philosophy only by Sotion (*Dox. Gr.* 147) in accordance with what was in his time current practice in the schools. We have no good grounds for believing that in the Presocratic period a succession master—scholar was normal or necessary, or that schools existed before the Platonic Academy (which was formally a θίασος or cult society). Philosophers may of course have belonged to ἑταιρεῖαι, political or religious societies.

[14]The four *Lives* are here grouped together as an end-product, as in a sense they are. Their differences of character, however, are considerable and determine differences of use. Diogenes Laertius is a third-century compilation, of value to us for the sources from which it is compiled. Porphyry is a scholar as well as a philosopher. Though his Neoplatonist bias is obvious in his choice of sources, he cites them and the extent of his own elaboration is small. Iamblichus is a teacher and an adept of philosophico-religious practice, zealous to convert. He is a great excerptor but rarely acknowledges his sources, and this not with intent to deceive but simply because it seems to him material not from whom but what he borrows. He does not hesitate to rationalize, explain, amend.

The *Life* (cod. 249) in the *Bibliotheca* of Photius (ed. I. Bekker [Berlin 1824], see O. Immisch, *Agatharchidea.* (*Sitz. Heid. Ak.* 1919) is as yet inadequately edited. The primary problem is to determine the period to which it is to be attributed, probably not an early one. It has a general peripatetic-stoic colouring and owes much, indirectly, to Aristotle. From monad and definite dyad derive point, line, surface, and solid but a distinction is drawn between conceptual monad and mathematical one. The soul is in life a quantitative part, but after death it transmigrates. (Either the author or Photius himself qualifies this doctrine as absurd.) (See K. Reinhardt, *Poseidonios von Apamea* [Stuttgart 1954]; *RE* "Poseidonios" 763–768; Praechter, 518).

Photius is as interesting, if not as coherent, as the *Hypomnemata* of Alexander Polyhistor preserved in Diogenes Laertius and might in part derive from sources of the same period. Even if it were adequately edited, however, it would add nothing to our purpose except for a classification of Pythagoreans, more elaborate than anything we know and so probably of later origin.

[15]On Aristotle's monograph *On the Pythagoreans* see my article *TAPA* 64 (1963), the conclusions of which I summarize here. Ross fr. 1.130: the first four lines need not derive from Aristotle. Ross fr. 5.134=*D. L.* 8.33 clearly belongs to Alexander Polyhistor and not to Aristotle. Ross fr. 135: this fragment is to be attributed, as by Ross, to Aristotle. Ross fr. 17.143: this fragment is to be rejected, Aristotle's name appearing in it only by emendation.

3

THE PYTHAGOREANS
IN THE FIFTH CENTURY

IN the many discussions of Pythagorean doctrine in his treatises, Aristotle refers infrequently and only incidentally to individual Pythagoreans, and never to Pythagoras. As a rule he refers collectively to "the Pythagoreans." To what collectivity are we to suppose him to refer? To this troublesome question there are as many answers as there are historians of philosophy. The simplest solution is to say that "the Pythagoreans" are a brotherhood or religious society or sect having a body of doctrine to which the "brothers" subscribe. This supposed brotherhood will be discussed at length in a later context (138–140). Suffice it for the present to say that there is no evidence for a religious or philosophical brotherhood (though there is for a political association), that there is no parallel for such a quasi-monastic institution before the Christian era, that there is no evidence for "schools"— much less for brotherhoods—centering around early thinkers, and that the very notion of an orthodoxy runs counter to the ethos of Greek thought.

If the hypothesis of a brotherhood is to be rejected we must attempt to solve our problem by examining what our sources tell us of fifth-century Pythagoreanism.[1] Perhaps they will reveal the identity of Aristotle's Pythagoreans. In the fragments of the Presocratics we find numerous references to persons as Pythagoreans, and to their opinions as Pythagorean. Sometimes, though rarely in the case of earlier Pythagoreans, we find references to their writings. It is difficult not to assume that the persons referred to are historical, having recognizable views that can be reconstructed with the aid of conjecture. But on closer examination we find that all our sources are post-Aristotelian. From the fourth century onwards the lacunae in the history of Pythagoreanism began to be filled by tendentious writers. When the Neopythagoreans annexed the mathematical disciplines as their province they equipped early Pythagoreans with mathematical achievements, and Pan-Pythagoreans like Iamblichus simply swept everything they could into the Pythagorean net, as is evidenced by his all too catholic list of Pythagoreans (*VP* 265-267). Thus in tracing the development of early Pythagoreanism we must proceed with caution.

When Pythagoras migrated from Ionia to Magna Graecia he arrived in a new world as yet almost untouched by the Ionian enlightenment.[2] It was a world that Xenophanes, an Ionian and a contemporary, found not uncongenial—a world of great wealth and vitality, exhibiting, at least in the land-owning and mercantile classes, the luxuries and excesses that accompanied material prosperity. But the city states on the Ionian Sea were politically turbulent. Migrations from Asia Minor, if they brought with them displaced intellectuals, also brought factions, border clashes, and disputes about territory. It is unlikely that Pythagoras found a climate favourable to philosophical pursuits and orderly inquiry. He did however, find a favourable soil in which to implant the political and moral ideas that were a concomitant of his philosophical theories. That he attempted to teach those theories we need not doubt, but that his practical doctrines commanded more ready acceptance must not surprise us.

We do not know what was his role in Croton, the city in which he established himself: he may have come from Ionia with a patrimony and acquired land—the governing aristocracy of Croton were largely landowners (Dunbabin 361)—or he may have engaged in trade. It seems unlikely that he lived by his teachings. To do so he would have had to be a rhapsode or reciter of poetry, like Xenophanes, or a forerunner of the itinerant sophist-teachers. Somehow he gained adherents and political influence in Croton, and his faction was dominant for a time—we do not know how long. But dissensions arose as he had predicted (*Fr. Sel.* 130) and he departed for Metapontum, where he died about the end of the sixth century.

These dissensions, however, cannot have been more than an episode, for the Pythagoreans had the upper hand in Magna Graecia throughout the first half of the fifth century. They may have been little more than a dominant political faction using the name of Pythagoras, as their opponents used the name of Cylon.[3] Their domination came to an end about the middle of the fifth century, when they were killed, exiled, or dispersed. After that, though there may have been some Pythagorean activity in Magna Graecia of which we know nothing, it is unlikely to have been scientific activity. A few exiles collected around Lysis and Philolaus in Thebes, and there was a small group, not of

Italiot origin and of no great consequence philosophically, in Phlius. At about the end of the century Philolaus appears to have returned to Tarentum where political circumstances had again become favourable. The so-called Pythagorists were expelled from other parts of Magna Graecia about 390 B.C., but Tarentum continued to offer Pythagoreans a haven. It became a centre of importance for them when Archytas, a professing Pythagorean, became its *strategos*.

This summary account of Pythagorean political history, though it glosses over the lacunae in our knowledge, suffices for a consideration of the philosophical and scientific development. When we turn to that development we discover to our astonishment that the Pythagoreans —whether as brotherhood, or school, or as individuals professing that name—made little or no contribution to philosophy during the century that elapsed between the death of Pythagoras and the time of Archytas. In that period there are only two Pythagoreans with any claim to scientific eminence, Hippasus and Philolaus. The Neopythagoreans, and later Iamblichus, made every effort to increase their number, both by annexing thinkers of a similar tendency—for instance Parmenides—and by tricking out with fictional fact names that were nothing but names. All their best efforts succeeded in recovering no Pythagorean of repute within the century. Proclus concedes as much in his sketch of the history of geometry (*In pr. Eucl. El.* Fried. 64 = Wehrli, *Eudemus* 133). There he imputes great merit to Pythagoras, alleging that he erected geometry into a *paideia*, and ascribing to him the greatest mathematical achievements. But despite his Pythagorean bias he cannot cite another Pythagorean mathematician between Pythagoras himself and Archytas. Thus any reconstruction of fifth-century Pythagoreanism must be built around the persons of Hippasus and Philolaus.[4]

Hippasus[5] is a puzzling figure concerning whom our most trustworthy source is Aristotle, and he tells us very little. The only reference occurs in his account of early opinions on first principles and causes. There he says that "Hippasus of Metapontum and Heraclitus of Ephesus make the first principle fire" (984a 7). But, Simplicius (*Phys.* 23.33 = *Dox. Gr.* 475 = *Vors.* 18.7) obviously alluding to the *Metaphysics*, tells us that "Hippasus of Metapontum and Heraclitus of Ephesus make the first principle one, in motion, limited; but for them it is fire, and they assert that existing things come to be from fire by condensation and rarefaction, and are again broken up or dissolved into fire, that being the only substrate of the physical world." What Theophrastus (for Simplicius is citing the *Physical Opinions*) adds to Aristotle's information certainly misrepresents the position of Heraclitus. In saying that, for Hippasus, the first principle is "one, in motion, limited," Theophrastus may only be attempting to reconcile Hippasus' position with the fact that he is reputed to be a Pythagorean. At all events the connection established by Aristotle between the two thinkers remains a commonplace of the doxography. Everything else we know of Hippasus either involves contradiction or is subject to doubt.[6]

There are three distinct problems regarding Hippasus to which we must offer a solution if we are to attempt to suggest the role he played in politics and in thought. At what date did he live? Was he a dissident Pythagorean? Did he discover (and promulgate) the so-called Platonic figures and the secret of irrationality?

As Mondolfo remarks (ZM 2.626) we can hope to explicate the conflicting evidence only if we can first settle the problem of chronology. How conflicting the evidence is, and how easily it can be made to warrant scepticism, Frank (261–263) has clearly shown. The fact that Aristotle associates Hippasus' name with that of Heraclitus would seem to suggest that they were roughly contemporary. It is unlikely that he would have done so if Hippasus had been a thinker of the early fourth century. Thesleff (28.n.2) points out that the Phlian tradition of a Hippasus as one of Pythagoras' forefathers "indicates that Hippasus the Pythagorean was properly considered as somehow related to Pythagoras." It may at least indicate that they were believed to be roughly contemporary. And finally, the doctrine that the first principle is fire is likely to be an early one—earlier than any theory of the elements. For these reasons it seems preferable to regard Hippasus as flourishing in the first half of the fifth century or earlier.

There are three principal problems concerning this nebulous Hippasus, and each of them has occasioned much controversy in recent years. Only Iamblichus gives us details of his life and doctrine. What were Iamblichus' sources? What grounds has he for his account of the division of the Pythagorean brotherhood into *mathematici* and *acusmatici*?[7] Are we to believe Iamblichus' accounts of Hippasus' mathematical achievements?

For Iamblichus, Hippasus is a romantic figure, having a key role both in a democratic reaction against "the oligarchic party in the school" and in a split occurring within the Pythagorean order (*VP* 257). He cites no authority for his account, but here as elsewhere he may owe something to Apollonius of Tyana, though many of the details are probably due to his own penchant for novelistic narrative.

He may also have been using the *Epitome* of Heraclides Lembos. Diogenes Laertius remarks (8.7): "Heraclides states that the *Mystic Account* attributed to Pythagoras was written by Hippasus, with slanderous intent towards Pythagoras." Diels (*Dox.Gr.* 150–151) suggests that Heraclides' source for the list of Pythagoras' writings that precedes this remark is Hermippus of Smyrna (*ca.* 200 B.C.). Hermippus wrote *Bioi* on the basis of Callimachus' *Pinakes*. As a librarian he gave an orderly account of the holdings of the Alexandrian Library but, as Praechter remarks (16), "he was also a worthy successor of Aristoxenus in accepting and fabricating malicious gossip." That an Alexandrian librarian would doubt the authenticity of writings attributed to Pythagoras is probable, but he must have had some grounds for the attribution to Hippasus. As he often depends on the tendentious constructions of Aristoxenus, and as Aristoxenus recounts the conspiracy of the Cylonians, though without mention of Hippasus (Iambl. *VP* 248 = Wehrli *Aristoxenus* 18), Hermippus may derive his tale of Hippasus' opposition to Pythagoras from Aristoxenus. Now we know that Aristoxenus, though he did not explicitly divide Pythagoreans into *mathematici* and *acusmatici*, did suggest that some of the Pythagoreans were philosophers and that others merely practised external observances. He may have connected Hippasus with the second group, as having been expelled from the inner circle on account of his Cylonian activities. This does not exclude the possibility that, for Aristoxenus, Hippasus was little more than a name, his opposition to Pythagoras being an inference from the fact that his first principle, fire, was un-Pythagorean. As we can make no sense of the conflicting and obviously elaborated accounts in Iamblichus our only resource would appear to be some hypothesis such as I have offered.

Our second problem is Iamblichus' account of the division of the Pythagorean "brotherhood" into *mathematici* and *acusmatici* (*VP* 81–88; *c.m.sc.* 76 Festa). Iamblichus' lively tale of how that division occurred is full of contradictions (Burkert 187–196). His basic tendency is apparent in the fact that whereas in his sources he found Hippasus as an *acusmaticus*, he must, on account of the mathematical achievements attributed to him, rebaptize him *mathematicus*. Burkert (190–191) proposes to refer the account to Aristotle, on the grounds that the *acusmata* (whence *acusmaticus*) derive from the Aristotelian tradition. But the terms are not Aristotle's, and Porphyry (*VP* 42 = *Fr. Sel.* 135) can refer to the *acusmata* as *symbola* in quoting a series deriving from Aristotle. It would seem more probable that Iamblichus' source,

here as in so many instances, was that from which he borrowed the
title for his book, Aristoxenus. Aristoxenus was no doubt aware of the
crass contrast between the ideal of the Pythagorean sage he was seeking
to depict and the dirty, barefoot, vegetarian Pythagorists of the
Middle Comedy (*Vors.* 1.479–480). He could not deny that they
"belonged," but somehow he must present them as second-class
Pythagoreans. He will have felt no compunction in inventing a suitable
tale around a nebulous Hippasus. (Diels, *Elementum.* 63, remarks that
"the confusion of Hippon, Hipponax, Hippys, and Hippasus in our
tradition is an almost inextricable one.") This Hippasus, in that he held
fire to be the first principle, was already stamped as deviant if not
dissident. Aristoxenus may himself have added the betraying of
mathematical secrets. He was not inclined to the excessive mathematical emphasis of the Academy. In any case he must have had some
hand in creating this early, and disreputable, forerunner of the *acusmatici*, though he himself did not use the terms *mathematici* and
acusmatici.

As to the mathematical achievements of Hippasus, our tradition
presents even greater problems. He is said (Iambl. *V.P.* 88 = *c.m.sc.*
25 = *Vors.* 18.4) "to have constructed and made public the sphere of
twelve pentagons," and on the authority of Aristoxenus (Schol. Plat.
Phaedo 108D = *Vors.* 18.12) to have experimented in musical sounds.
Iamblichus (*Vors.* 18.15 = *in Nic. Ar.* 100.19), apparently considering
Hippasus a contemporary of Archytas, adds that Archytas and
Hippasus and their circle used the term "harmonic" of one of the
proportional ratios previously known as "subcontrary." He is *not*
said to have inquired into irrational numbers and incommensurability.
Iamblichus imputes this as a crime to some other anonymous Pythagorean (*VP* 88 = *Vors.* 18.4). Von Fritz (*Annals Maths.* 248–257)
has claimed for Hippasus the discovery of incommensurability on the
basis of his experiments with disks and tumblers. As von Fritz himself
concedes, the interconnection "is, of course, very indirect" (248)—so
indirect in fact that even if we are disposed to consider the account of
the experiments historical, their connection with incommensurability
seems highly problematical. At one stage of his argument (252), von
Fritz states that "Proclus credits Pythagoras with a formula which
makes it possible to form any number of different, rational, right-
angled triangles by finding pairs of numbers the sum of the squares
of which is equal to a square number." What Proclus actually says
(*In primum Eucl. El.* Fried. 426 = *Vors.* 58.19) is: that "the square of
the hypotenuse of a right-angle triangle is equal to the sum of the

squares on the other two sides"; and he adds in a comment, the reading of which is corrupt, but the sense of which is clear, that if we wish to lend an ear to the narrators of ancient history some of them attribute this discovery to Pythagoras and say that he sacrificed an ox on the occasion. Heath (*Euclid* 1.36–37, 343–344, 350–352) and van der Waerden (*Science Awakening* 100), both of whom would like to attribute the discovery of irrationals to Pythagoras himself or to early Pythagoreanism, point out that this tale is impossible and cannot derive from Eudemus. On these and on other grounds the thesis of von Fritz, attributing mathematical inquiries to Hippasus, seems to me untenable.

Iamblichus (*V.P.* 88 = *c.m.sc.* 25 = *Vors.* 18.4) tells us that Hippasus was the first to promulgate and to construct the sphere of twelve pentagons. As usual Iamblichus gives no indication of the source of his information, but it cannot derive from Eudemus. Proclus' version attributes the discovery of irrationals and of the Platonic figures to Pythagoras. We have no reason to believe that Hippasus was even mentioned by Eudemus. In any case it is recognized that Proclus rewrote the survey, giving greater importance to Pythagoras and the Pythagoreans. Van der Waerden (*Science Awakening* 90–91) has remarked that "what the Catalogue says about Pythagoras is unreliable," and this was shown in detail by Eva Sachs (28 ff.). So we conclude that even if Proclus had mentioned Hippasus—and the nature of his account of Pythagoras' mathematics makes this improbable—he probably altered the Catalogue to give importance to the Pythagoreans and would not be a credible witness. So the statement of Iamblichus must either depend on some later source or be a product of his own fertile imagination. If we wish to ascribe the discovery of irrationals and the construction of the dodecahedron to early Pythagoreanism they might as well be attributed to Pythagoras.

Hippasus is merely a peg on which the historians of mathematics hang their hypotheses. The real problem is to determine the time of the discovery of the irrational and of three of the five Platonic figures—square, tetrahedron and dodecahedron. No one doubts that these three figures were known (and "drawn") probably already in the sixth century. But the mode of mathematical thinking in the sixth century was not that of Euclid. We cannot suppose that earlier thinkers had elaborated methods enabling them to set up axioms, prove their theorems, and relate them to one another in a body of scientific knowledge that could be called geometry. It seems probable that the stricter methods which geometry implies for us were developed only towards the end of the fifth century.

As to irrationals, our problem is to ascertain when the irrationality of $\sqrt{2}$ was discovered. The dramatic date of the *Theaetetus* may be taken as about the date when Theodorus was making his inquiries into the surds from $\sqrt{3}$ to $\sqrt{17}$, though Plato may have put the date so far back merely to enable Socrates to appear as an interlocuter. In any case 400 B.C. is the earliest date. The irrationality of $\sqrt{2}$ is not mentioned and we assume it must have been discovered before Theodorus. How long before Theodorus? There are two possibilities:

1. The discovery was made early in the fifth century, either by Pythagoras or by Hippasus or by some other person (von Fritz's assumption, *Annals Math.* 245, n.1, that Proclus did not write ἀλόγων is gratuitous). This dating gives us the legend that the discovery so appalled the Pythagoreans they shrank from further inquiry for the best part of a century. Greek thinkers are not usually so easily appalled.

2. The discovery resulted from, or became mathematically important through, the critique of Zeno or some such critical approach, and then became a problem both for arithmetic and for geometry (*infra* Appx. II).

If we are to accept the first of these hypotheses then it does not greatly matter whose name we attach to the discovery. That of Hippasus, of whom we know next to nothing, will do; but the fact that he held fire, rather than number, to be the first principle speaks against him. If on the other hand we say, as I think we must, that mathematical speculation about such problems as the irrational is foreign to the whole period before Parmenides and Zeno, and that the problem of the irrational and incommensurability only makes sense as a mathematical problem, then we cannot connect it with Hippasus.

To conclude, we know that Hippasus of Metapontum held that the first principle was fire. We infer that he was a Pythagorean and a dissident. We assume that, as he is paired with Heraclitus in holding fire to be the first principle, he was either influenced by him (and probably a contemporary of his) or arrived at this theory independently. If he arrived at the theory independently he must have been either a contemporary or earlier, and then perhaps contemporary with Pythagoras). The rest of our tradition is unreliable, and cannot be used to add to our knowledge of Hippasus or of early Pythagoreanism.

If Hippasus, in the first half of the century, is a legendary figure of whom we know next to nothing, Philolaus,[8] in the second half of the century, is a thinker of whose historical existence we are assured; but the authenticity of his fragments has been a matter of heated controversy for over a century now.[9] The view that commands widest acceptance is that, towards the end of the fourth century, when many

Pythagorean pseudepigrapha were written, someone set himself the task of writing a book purporting to be a treatise *On Nature* by Philolaus. This forger may have used genuine writings of Philolaus, but he has one eye on the Academy, whose curiosity about things Pythagorean was intense. He has produced a brilliant and convincing document, telling the fourth-century Platonist (as it also tells us) precisely what he would most wish to know, with that hierophantic concision that Plato had taught them to regard as archaic. But even if we could regard the fragments as genuine, in whole or in part, they would not enable us to solve our problems. For they reveal a thinker of no great stature, whose interests are peripheral.

For our purposes the detail of Philolaus' doctrine is less important than his role in the history of thought. We would wish to regard him as an exponent of Pythagorean tradition whose doctrines probably had been modified in reaction to Parmenides and Zeno. Our fragments yield little or no positive information. So let us consider the tradition negatively, asking ourselves in what respects it does not tell us what we should expect to be told.

1. There are, for Philolaus, no "secret doctrines," and there is no suggestion that in his teaching or his publication anything was held back or treated as arcane. Nor is he ever said to have been drowned at sea for promulgating secrets.

2. Tradition gives him, as it gives many philosophers, one constant companion, Eurytus. But we hear nothing of a "brotherhood," or of *mathematici* and *acusmatici*, or of any political activity. (The exasperating doggerel in Diogenes Laertius [8.84 = *Vors.* 44 A 1] confuses Philolaus with Dion.)

3. There is no suggestion of an *ipse dixit* orthodoxy. It is said (*Dox. Gr.* 283 = *Vors.* 44 A 9) that Philolaus subscribed to the notion of *peras/apeiron* as first principles; but except in the B-fragments (B 1–3), where that doctrine is given a characteristic twist and the terminology is altered, he makes nothing of the notion. He departs radically from the basic doctrine described by Aristotle if, as Zeller (*ZM* 451) suggests, he was responsible for the Table of Opposites of the *Metaphysics* (986a 22–26).

4. Lysis represents what we expect in a Pythagorean, the ethical hero and sage. Plato (*Phaedo* 61D) suggests that Philolaus may have argued against suicide, but otherwise we hear nothing of ethical teachings or moral precepts.

5. Central fire plays an important role in his astronomical theories, and his medical teachings (44 A 27) suggest an emphasis on fire/heat.

They do not suggest that fire was his first principle, as it was that of Hippasus. But fire plays no role in what Aristotle represents as central Pythagorean doctrines.

6. Though he may have had mathematical and para-mathematical interests Philolaus was not a mathematician.[10]

If we turn from the negative to the positive aspects of Philolaus' teaching we find him represented in the doxography as having almost exclusively astronomical interests.[11] This doxographical emphasis must be due to Theophrastus. Aristotle mentions him only once (*Eth. Eud.* 1225a 30 = *Vors.* B 16) in an ethical context. The *Theologoumena Arithmetica*, and his dedication of angles of the triangle to gods (44 A 14) suggest arithmological interests. From a fragment of the *Iatrika* of Menon (44 A 27–28) we know that he propounded physiological theories. All this suggests a wide range of interest and free speculation in disparate fields that are not always number-related. If we are surprised to find intuition used as a tool of inquiry in the last half of the fifth century, we need only remind ourselves of the success it encountered in the fourth, in the person of Heraclides Ponticus.

Philolaus' companion, Eurytus, came from one of the cities of Magna Graecia (*Vors.* 45.1). He deserves mention only because of a curious anecdote that casts light on the mathematics of the time. Archytus, according to Theophrastus (*Metaph.* 6a 19 = *Vors.* 45.2), once remarked, obviously not without malice, that one must pursue an idea to its final conclusion, as did Eurytus. Other thinkers set up a theory of a One and an indefinite dyad, from which they generate numbers, plane surfaces, physical magnitudes. They add that space and the boundless void come from the dyad, while soul and some other things come from numbers and the One. But Eurytus, says Archytas, was different; he specified the number of man, horse, and so on.

Here Archytas is glancing critically at thinkers who propound some version of the point–line–surface–solid theory. Who these thinkers are who held theories so similar to those of Plato and the Academy and yet differing from them we do not know. Indeed we are surprised to find Archytas alluding to such theories. But his point is that, for all their subtlety, they lack the practical applications exhibited by the single-minded Eurytus.

Aristotle (1092b 9) uses the same illustration in asking: Are numbers causes in the sense that points are causes of solids? Eurytus, he says, used to specify the number of man or horse, representing by pebbles the shapes of animals and plants as do those who represent triangles and rectangles. Alexander (826–828) explains in detail how, given the number of man, Eurytus would create a sort of mosaic portrait by the use of coloured pebbles. He would probably do so in outline, after the manner of mythical figures seen in constellations, and the original number would be arrived at arithmologically (985b 23–986a 12).[12]

In this anecdote Archytas can only be poking fun at the methods of earlier Pythagoreans. It does not, however, encourage us to believe that the Pythagoreans of the time were mathematicians pursuing scientific inquiries.

I have reviewed the tradition of fifth-century Pythagoreanism, in order to discover what foundation it affords for the elaborate structures of the Neopythagoreans and of some modern scholars. I can find no grounds for believing that a "brotherhood" existed, and none for thinking that any Pythagorean or Pythagoreans pursued scientific or parascientific inquiries that might have debouched in the mathematical disciplines. Archytas, an innovator also in other fields, appears to have been the first Pythagorean mathematician. Between Pythagoras and Archytas the tradition reveals neither an apostolic succession of persons nor a conservative orthodoxy of thought. We might then be disposed to conclude, as does Frank, that scientific Pythagoreanism is a legend foisted on us by a later age and that Aristotle's account of Pythagorean thought is to be referred to Archytas and his school.[13]

Frank's thesis, novel and important as it was in its time, is now conceded to be untenable. Aristotle was well able to distinguish between the Pythagoreans and Archytas, on whom he wrote a monograph, fragments of which remain. What we know of the thought and the mathematics of Archytas bears little or no relation to Aristotle's account of Pythagoreanism in general character, themes of discussion, or methodological approach. Archytas was a mathematician who dealt with the mathematical problems of his times. He was not an antiquarian and did not archaize. But the Pythagoreans of Aristotle's account propounded a cosmology. The problems they faced, and the attitude they assumed to these problems, were not those of the early fourth century but of a much earlier time. If we refer the account to Archytas we must leave out of our reckoning the person the name implies—Pythagoras. Yet we are agreed that there was a person behind the legend and even Frank (78–80) concedes that he may have concerned himself with numbers and "number mysticism."

Who then were the Pythagoreans of whom Aristotle speaks? I would suggest that Aristotle refers, however cautiously and indirectly, to Pythagoras himself. The information that he was able to gather, and that he collected in his monograph *On the Pythagoreans*, must have attributed to Pythagoras not only a legend but also doctrines. If these doctrines circulated as those of "the Pythagoreans," their origin, or some part of their origin, must have been attributed to Pythagoras. It seems probable that a body of doctrine, relatively small and coherent, was in circulation as Pythagorean—a nucleus regarded as common to Pythagoreans and deriving from Pythagoras himself—and that Aristotle felt it the part of caution to ascribe it anonymously to "the Pythagoreans." It probably derived from Pythagorean tradition in Magna Graecia.

We have no means other than internal evidence by which to ascertain the author of the doctrines Aristotle reports. Our examination of the evidence may serve incidentally to recommend the notion of Pythagoras as author. But our principal object is to establish the character and features of the Aristotelian account, as being of primary importance for Platonism and Neoplatonism. One objection however must be raised and met before we proceed. If Pythagoras himself was the originator of the theories Aristotle reports, and if Pythagoreanism in some form was an active force during the fifth century, must we not assume, and be able to discover, evidence of its impact?

The hypothesis of an oral transmission, in a form roughly similar to that reported by Aristotle, of Pythagoras' own physical teaching is a possible one. It is not possible that, given some such teachings, the thought of the fifth century should not reflect them, directly or indirectly. But there is little general agreement about the history of thought in that century. What are landmarks for one scholar are mirages for another. All that can be done is to offer a brief review of development, in the form of categorical statement, showing how the Pythagorean doctrines could fit in. For our present purposes it suffices to show that a continuing Pythagorean tradition *can* have been present then.

The key figure is Parmenides. Parmenides was born, according to Apollodorus, about 540 B.C. or, if we take the date to be inferred from Plato's *Parmenides*, about 515 B.C. He is said to have "heard" Xenophanes, a critic of Pythagoras, but then, departing from him and his teachings, to have "followed" Ameinias, a Pythagorean to whom he dedicated a tomb. What we may take as certain is that Parmenides could not have been born and have lived his life in Magna Graecia without being familiar with Pythagorean doctrines.

The tone and structure of Parmenides' poem is understandable only if we see it as a reaction—a positive and almost violent reaction—

against some preceding teachings. This is peculiarly apparent in the proem. If he were about to expound his doctrines after the manner of the Ionians there would be no need of the supernatural apparatus, no need of the solemnity of verse. We can only suppose that after long wrestling with a doctrine for him invested with authority, he was driven in part to modify, in part to reject it. He feels himself, however, impelled to seek and claim for this rejection an authority higher than that of any human teaching, the authority of truth by divine revelation.[14]

The argumentation that follows the proem has this same character. If we see in it the beginning of logic, it is not because Parmenides was displaying a new technique but because, in anguished examination of a hypothesis he himself had once accepted, he has felt himself compelled to pose questions, to meet objections, to ask himself "How do we know this?"

If the thesis against which Parmenides argues is that of Pythagoras, he is saying in effect: We can know nothing about a stage earlier than the coming-to-be of our universe. Indeed we cannot know that it came to be. All we can say is that it *is*. From the fact of its existence we can deduce certain attributes, and they exclude the possibility of further change, of the coming-to-be of particulars, of a plurality of this unity, and of any *harmonia* or *logos* of parts. This is as far as you can get in your investigation of truth, of what we may be said to know and to know as existing. You must not confuse this Being with the report of the senses if you wish to go farther and describe the world of sense. Nor must you introduce any notion of non-being. That can only lead you astray. Confine yourself to a coherent and plausible description of what you see and hear and (he may imply) don't indulge in fancies like number-things in which Being and the perceptual world are confused.

It was against the scandal of this two-world thesis of Parmenides that subsequent thinkers reacted. They rightly disregarded the *Doxa* solution, which Parmenides himself had rendered largely outmoded, and struggled with his doctrine of one Being. His arguments, novel both in form and in substance, were so convincing to his immediate successors that they did not at first attempt to attack the notion of a One Being that was our universe. Empedocles denied that it was internally a unity, declaring that it consisted of four elements, each in substance atomic, and two forces (likewise elements and somehow corporeal) that kept the universe in constant cyclic process.

Empedocles' world sphere is externally that of Parmenides, and for him as for Parmenides there is no coming-to-be or passing-away. If he may be said to revert to theories of Pythagoras it can only be in the sense that he sees his cosmos as a vast and living complex. Of this cosmos man, beasts, and plants are parts as consisting of the same elements and subject to transmutation into these elements. But just as Pythagoras cannot have seen men as numbers walking, for a man can be a number only if the numbers of which he consists are his unseen *physis*, the expression of a physical but not visible *harmonia* or proportion, so for Empedocles the human person is an expression of proportion between invisible elements—a right proportion or *harmonia*.

The origins of the Atomists theories can be explained without recourse to a hypothesis of Pythagorean influence. But that they may have had reference to doctrines of Pythagoras, such as those mentioned by Aristotle, is rendered plausible not only by the obvious and admitted similarities of monad and atom, but also because our tradition tells us of an interest shown by Democritus in Pythagorean doctrine, and indeed of a book of his having the title *Pythagoras*. So it is possible that Pythagorean doctrine was present and working as a leaven in Atomist theories. It need not surprise us that it did not produce mathematical inquiry in the strict sense. It could produce only curious number speculation until the development of mathematical method, and mathematical method was not evolved by the Pythagoreans.

It is in Plato, however, that we should expect to find most clearly reflected the theories of "the Pythagoreans." Aristotle (987a 29–31) tells us that Plato's thought, though it had its own peculiar characteristics, was in most respects based on the theories of the Pythagoreans; and by Pythagorean theories he must mean those theories he himself has described in passages immediately preceding, principally theories having to do with number. But every theme that Plato uses undergoes a sea-change, a process of re-thinking and re-imagining that makes it impossible to distinguish between tradition and innovation. His doxographical hints regarding the Eleatics and Heracliteans are relatively many, those regarding the Pythagoreans few. Perhaps the clearest reference is in the *Philebus* (16c): "This is the *technê* I mean. To my mind it is a gift of the gods which somehow they sent us down by means of a Prometheus, with a kind of clearest fire; and the ancients, being better men than we and not so far removed from the gods, have bequeathed us the tradition that things that are said to be proceed from a one and a many, and that they have as original constituent a Limit and an Unlimited." In the theory Plato here presents, the Prometheus is likely to be Pythagoras—though not all scholars agree—and the contrariety *peras/apeiron* must be Pythagorean.

Many other doctrines, we are told from time to time, must be of Pythagorean origin, both in the *Philebus* with its numbering of harmonies and its emphasis on the quantitative, and in other dialogues; for example, in the geometrical elements of the *Timaeus*, the numerical harmonies of the world-soul, and the doctrine of *Homoiosis théô*. In no single case is Pythagorean origin undisputed, though in general a Pythagorean element is conceded. Apart from Aristotle's account we have none but subjective means for determining the impact of Pythagoreanism on Plato. So if we wish to determine the nature of Pythagoreanism in the fifth century, its impact on Presocratic thinkers and on Plato, its influence on the Early Academy and on the development of Platonism, and its role in the Neopythagorean revival, Aristotle's account is a crucial document and demands our careful and critical scrutiny, first of all to determine *what Aristotle says*.

NOTES

[1]The fragments of Pythagoras and the Pythagoreans are, perhaps inevitably, the least satisfactory part of the *Vorsokratiker*. Diels has grouped together with Pythagoras certain "Altere Pythagoreer." Of these Cercops and Brotinos belong in an Orphic context; Petron is merely a name attaching to a curious theory; Calliphon and Democedes are Crotoniate physicians who have been annexed to the list; Parmiskos, a Metapontine (and so Pythagorean), is known to us only through a Delian anecdote; Hippasus is the only one of the group whose connections with Pythagoreanism are established. Later Pythagoreans Diels again groups together (44–57). Not all of these are philosophers (Damon and Phintias) and many are simply names that garnish the "school." Finally he has a long omnium-gatherum chapter (58) in which he has put the catalogue of Iamblichus, anonyma, the *symbola*, fragments of Aristoxenus, and the Pythagorists.

The fragments as published by Cardini are easier to use and well edited but, if taken at face value, much more misleading. Miss Cardini is as ready as Iamblichus to baptize as a Pythagorean anyone having the remotest connection with that "brotherhood."

[2]As the biographical details have no firm historical foundation they are discussed in App. 1, together with the problem of chronology.

[3]Dunbabin, *The Western Greeks* (357–375) discuss Pythagoreanism against

the background of the history of Magna Graecia during the period. He sees Pythagorean influence as exercised through *hetaireiai* (361) or political clubs the tendency of which, in Croton as elsewhere in Magna Graecia, will have been oligarchic. He points out that these clubs are already mentioned in connection with the defeat of Sybaris in 510 B.C., though their dominance must have come only in the first half of the fifth century, and that Milo, the victorious Crotoniate leader of 510 B.C., six times an Olympic victor, was apparently an adherent of Pythagoras; his house later became the meeting-place of the club (Iambl. *VP* 249).

In the great dearth of information about the history of Magna Graecia during the period, Dunbabin (356, 486) emphasizes the importance of the incuse coins; from these he concludes that Sybaris was the dominant power from about 540 B.C., shortly after the beginning of coinage—about 550 B.C.—down to the time of her destruction in 510 B.C., and that Croton was dominant thereafter. On this coinage see App. 1.

Dunbabin (359) dates the Crotoniate disaster at the Battle of the Sagra as 540 B.C., but it is to be noted that he is dating back a decade from the presumed date of Pythagoras' arrival 530 B.C. He notes a gap in the roll of Crotoniate victors at Olympia between 548 and 532 B.C., and argues that this may reflect the city's decline after the Sagra. But it may simply reflect either casualties or a generation with no outstanding athletes. Dunbabin accepts (361) the stories of moral regeneration worked by Pythagoras, productive of a powerful state. If Pythagoras produced any such moral regeneration in an area not famed for moral rigidity his moral ascendancy must have been as great as that of Lycurgus or Solon. Dunbabin does not attempt to assess the part that religious trends may have played. It is easy to over-emphasize them. It is perhaps not without significance that Phayllos of Croton, an Olympic victor (Dunbabin 85,375), at the height of Pythagorean ascendancy, should have dedicated a stele to Zeus Meilichios.

In general Dunbabin's sober and cautious account skirts the miraculous and Pythagorean bias more successfully than does that of K. von Fritz, *Pythagorean Politics in Southern Italy*. Von Fritz deals with the political evidence cautiously (92) and his dates for political events seem acceptable. He is less cautious with doxographical evidence, arguing from it that Pythagoras and his "brotherhood" maintained a tight oligarchic control over Croton. His authorities for this thesis are Dicaearchus and Aristoxenus, both of whom are admitted to have slanted or fabricated their evidence in order to portray Pythagoras as their ideal of the sage. The monograph of E. L. Minar makes more use, and more uncritical use, of late sources.

[4]See n. 1. A role is often assigned to Alcmaeon who, though not himself a Pythagorean, is to be regarded as of the same milieu (I. Wachtler, 83–86). But we have no grounds for regarding Alcmaeon's ideas as derivative or even as very similar. Aristotle (986a 27–34) says that, like the Pythagoreans, Alcmaeon recognized a primary contrariety, but differed from them in the kind of contraries specified. Aristotle is unable, so he says (thus suspending judgment), to determine

whether the authors of the Table of Opposites derived their ideas from Alcmaeon or vice versa. The Table of Opposites is probably late fifth-century (infra 44–52, nn. 5, 7). From Aristotle's remark we can infer nothing as to the relation between Alcmaeon and Pythagoras. Ross's excision of Pythagoras's name from the passage seems to me fully justified (cf. Guthrie, 341–359).

Of the Diaspora Pythagoreans, none made contributions to thought before Archytas except Philolaus and, if we will, Eurytus.

⁵Diels (*Vors.* 18) gives all the passages relevant to Hippasus. Guthrie (320–322) discusses them cautiously. Von Fritz has an important article on the discovery of incommensurability by Hippasus of Metapontum (*Annals. Maths.* 242–264) which I have discussed in connection with the problem of incommensurability (App. 2). Von Fritz assumes the existence of Pythagorean mathematics in the fifth century, and therefore of Pythagorean mathematicians. If one makes this assumption it is not difficult to find supporting evidence. In his assessment of the mathematical evidence he sometimes assumes that because a fact was known early, the proof—and the method which that proof implies—were also known. An example of the fictional manner is van der Waerden (*Science Awakening* 106–107) on Hippasus.

⁶K. Reinhardt, *Parmenides* 229, suggests that Heraclitus, Alcmaeon, and Hippasus are thinkers between whom a relation must exist, the connecting link between Heraclitus and Hippasus being fire as the soul of microcosm and macrocosm. This notion finds expression in the doxography (*Dox. Gr.* 388) where first Parmenides and Hippasus, then Parmenides, Heraclitus, and Hippasus are said to have held that the soul was "fiery." (Iamblichus, however, in his *De Anima* (*Vors.* 18.11—Festugière, *La révélation* 3.182) says that Hippasus held it to be number.) Burnet suggests (293) that the notion of fire may be connected with the central fire of Philolaus, and that in a later Pythagorean doctrine of the elements there were features not identical with but suggesting the theory of Plato's *Timaeus*. There is, however, nothing to justify the projections of such doctrines into early Pythagoreanism, nor are we justified in assuming that for Hippasus the first principle was fire because the soul was fiery. Cherniss (312 n.82) suggests that *De Anima* 416a 9–18 refers to a theory that "the soul is fire" and to Heraclitus. Since Heraclitus and Hippasus are paired as holding that fire is the first principle it may be a doxographer's inference that for Hippasus also the soul is fire.

⁷Von Fritz in his "Mathematiker und Akusmatiker" (11 ff.) discusses the tradition that there were in the "brotherhood" two classes. The evidence he uses is almost entirely late. Iamblichus knew, and probably instituted in his own school, practices and classes of adepts such as he projects into the sixth and fifth centuries. The picture Eunapius paints of Iamblichus (*V. Soph.* Iambl.11; *ZM* 3,6.1–6) bears a marked resemblance to the picture Iamblichus paints of Pythagoras.

A. Rostagni, *Scritti Minori.* 35–56, in a discussion of the orations attributed to Pythagoras, considers the speeches as rhetoric in the manner of Gorgias and documents of that time. They are indeed exercises in rhetoric, but not fifth-century rhetoric.

[8]Philolaus is generally conceded to have been about the same age as Socrates, i.e. born 470–60 B.C. Apollordorus of Cyzicus, a Democritean, says (*D.L.* 9.38) that Democritus (born 460–57 B.C.) "associated with Philolaus," and this suggests rather a contemporary than a later generation. He had been living in Thebes before the dramatic date of the *Phaedo* (61E) but had by then already left, probably to return to Tarentum. Two apocryphal tales assume his return there: one (*D.L.* 8.85) suggests that Plato got the writings of Philolaus from a disciple of his imprisoned in Syracuse, the other (*D.L.* 3.6), that Plato visited Philolaus and Eurytus in Magna Graecia after Socrates' death. He must then have lived from 470–60 B.C. to after 399 B.C. and have been a contemporary of Socrates and Democritus, a younger contemporary of Zeno (born *ca.* 490), Empedocles (born *ca.* 485?), and Anaxagoras (born *ca.* 500?).

[9]That Philolaus did in fact publish writings there can be no doubt (*Theol. Ar.* 82.10); the fragments may ultimately derive from that book or those books (*Vors.* 44 B frs.). Diogenes Laertius (8.85), on the authority of Hermippus, mentions only one, as does Timon (*Vors.* 44 A 8=Gell. 3.17.4). The three books of *D.L.* 3.9 are not written by Philolaus but bought from him. It is worthy of note, however, that the writings reflected in the doxography are almost entirely connected with astronomy, and that the *Theologoumena Arithmetica* reflects number speculation. Neither has much in common with the fragments.

The case against the authenticity of the fragments (*Vors.* B 1–19) is well stated, in summary form, by Raven (*KR* 308–311) with reference to the principal discussions, pro and con. Thesleff (41–45) outlines the course of the controversy. The suggestion of Frank (334) that the fragments have their origin in a forgery of Speusippus' is improbable. They echo neither what we known of Speusippus' own teachings nor what we read in the *Theologoumena*. It is difficult to believe that Speusippus would have indulged in such a mystification, for which we have no known parallel. It is easy to point out inconsistencies and gross overstatement in Frank's case, as does Guthrie (332), but Cherniss observes (386) that his analysis of the fragments "makes it superfluous to restate the overwhelming case against them."

Among German philologists, however, from Boeckh onwards, there has been a hankering after the reinstatement of Philolaus; and Burkert (225–256) has now presented a strong case for considering genuine some of the fragments— B 1–7, B 13, B 17. I have attempted below to evaluate them as genuine fragments (112–117) though I cannot find wholly convincing Burkert's argument that the fragments need not stand or fall together.

[10]Plutarch (*Quaest. Conv.* 718E = *Vors.* 44 A 7a) tells us that "according to Philolaus, geometry was the fountainhead and homeland of the other sciences," because (Diels' quotation should continue) "it turns the mind away from sense perception and leads it upwards." Even if this platonizing apophthegma is genuine it does not necessarily point to mathematical pursuits. Eva Sachs (41–49) has disproved the notion that Philolaus taught the five elements and five Platonic solids. The geometrical derivation theory ascribed to him by Nicomachus (*Theol. Ar.* 74.10 = *Vors.* 44 A 12) is Platonic in its assumptions and Neopythagorean in its elaboration (Burkert 229) of the point–line–surface–

solid theory of derivation to which reference is made later in the same context
(*Theol. Ar.* 85.22). It is difficult to imagine what might properly be called
mathematical pursuits in Thebes at the time of Philolaus. His astronomical
theories are *a priori* constructs. The evidence does not suggest that he was a
mathematician.

[11]The following fragment might appear to be an exception: "There being five
solid figures, also called mathematical figures, Pythagoras asserts that earth
is formed of the cube, fire of the pyramid, air of the octahedron, water of the
icosahedron, and the sphere of the universe from the dodecahedron." (*Dox. Gr.*
334 = *Vors.* 44 A 15). This excerpt from Aëtius, in the parallel columns of
Doxographi Graeci (334) follows—both in Ps. Plutarch and in Stobaeus—a
paragraph describing the generation of the physical elements. Our excerpt merely
completes that account, which deals with Plato and not Pythagoras. The name
of Pythagoras is missing in Stobaeus, and the excerpt makes good sense without
it. As the doctrine is clearly Platonic, and could not by any stretch of the
imagination be extended to Pythagoras, Diels must be printing it here (referring
it as he does to B 12) because he intends us to infer that for Pythagoras we
should read Philolaus. But if we do not accept the Philolaus fragment as genuine
we will prefer to understand that it refers to Plato. This excerpt then does not
justify us in imputing any theory of the regular solids to Philolaus. And no more
does A 13, where Iamblichus tells us that Speusippus, in the first half of his book
on Pythagorean number, treated of the five figures that are assigned to the
cosmic elements.

We are therefore thrown back on a fragment (B 12) that we cannot consider
to be authentic. It reads: "The bodies (i.e. elements) of the sphere are five in
number: within the sphere fire, water, earth, and air, and the vehicle of the
sphere (i.e. *aither*) as fifth." This passage, which has given rise to endless debate,
is perhaps best discussed by Eva Sachs (42–48). The questions for our purposes
are: (1) When were the five Platonic figures first constructed, inscribed in the
sphere, and treated on the lines of Euclid XIII? (2) When were the five regular
solids equated with the four elements of Empedocles, plus *aither*? To these
questions Guthrie (266–273) seeks to answer that an empirical knowledge of the
figures is possible even for Pythagoras—or for Hippasus to whom it is also
attributed; and, for the second question, that the correlation with physical
elements "may have originated with Philolaus, but on that one can hardly be
positive" (273). We are not, however, interested in fore-runners or partial
anticipations of these theories, but in when the theories were advanced as
scientific ones, and advanced not as a casual aside but as a thesis integral to the
thinker's thought. So our answers to the questions, as it seems to me, must be
that the five Platonic figures were not treated as involving interrelated problems
of geometry before Theaetetus, and were not equated with the five elements
before about the time of Plato. As to the arithmological fragment B 11 see
Frank 313, n.1.

[12]J. E. Raven, *Pythagoreans and Eleatics* 101–111, makes an interesting attempt
to reconstruct Philolaus' theories as a reply to the critiques of Zeno. Ingenious
as is his interpretation of Eurytus' curious method, I cannot find it convincing.

Nor am I persuaded that Philolaus would feel himself obliged to evolve an answer to criticisms the impact of which he may not have felt. If he left Magna Graecia and settled in Thebes, not an intellectual centre, about the middle of the century, he may have known little of the debate that ensued.

I suggest that Eurytus, like Petron (Plut. *de def. or.* 422 B = *Vors.* 16 = Wehrli, *Phainias von Eresos*, fr. 12) who may have been a contemporary, derives his theories from astronomical practices and makes his number count have some "mystical" significance.

[13]The fifth-century emigrés are not to be confused with the Pythagorists who appear in the Middle Comedy in the fourth century (*Vors.* 1. 478–480). These cannot have emigrated because of political pressures, as von Fritz (*Pythagorean Politics* 92) would appear to suggest. The political pressures Dionysius II exercised were not directed against Pythagoreans, and in any case they could have taken refuge in Tarentum or in eastern Magna Graecia, where they would have been out of his reach. Why they should have emigrated to mainland Greece we do not know. They appear to have been mendicants, but whether they lived by their mendicancy and were itinerant does not appear. Some of them at least, appear to have had intellectual pretensions (*Vors.* 1, 480.11) as did some of the Cynics with whom their mode of life had much in common. If their discipline had religious aspects they do not appear to have caused scandal as did the Orpheotelestai, who sold "pardons."

In the fourth century we begin to encounter ascetic disciplines that are unlikely to be of Pythagorean, and that may be of foreign, origin. Nevertheless ascetic practices were, as we know from Aristotle, a characteristic of Pythagoreanism. These practices may have become an end in themselves, as in the case of the Franciscans, and may have led to the exaggerations which the writers of comedy found at once laughable and revolting. The phenomenon must have been fairly common (and perhaps also novel) to excite the attention of the writers of comedy.

[14]The subordinate clause in the first verse of the proem (28 B 1) ὅσον τ'ἐπὶ θυμὸς ἱκάνοι is crucial for any such interpretation as mine. Diels-Kranz translates: "soweit nur die Lust mich ankam." K. Deichgräber, *Parmenides Auffahrt zur Göttin des Rechts* (Akad. Wiss. Mainz 1958) 641, 652, translates "soweit das Verlangen jeweils gelangt." M. Untersteiner, *Parmenides—Testimonianze e Frammenti* (Florence 1958) "conforme allo slancio della mia volontà." H. Fränkel, *Wege und Formen*. 158–159: "Die Rosse, die mich bringen soweit jeweils mein Wille vordringt, anlangt." I would prefer to understand the passage as does Fränkel. It is the *desire* of the poet that motivates the journey and urges on the horses. He is not simply undertaking a journey of instruction. His *Thymos* demands to *know*.

It is worthy of note that in the allegorical interpretation of Sextus Empiricus (Math. 7. 111 = *Vors.* B 1) where the mares are irrational impulses, the maidens the senses, and so forth, the clause is omitted. It must be passed over in any such interpretation. Parmenides expresses himself figuratively. He wishes us to understand him literally: under the pressure of his own internal impulses he undertakes the voyage in spirit.

4

THE OPPOSITES

WHEN Photius in his *Bibliotheca* (1.438) tells us that Plato was the ninth and Aristotle the tenth successor of Pythagoras in the headship of the Pythagorean school he is exaggerating to the point of absurdity a tendency prevalent in the Greeks' accounts of the history of their thought. They tended to represent it as a steady, orderly progress from an early dawn to the full light of philosophical day. Even Aristotle in his doxographical excursuses, though he sometimes recognizes that the chronological is not always the logical order, nevertheless presents the thought of his predecessors as an orderly progress towards his own solutions. And the practice of Theophrastus, as it is observable in the doxography, is similar. This tendency towards system is exaggerated in the writers of *Successions*, and again in the period of syncretism. By imposing a rigorous order on the history of thought they distort its perspectives.

This distortion, serious in the history of later philosophy, is fatal to accounts of the Presocratics whose thought cannot be forced into any orderly pattern but resembles rather a series of frontal assaults on a stronghold impregnable to the means of the assailants. Parmenides began the revolution in approach. He defined his objective, and he evolved methods of attack. He initiated, if not an orderly progress, at least a dialogue in which thinkers reacted to one another's thought. After him all philosophers had to take account of the problems he raised and, in a measure, adopt his methods.

When we consider the thinkers that preceded Parmenides we cannot assume that we know the questions they were asking nor, except in a very general way, the assumptions they made in devising their answers. Their answers were disparate. Thales declared the primary *physis*, the nature or substance of the physical world, to be water; Anaximander, the Unlimited; Anaximenes, air or vapour; Pythagoras, number; Heraclitus, fire.[1] Each thinker names one *physis* not as matter or substrate of a world they conceived as a cosmos, but as a key to its understanding.

It is difficult for us to understand why these early thinkers, observing the stars in their processions, watching the changes of the seasons, observing the cycle of growth, maturity, and decay or death, seeing the changes and chances of human existence, should from such observations and reflections argue to a unity of substance in the plurality of existents and behind constant change. Centuries of habituation to the formal language of thought have rendered foreign to us their modes of thought. Nevertheless we at once recognize their idiom as essentially different from that of Parmenides. This gives us an important criterion for judging whether Pythagorean thought as represented by Aristotle is pre-Parmenidean or post-Parmenidean.

In any attempt to penetrate the thought of the early thinkers, however, an understanding of their means is as important as an understanding of their objectives. We have already pointed out that they made one important assumption—that that world was an orderly one. They made two other equally important assumptions, or, rather, they accepted as axiomatic and used two current notions, that opposites reacted to one another and that like attracted like. These two notions were not peculiar to thinkers. They were the common property of all minds. Proverbial wisdom knew that birds of a feather flock together, as surely as it recognized the opposition between day and night or hot and cold. Both notions are used by early thinkers in constructing their theories of *physis*, as part of the texture or pattern of their thought. They are not themselves formulated, but are rather a means to formulation.

The notion of likes in the sixth century extends to identity—similarity of kind or structure—similar things having an inherent tendency to form aggregations. It is a notion that is gradually clarified and formulated more precisely, but it is a simpler and less ambiguous one than that of opposites and so its apparent importance is less. We hear only occasionally and incidentally of likes.[2] Every thinker wrestled with the problem of opposites[3] and how they functioned. It was obvious that in our universe, as an inherent characteristic of its *physis*, pairs of contraries were ranged either in balance with one another, or in hostile opposition to one another, or as following one another in cyclical succession—hot and cold, war and peace, day and night. Our universe being a living one, its life was conceived as characterized by change, but change after an order or pattern in which contrary forces by their interaction produced all the variety of the visible world.

These "laws" or patterns of physical behaviour were not themselves the subject of investigation by sixth century thinkers. They were seeking for *archai*, sources or first principles that could be regarded as the key to the explanation and understanding of nature. These principles were naturally physical ones, and often physical existents such as earth, air, water, fire.[4] They were thought of as attracting their likes and interacting with their opposites. But the early thinkers saw that by subjecting one first principle to the operations of "love" and "strife" they could not produce an orderly universe or "cosmos." They attempted to escape from their dilemma in differing ways.

Anaximander (12 B 1) spoke of the elements "making reparation" to one another, and so preserving the order or balance of the universe while admitting cyclical process. He was compelled to recognize, however dimly, that there must be not only a substrate but also some form of causation. The solution of Alcmaeon of Croton (*Vors.* 24) is a similar one, but for him the cosmic forces were in *isonomia* or balance rather than in conflict. His opposites were the homely ones of the physician—wet and dry, hot and cold, bitter and sweet—and between these the balance which is health must be kept. This balance must be maintained not only for physical well-being but also in the *isonomia* of states and in the process of the cosmos.[5]

The shift from the search for *archai* to the recognition of physical law is complete with Heraclitus. He believed that our universe is one, that its unity is observable in a *logos* or formula of structure and that this universal formula is accessible to those who "use their minds."[6] "If you are a sensible, wide-awake person and will listen to me" thus we may paraphrase the famous first fragment (22 B 1) "I can explain to you the *logos* of our universe, its formula or law." The *logos* he enunciates is in substance that of contrariety. In human affairs and in the physical world the secret is to recognize the existence of inter-acting opposites and the fact of conflict. Because he made it central in his theory contrariety assumed a greater importance after Heraclitus. But he was merely making explicit the assumptions of all the natural philosophers that preceded him, and so also of Pythagorean thought. All thinkers felt themselves bound to "give an account" of the opposites. None erects them into first principles as the *physis* of our world, so creating a real dualism of first principles. As on Olympus, for all its dissensions and conflicts, there was one ruler and one only, so in Presocratic thought there is one *physis*. The importance given by Aristotle to the opposites in his account of the Pythagoreans must not mislead us into thinking that their opposites were the first principles of a dualistic cosmos. Their cosmology had to take the form of a generation in time and so the opposites, for them as for other Presocratic thinkers, had to precede their *physis*. But they preceded it as the two opposed forces the interaction of which produced its life.

Aristotle's emphasis on the Pythagorean opposites is in part due to the importance they in fact had. It is also due to the role contrariety assumed in his own system, inclining him to read back into the thought of his predecessors some anticipation of his own neat solution of the problem. But opposites were no peculiar mark of early Pythagorean thought. Indeed it would appear that they were less concerned with contrariety than other thinkers of their own time, except in one important respect. The idea of Limit/Unlimited appears to have been fundamental. From that one pair of contraries they generated both the universe and number.

In the introduction to the *Metaphysics*, Aristotle surveys the theories of his predecessors in the light of his own doctrine of the four causes. After a general discussion of the role of number in Pythagorean speculation (985b 23–986a 13) he continues (986a 13–21):

The object of our survey is to discover also in their case what first principles they posit and how they fit into the scheme of causes we have outlined. Now they too clearly consider number to be a first principle, both as material substrate for existing things and as modifications and states of these things. They consider that the elements (*stoicheia*) of number are the Odd and the Even, the former being limited and the latter unlimited. The One (unity) proceeds from both (it being both odd and even), number proceeds from unity and, as we mentioned, the whole universe is number.

In so far as it concerns number and number theory, this passage will be discussed later (pp. 76 ff.). For the present we note that it mentions a pair of opposites, Limit/Unlimited, under which is subsumed another pair, Odd/Even. Aristotle then continues 968a 22:

Other Pythagoreans say the first principles are ten, each of them a pair of opposites, arranged in a so-called Table:

Limit	Unlimited
Odd	Even
Unity	Plurality
Right	Left
Male	Female
At Rest	In Motion
Straight	Curved
Light	Darkness
Good	Evil
Square	Oblong

Aristotle goes on to say that for Alcmaeon also, pairs of contraries were first principles of "most *human* things" but that he did not define their number. As Aristotle remarks (986a 28) his theory of opposites may have influenced contemporary Pythagoreans, or they may have influenced him. But we need not conclude that there was any close similarity between the theories in their detail, or that they were meant to explain the same things.

We have then two differing Pythagorean accounts of the opposites, the first a short list—Limit/Unlimited, Odd/Even—the second a table of ten pairs. There is no necessary conflict between the lists, the one being an amplification of the other; nor, as Cherniss remarks (225, n. 35), are Aristotle's conclusions (986b 4–8) affected by an expansion of the table so long as the basic Pythagorean opposition of Limit/Unlimited and Odd/Even is respected. Zeller (*ZM* 1, 2, 452, n. 2) suggests that the varying amplifications of which we have knowledge were inevitable developments. Simplicius (*in Arist. Phys.* 429.7) knows of several such amplifications. The way in which Aristotle introduces the longer list—"others of these same Pythagoreans"—suggests that he is here speaking of a group within a larger body, and perhaps of a single person, as he sometimes uses the indefinite plural for the singular. The list itself exhibits no logical sequence nor structure. We have first the primary oppositions (pairs 1 and 2). There follow unity and plurality (3), four pairs that may be cosmological (4–8), an ethical pair (9), and a geometrical pair (10). The table would appear to have been padded out to the perfect number of the *tetractys*. It is significant because of the ethical character that has been given to contrariety, all those subsumed under Limit having an obviously "good" colouring, those under Unlimited "bad." That the opposites were so interpreted in the Pythagoreanism of the fourth century we need not doubt. It is improbable that the original pairs were all so qualified.

In the *Nicomachean Ethics* Aristotle makes two further incidental references to a Pythagorean Table of Opposites (*E.N.* 1096a 3–b 7):

It might be asked what they mean by a "thing itself." The definition of "man itself" and "man" is one and the same, that of man. In respect of man they do not differ. It follows that there will be no difference between "good itself" (*autagathon*) and good. Nor will the "good itself" be more good if it is eternal. Long-lasting whiteness is no whiter than shortlived whiteness. The thesis of the Pythagoreans is more plausible. They place the One in the column of goods of their table. Speusippus appears to have followed them here.[7]

Aristotle's concise reference here is somewhat obscure. He is arguing against the Theory of Ideas and against the primacy of the *autagathon*. The Good, he says, should not be identified with Unity and Being. It is better ranged under Limit in the "good" half of the Pythagorean Table of Opposites, not necessarily as an attribute of Limit but as a first principle posterior to Limit and Unity. Such was the solution of Speusippus (1091a 33–34) and of the Pythagoreans (1072b 31). Aristotle is not accepting their solutions, but he is saying that they are preferable to Plato's theory that the Idea of the Good is prior to all other ideas. Aristotle appears to have conflated two notions: that the table exhibits a good/evil tabulation of opposites, all the terms in the left-hand column being essentially good; and that the Good, though a first principle, is subsumed under the primary principle, Limit, and so is posterior to it if not in time, as it was for Speusippus, then in hierarchical order. From Limit/Unlimited and Odd/Even come numbers as physical existents, and with these or subsequent to them come Good/Evil not only as predicates of the opposites in their respective columns but as designating things to be sought or shunned.

This same Table of Opposites, or some variation of it (for we need not suppose it to be canonical except for the first two pairs), is again alluded to in the *Ethics* (*E.N.* 1106b 27–30):

So virtue is a sort of mean, aiming as it does at the median position (between two extremes). Further, one can miss this mark in many ways. For Evil is in the column of the Unlimited in the Table of Opposites, according to the theory of the Pythagoreans, whereas Good is in the column of Limit. But you can hit your mark in one way only.

In Aristotle's own ethical theory the aim of ethical conduct is presented as some one point that is median, but not necessarily the middle, in the whole locus or area lying between contraries. These contraries are not Good and Evil but the excess and defect of ethical qualities such as extravagance and niggardliness. He is here suggesting that it comes to the same thing if we regard the ethical quality at which we aim as a Limit, and both excess and defect as unlimited. He is not implying that this is Pythagorean ethical theory, but only that their Table of Opposites could be interpreted in this sense.[8]

In these two passages of the *Ethics* Aristotle appears to be using the Pythagorean Table of Opposites for his own dialectical purposes. He does not profess to be expounding Pythagorean doctrine, but merely alludes to it for incidental confirmation of his own theories. We conclude that the Table had sufficient currency in Aristotle's immediate circle to make the allusion intelligible, and that whatever the precise nature of the Table, Limit/Unlimited remained the primary pair.

In regard to the Pythagorean opposites therefore, and their Table we may conclude that Limit/Unlimited is the primary pair and that under it is subsumed Odd/Even, Odd corresponding to Limit and Even to Unlimited. As Odd/Even pertains rather to number theory than to the basic opposites we shall consider for the present only Limit/ Unlimited, the primary pair in Aristotle's account.[9] What he himself understands by Limit emerges from his definition of *peras* (1022a 4–13) as (1) the limit or boundary of a given thing, (2) its form or figure (*eidos*), (3) its extreme limits—*terminus ad quem* or *a quo*, (4) its essence or being. Aristotle adds that it has as many meanings as *arche* (first principle) with which it is often synonymous. Of the meanings here given, form or figure (*eidos*) suggests the Pythagorean term *chroia*,[10] and *chroia* appears to be equated with *peras* in one of Aristotle's few discussions of Pythagorean cosmology (1091a 12–18):

It is absurd and indeed impossible to erect a theory ascribing coming-to-be (*genesis*) to eternal things. Yet without a doubt the Pythagoreans do so. They say that when the One has come into existence, by being put together from plane surfaces or surface limits (*chroia*) or seeds or some unspecified constituent, at once Limit draws in to itself and limits the nearest parts of the Unlimited.

This theory that Aristotle summarily dismisses is a cosmological one, and as such not immediately relevant to our inquiry into the nature of the primary opposition. What we may note is that Limit is conceived of as an active force operating on (a passive) Unlimited to produce the One, our physical world (*supra* 47). Then, the One having come to be, Limit persists in its active role, drawing in to itself the nearest part of the Unlimited, elsewhere (1048b 10) equated with the Void. At the same time, under the guise of *chroia*, Limit has the further role of surface or limit of things. It is at once a cosmological first principle, a principle creating discrete quantities (Burnet *EGP* 108) and the exterior surface of these quantities. So though Limit/Unlimited is not the Pythagorean *arche* in the sense of being the *physis* towards the knowledge of which their inquiry is directed, it is in another very real sense a first principle as productive of that *physis*.

In summarizing his review of his predecessors' theories Aristotle concludes that all of them recognized one or more material causes, and some few an efficient cause or cause of motion. He continues (987a 10):

Up to but not including the Pythagoreans of Magna Graecia (οἱ Ἰταλικοί) doctrines of cause were rather obscure. . . . The Pythagoreans, though they also recognized two causes, made this significant addition peculiar to themselves that they held the Limited and the Unlimited not to be constituted of some other thing like fire or earth or another such (element); but that the Unlimited itself and the One itself were the substance of the things of which they are predicated, and consequently that number was the substance of all existing things. This, in general lines, was their teaching as to (material) cause. They also initiated discussion and definition of essence, but their method was excessively simple, and they defined superficially. They used to consider as essence of a thing that term of which it is primarily predicated, (which is) like considering dyad and "double" to be the same because "double" is a primary predicate of two. But "double" and "dyad" cannot be identical in essence or unity will be a plurality, as was a consequence in their case. . . . [11] After the system mentioned came Plato's, which followed for the most part the same lines as the Pythagoreans' but had characteristics of its own.

Here Aristotle is forcing Pythagorean doctrine into the pattern of his own four causes. In labelling as material cause everything that constituted, or contributed to the constitution of their universe, he is guilty of over-simplification. When he interprets their equation of things or concepts with numbers as an anticipation of definition of essence, he is being arbitrary. But what is important for our present purpose is what he has to say of their material cause. He says that (15–16) Limited (*peperasmenon*—that which has been limited) and Unlimited, a pair that has no other "matter" constituting it is the Pythagorean material cause. But immediately thereafter (18) the pair is referred to as the One and the Unlimited. So "that which has been limited" is the One.

Earlier (986a 17–21) when the procession of Pythagorean *archai* was described, the following order emerged:

Limit—Unlimited
Odd (Limited)—Even (Unlimited)
The One (even-odd)
Numbers that are things

In the present passage the One (as limited) is paired with the Unlimited. We infer that Aristotle distinguished between the primary cosmological opposites *peras* and *apeiron* and the opposites that are material cause in our physical world. These latter are the One as product of the primary opposites and the Unlimited or Void. This void is external to the One and is breathed in to "delimit the *physis*" of number (*Phys.* 213b 22–29). These two are the material cause of our world and there is no other "matter" such as fire or earth. So the primary contrariety, Limit/Unlimited, appears in three roles. In its cosmogonical role the interaction of these contraries produces the physical world. In its physical role they are the material cause of our world. In its quantifying role, they are the existents of our world and the space separating them.

Let us attempt to sum up what Aristotle tells us of the Pythagorean opposites. In the first place he tells us that the notion of opposites was not peculiar to the Pythagoreans, but was characteristic of all his predecessors. "For they all, even when they assumed them without due process of reasoning, nevertheless taught that the elements[12] and what they called first principles were opposites, as if under the compulsion of the truth itself." (*Phys.* 188b 27–30, n. 12).

In Aristotle's own thought there are four causes, or conditions necessary for the existence of things and necessary for our knowledge of them. His contraries are adjectival to the substance in which they inhere. He thought that all his predecessors had been groping towards some such formulation, and that the Pythagoreans had approximated it more closely than some. Their basic opposition can be construed as adjectival of the One. But Aristotle has not contented himself with giving us only such details as fit in with his own theory. In general lines what he tells us is as follows:

1. For the Pythagoreans the primary opposition is Limit/Unlimited. This pair of opposites is a presupposition of our world. It characterizes our world as inherent in the One, which is even-odd. Within our world it delimits number things.

2. Under Limit/Unlimited is subsumed Odd/Even, and at least in some aspects or functions the two pairs of contraries are identical. The role of Odd/Even is to mediate the production of numbers—that is, of things.

3. At some unspecified date (it would appear to have been as a subsequent development), to the primary opposites were added other pairs up to the number of ten. There were several lists, no one of which was canonical. These expanded lists had ethical connotations, the Limit/Odd column being good and the Unlimited/Even column being bad. This does not imply a good and evil dualism in the cosmos, but rather a classification of goods to be pursued and evils to be shunned. Aristotle regards the two primary pairs as the basic Pythagorean opposites, and there is no suggestion that they may have been ethically qualified. The Table of Opposites he regards as an expanded list attributable to "others of these same Pythagoreans."

4. The opposites are present in our world as an existing order in two ways. They are present in the One as limited and in the surrounding void as unlimited. And the One itself is a product of Limit/Odd and Unlimited/Even. From the One proceed the numbers that are the

existents of the physical world. They are discrete quantities as separated by the Unlimited breathed in to this end from the surrounding void.

How credible is the Aristotelian report? That *peras/apeiron* is the basic contrariety we need not doubt. If we question the further developments of that fundamental notion we must nevertheless concede them probability. It may be further urged that there is no conflict with the *peras/apeiron* theme as developed in the *Philebus*, nor with the theory vaguely outlined in the Philolaus fragment (*infra* 112–117). Nor is there any Platonic contamination of One and indefinite dyad, or of point, line, surface, solid. These however are negative arguments, of use only to buttress a conviction that, unless we can bring a good case against one or several aspects of his report, Aristotle is our best and most credible witness.

A major difficulty of interpretation remains. Who are the Pythagoreans of whom Aristotle speaks? When he speaks of "the Platonists" we know by and large what he means, even if we are still disputing whether and up to what period Aristotle included himself among them, and if members of the Academy who did not subscribe to the Theory of Ideas are to be considered Platonists. Likewise when he speaks of "the Eleatics" we understand his reference. In both cases he is referring to a recognized master whose doctrines are known, and to contemporaries, of whose doctrines we assume him to be informed.

Our immediate object is to establish the nature of Aristotle's report on the Pythagoreans. Our final object is to situate this account in the perspective of the history of thought, and we ask: "Who were these Pythagoreans of whom Aristotle speaks?" We suggested earlier that he may have reference to doctrines of Pythagoras himself. Our consideration of the Pythagorean opposites suggests that that doctrine too must have an early origin.

NOTES

[1]Burnet *Early Greek Philosophy* 10–12, and app. 363–4 discusses the meaning of *physis*, concluding that it means *stuff* or *primary substance* and denying that in origin it can have meant *growth*. D. Holwerda, *Commentatio de vocis quae est physis vi atque usu* (Groningen 1955), in an exhaustive study of the uses of the word, concludes that its primary sense is *being*, whereas Kahn 201 n. 2 argues that the primary sense is *growth*. Aristotle, in defining the term *physis* (1014b

16) seeks to give *growth* as an original meaning on the strength of a long upsilon. The quantity of the vowel is variable, Chantraine (*Gramm. Hom*². [Paris 1948] 1.372) suggests for metrical convenience. The word had acquired such programmatic importance for sixth-century thought that it meant in part what each thinker made it mean, but the meaning certainly included the idea of *primary substance*, usually of a primary substance that *had come to be.*

²The notion of "likes" is clearly expressed in the epic, but the notion of opposition is formulated only later. The prepositional ἄντι which appears in the Latin *ante* as meaning "before" in time or place or importance, has little or nothing of this meaning in the epic. What would appear to be its original Greek sense of "over against" or "face to face" is to be seen in the adverbial forms ἄντα, ἄναντα, ἐς ἄντα (Chantraine, *Gramm. Hom*.² 91–92, 148). A man cannot ἄντα μάχεσθαι (*Il.* 19.163), (in the sense of fighting face to face) all day long without food. Opposing forces face one another—ἐναντίοι ἔσταν Ἀχαιῶν (*Il.* 5.497). The confrontation is not necessarily hostile. Patroclus sits in silence facing Achilles οἷος ἐναντίος ἧστο (*Il.* 9, 190), as in Sappho (2, 2), the lover sits facing his love ἐναντίος τοι ἰσδάνει. The prepositional ἄντι occurs in Homer only ten times, whereas the adjectival forms occur over a hundred times, ἄντιος being about twice as frequent as ἐναντίος. It is therefore well on the way to establishing itself as a predicate expressing confrontation, often hostile; but as a term having a technical sense we meet it first in Parmenides (*Vors.* Wortindex; 28 B 8.55). It is used of his opposites, fire and night, occurring in the form τἀντία and adverbially. This does not mean that the notion of contrariety was not present earlier, but it seems probable that it was not an explicit notion before Heraclitus.

Plato (*Lysis* 215c) refers to the passage in Hesiod (*Op.* 11–26) in praise of emulation, where potter is said to vie with potter, etc. and points out that it implies a contradiction of the principle of like to like. Plato's use in the *Lysis* of the notion of likes and opposites is meant as paradox. The word ἐναντίος as well as the popular notion had the precise connotations Aristotle defines (Bonitz, *Index*).

Kahn, 126–133, discusses the opposites, especially in the Hippocratic treatises. He is particularly interested in their role as *dynameis* (τῶν γὰρ ἐναντίων τὰ ἐναντία ποιητικά. Arist. *Pol.* 1307 b29) in the qualitative explanations of *physis* characteristic of Ionian thought, explanations that culminate in Aristotle's *De Generatione*. I have attempted to suggest that the applications of the notion are much wider, and that its origins are popular. Festugière, *L'ancienne médecine* xxiii–xxvi, has pointed out the protest in that treatise against the adoption of physical theories in medicine. The theories resulting from this adoption were built on four elements and usually four opposites. H. Fränkel, *Dichtung und Philosophie* 603–605, surveys the widespread uses of the notion of contrariety in early Greek thought, reviewing its occurrences in the poets as well as the thinkers of the archaic period; its recognition in life and the experience of the person, as well as in the constitution and events of the physical world. He discusses its special functions in Pythagorean thought (314–318).

³Opposites play a major part in Aristotle's report of Pythagorean doctrine.

The notion of "like to like" though not equally stressed by Aristotle is of equal importance for Presocratic thought. It is less clearly defined. Some ambiguity is inherent in the origin of the word. Boisacq *s.v.*-skr. *samah*, εἰς (Gort. ἕνs) ἅμα *simul semper*, ὁμός, ὅμαλος, ὅμοιος *similis*. For the variant ὁμοῖῖος Chantraine (1.168). ὁμός in the epic has the sense of "joint," "shared," "common" (Lat. *communis*). Zeus and Poseidon were of ὁμὸν γένος ἠδ' 'ιὰ πάτρη (*Il.* 13.354). That sense is obvious in ὁμογάστριος (*Il.* 21.95; 24.47). But already in the epic ὁ αὐτός begins to be used for identity (Monro, *Hom. Gramm.* sec. 252), and thereafter ὁμός falls into disuse except in compounds. So in the epic we have the beginning of a differentiation between identity and similarity.

ὅμοιος can be used in the epic as a synonym for ὁ αὐτός, but by far its most common use is to institute a comparison and declare things or persons to share a common characteristic in virtue of which they are declared to be "like." Even the notion of the attraction of likes is already present in the *Odyssey* (17.217):

νῦν μὲν δὴ μάλα πάγχυ κακός κακόν ἠγηλάζει
ὡς αἰεὶ τὸν ὁμοῖον ἄγει θεὸς ὡς τὸν ὁμοῖον

It is worthy of note that in the epic ἴσος can be used as a synonym for ὅμοιος (*Il.* 1.187; 23.632). Thales is said to have called equal angles ὁμοίαι (*Vors.* 1.486, 36–45) and this usage is to be found in Euclid (3. def. 1, 6. def. 11, etc.).

The notion of *Homoiai* is an important one throughout Greek thought. Aristotle defines his acceptance 1054b 3–13. For the role of likes and opposites in perception Theophr. *De Sens.* 1 ff. = *Dox. Gr.* 499.

[4]Kahn, 119–126 and 134–159, has a discussion of the elements that is a valuable addition to Diels' basic study *Elementum* (Leipzig 1899). It is noteworthy that the Table of Opposites given by Aristotle (986a 22–26), even in the expanded form, does not include any of the four elements of Empedocles or the basic Ionian opposites hot-cold, dry-moist. The Pythagoreans seem to have adhered to their quantitative explanation of the *physis* and to have had no doctrine of the elements peculiar to them, as Aristotle remarks (990a 16–18). This may be taken to suggest that their scheme was pre-Empedoclean.

[5]J. Wachtler, 76–82, discusses the relevant fragment (*Vors.* 24 B 4). Wachtler argues that Alcmaeon was first and foremost a physician, that the Crotoniate medical school had made the city famous for its practitioners before the coming of Pythagoras, and that (88–89) Alcmaeon is not to be considered a Pythagorean, pointing out that *Metaph.* 986a 27 implies that he was not, and in support adducing Simplicius (*in de An.* 32.3–14) who uses the same argument. Alcmaeon's opposites are clearly physiological and qualitative. It does not necessarily follow that Alcmaeon was anti-Pythagorean or that he had no contacts with Pythagoreans. To draw such a conclusion one must assume that Pythagoras was the dominant figure in Croton and that anyone not with him was against him.

[6]Frs. 1, 114, 2. Kirk, 49, following Gigon, *Untersuchungen zu Heraklit* (Leipzig 1935) 11, arranges the fragments in this order. The pun ξυνόν-ξυν νόῳ makes it abundantly clear that the *logos* is accessible to *nous*. One is tempted to suggest that the *logos* (of commonsense) of Heraclitus is a reaction from a preceding mathematical *logos*, a number formula (Anaximander, Pythagoras), but there is

no evidence for an early Pythagorean *logos* doctrine. W. Bröcker, *Hermes* 84.3 [1956] 382–384, argues that Heraclitus B 126 is a part of Anaximander B1, because (a) it implies for Heraclitus a four-element doctrine (in contradiction with Heraclitus B 36 and B 76) and (b) a four-element doctrine is ascribed to Anaximander by Simplicius (*Physics* 24.13 = *Vors.* 12 A 9 and *Physics* 154.14 = *Vors.* 12 A 9a). Certainly it is difficult to fit the elements into Heraclitus' theory of opposites.

[7]Burnet, *Nicomachean Ethics* (London 1900) *ad loc.*, refers this passage to the συστοιχία of *Metaph.* 986a 22 and to 1072b 30 where it is suggested that the Good is posterior to the first principles and also better. Gauthier-Jolif, *L'Éthique à Nicomaque* (Louvain 1959) *ad loc.*, makes reference to all the passages in which Aristotle discusses the doctrines of the Good of the Pythagoreans and of Speusippus, pointing out that in the *Metaphysics* he criticizes these doctrines in other respects but that here he limits himself to recognizing a merit of their theories. Burkert 45–46 interprets the Table as bridging a fourth-century gap between Pythagoreanism and Platonism.

Ross in his comment on 986a 22, referring to other Pythagorean lists of opposites, reasonably suggests that "this precise list is of no special importance, but probably it acquired a certain vogue among the Pythagoreans owing to its recognizing just *ten* pairs of contraries." The fact that no list acquired canonical status, in Aristotle's time or later, suggests to me that the table developed late, and that it is only because we see "primitive" elements in it that we are inclined to think it early. It has already been noted that Zeller (ZN[6] 1.460) suggests attribution to Philolaus. See Mondolfo's note ZM 2.450–452.

Plutarch, *De Iside* 370E (or his source) has made an obvious effort to rationalize, and platonize, the table. He subsumes the other nine pairs under ἀγαθόν/κακόν, followed by unity/duality (dyad) and limit/unlimited. Plutarch has ten pairs, but as Ross *ad loc.* has noted, other lists had less than ten and the late list of Porphyry (*VP* 38) which is headed by monad/dyad, had only six.

Frank (254–255) has suggested that Aristotle took over the Table of Opposites from Speusippus, its author. This suggestion, as Cherniss (390–391) has remarked, is untenable. Aristotle can and does distinguish clearly between the doctrines of the Pythagoreans and those of Speusippus (1080b 11–18).

It has been argued by Raven, 39–41, that the pair light/darkness suggest the poem of Parmenides. Raven argues ingeniously, on the lines of Cornford, that Parmenides is rejecting a Pythagorean cosmogony with which he is familiar. This is in itself likely enough, but difficulties arise when we attempt to infer from Parmenides the nature of the cosmogony against which he is reacting. In particular, as regards light/darkness, it seems just as probable, if not more so, that some Pythagorean living after Parmenides (say Philolaus) included in a table of opposites the typical Parmenidean contrariety light/night in the form light/darkness.

Good/evil is included as the ninth pair. Its position in the list is not of much significance. The important fact is that limit is the first good principle, and the good is not identified with, nor found in close proximity to, the One or unity. This would make the table congenial to Speusippus, who argued that the good was the product of evolution rather than its cause (1072b 30–1073a 3 and 1092a 11–15). Aristotle tells us that Speusippus followed the Pythagoreans in placing the One in the column of goods, rather than making a One Good the first principle for all subsequent goods.

All that can be safely concluded is that there were some Pythagoreans of indeterminate epoch who had arranged pairs of opposites in a table of ten pairs. Their primary pairs were the pairs Aristotle elsewhere calls, simply, Pythagorean. The rest of the list would appear to have been drawn up, perhaps in the last half of the fifth century, by some person or persons of Pythagorean persuasion of an eclectic rather than systematic tendency. These persons took account of contemporary controversy but did not include the typical Milesian opposites nor those of Empedocles. The tendency of the compilers was obviously an ethical one. It seems unlikely that Aristotle was deceived as to the provenience of the table, which could well have been the invention of Philolaus or of the group at Phlius.

⁸Gauthier-Jolif *ad loc.* (2.1, 142–146) discuss at length Greek ideas of ἀρετή and of μεσότης as they influenced both philosophy and medicine. They reasonably suggest that "le Pythagorisme introduit dans le mathématique la notion de mesure, et c'est sans doute dans la théorie pythagoriciènne des proportions qu'apparait pour la première fois le terme même de mésotès." This may be true of the term and of the sense in which Aristotle uses it, but there are no grounds for suggesting that the Pythagoreans made the application of the term *mesotes*, with its precise meaning in a theory of proportion, to ethical opposites, thus anticipating Aristotle. It is more probable that they regarded the whole area of conduct as one of conflict between good and evil, and that *harmonia* was their ethical aim. If they used an ethical term it is probable that for them, as for most Greeks, it would have been "moderation."

⁹Zeller (ZM 1.2, 449–453, 485) considers Odd/Even to be the primary pair or at least to be indistinguishable from Limit/Unlimited and more important in the sense that from Odd/Even proceed the numbers. Ross (*ad* 986a 18) disagrees and remarks that Zeller "does not do justice to the ethical element in Pythagoreanism." But we have seen reason to believe that the primary opposites were not ethically coloured before they found a place in a Table of Opposites. Zeller, however, is interpreting 986a 15–21 arbitrarily because he believes that the numerical aspect of Pythagorean theory must be primary also in the first principles, and that therefore Odd/Even must be primary. But Aristotle says (986a 18–19) that the *stoicheia* of Odd/Even are Limited/Unlimited.

At 1004b 27–33 Aristotle remarks, in a passage that is quoted in support of the primacy of Odd/Even: "In each instance of contrariety one of the two contraries is a privative, and all contraries can be referred to Being/None-being, One/Many. For instance, Rest is subsumed under One, Motion under Many. Almost all thinkers agree that existing things and Being consist of contraries, some stating these contraries to be Odd/Even, others Hot/Cold or Limit/Un-limited or Friendship/Strife." Alexander (262, 4–5) identifies as Pythagoreans those holding the primary opposites to be Odd/Even. Those who hold them to be Limit/Unlimited "would be those who posit the One and the Indefinite Dyad as first principles," i.e. Plato. Ross in his commentary follows Alexander in this. But Alexander's is a cautious assertion, arrived at by elimination. He assumes that each pair is characteristic of one thinker. If he ascribes Limit/Unlimited to the Pythagoreans he is left with Odd/Even for Plato and the Early Academy. But Aristotle is not interested in the equation of pairs with philosophers, only with contraries (one of them being a privative) as first principles.

That the Pythagorean primary pair is Limit/Unlimited is all but explicitly stated in the *Philebus* 16c-d where Plato, alluding to Pythagoras, speaks of the Prometheus who brought from the gods the revelation that things have in their nature a conjunction of Limit and Unlimited. Hackforth, *Plato's Examination of Pleasure* 21, accepts this identification. Stenzel, *Studien zur Entwicklung der Plat. Dialektik*[3] (Stuttgart 1961) 101, remarks that the mention of the Pythagorean primary pair is enough for readers to identify the person referred to.

Ross (*ad* 986a 18) discusses how Odd/Even could be subsumed under Limit/Unlimited. The explanations of ancient commentators which he cites seem to me to have a Neopythagorean colouring. Euclid (*El.* 7.1) in a book that is generally conceded to be Pythagorean-inspired writes: "An even number is one that is divisible into two equal parts; the addition of a unit closes it again," Here even numbers are seen as closed and so limited by the addition of an odd number, such an addition making them odd.

[10]As Ross remarks on *De Sensu* 439a 30, the original meaning of χροιά is skin. By it the Pythagoreans meant surface, and were not identifying surface and colour, colour being a later meaning of the word. Cf. 1028b 16.

[11]There are two major difficulties in this passage. Is μέχρι (9) to be understood in a temporal sense? The preposition need not imply time (*LSJ*) and, as Alexander 46, 7–12 points out, to so understand it would make nonsense of the order followed in the preceding discussion. We must understand Aristotle to imply that the Pythagoreans are a terminus of his discussion as immediately preceding Plato.

As to Pythagorean definition, Aristotle must be referring to such definitions as are mentioned 985b 29–32, where justice, the soul, *nous*, opportunity are equated with numbers. It is questionable whether the Pythagoreans felt that they were defining, or that the number was the essence of the thing. Aristotle cites dyad and double as his example. It is understandable that two might be thought to be the essence of twofold, and a relation does exist between them. But how can "two" be the essence of infinity, birth, growth, etc. all at the same time. (*Theol. Ar.* 89). If this is what Aristotle refers to it could certainly be seen as making a plurality of a unity (the dyad). But the allusion is elliptical, and Alexander, too, is puzzled. He offers the above explanation (which Ross accepts because Aristotle speaks of a first or primary predicate). His alternative explanation is that if, e.g., friendship is equal times equal, it need not be 4, but can be cube numbers to infinity.

The only reason for Aristotle introducing here, in the context of a discussion of causes, an allusion to Pythagorean definition is (as Ross *ad loc.* suggests) that the Pythagorean definition implies a recognition of a formal cause of sorts, and that therefore they may be said to recognize *two* causes material and formal (987a 13).

There is another allusion to Pythagorean definition, 1078b 21-23, where it appears that they are said to define because they ask "What is X?"

[12]Diels, *Elementum* is the classic discussion of the use of the term *stoicheion—elementum*. His conclusion is that though Heraclitus knows the opposites hot/cold and wet/dry which are basic to the four-element theory of Empedocles (Diels 15) it was Plato who fixed the terminological use of στοιχεῖον (36) and Aristotle who applied it to the Empedoclean elements (34). This Aristotelian use became so authoritative that the Epicureans never used the term for their atoms.

Diels finds the etymological origin of the word in the military στοῖχος, file or row, from which—somewhere in the fifth century—the term στοιχεῖα was derived as denoting (a) the series of letters in the alphabet and (b) a rough device for measuring time by your own shadow. It was from the first of these two uses that Plato took the term and the analogy he uses so frequently in the dialogues.

Diels' account of the uses of the term and of developments in application and meaning has remained authoritative, but his etymology has encountered question. Recently W. Burkert (*Philologus*, 103 [1959] 167-197) has queried it on the grounds that the letters of the alphabet are a series of which each letter is a member, as soldiers in a file are members of that fighting group. But the transfer of a term applicable to such a series to the four physical elements is not easily explainable. He argues that there must be some other use, of which both are derivatives, and which had a meaning such as "base" or "basis" (168). He finds such a use in the *stoicheia* of mathematics (193) and suggests that the term was first used by Hippocrates of Chios in the second half of the fifth century. Its use, he maintains, was extended to the letters of the alphabet in the process of developing musical theory. It may be urged against Burkert's thesis that (1) Plato, for all his interest in mathematics, never in his many uses of the term shows any awareness of such a mathematical background (see esp. *Tim.* 48B), and that (2) the connection of military row or file with the Elements of Euclid seems more tortuous than the way from file to letters of the alphabet.

For our purposes we note that the notion of physical elements gains currency with Empedocles, and that the term στοιχεῖα is applied to them soon thereafter, certainly not later than the Platonic use. Now Aristotle, though he says that the στοιχεῖα of number are the στοιχεῖα of all existents (986 a 1), in reporting on Pythagorean first principles almost always uses the term ἀρχή, which according to Theophrastus (*Dox. Gr.* 476.4) is Anaximander's term. If the Pythagoreans alone of Greek thinkers of the fourth century held non-elemental and non-material entities to be first principles, then either there was among them a thinker of great independence of mind who took a line differing from, and not related to, that of all his contemporaries or (which is infinitely more probable) the Pythagoreans were conservative in their doctrines and preserved as their own a pre-Parmenidean, pre-Empedoclean theory that must have had its origin with Pythagoras himself.

5

PYTHAGOREAN COSMOLOGY

IN his discussion of the thought of his predecessors in the *Metaphysics* Aristotle finds them all to have anticipated in some measure his own doctrine of the four causes, "as if under the compulsion of the truth itself." But when, in the *Physics*, he comes to consider how they applied their principles in explaining the physical world, he finds their explanations defective. For him, natural process is to be explained, not by any one cause alone, but by a combination of causes, these being the necessary conditions of change. And change occurs not simply by the interaction of contraries, as the Presocratics sometimes supposed, but by the passage from privation to form in a material substrate. "By reason of inexperience they left the path" by which alone physical problems can be solved.

In the introduction to the *Physics* Aristotle gives all his predecessors short shrift; he glances at Plato only once and mentions the Pythagoreans not at all. For him they are not physical philosophers. In the case of the Pythagoreans this is partly because he discovers in their thought a confusion of the metaphysical and the physical (989b 29–990a 8). But there are other reasons why he should be, if not a hostile, at least a critical, witness. In the first place the Pythagoreans set out to explain how the world came to be (for "there is no doubt they generate it" (989b 34; 1091a 13)) not as a *creatio ex nihilo* but as an evolution from some indeterminate state to its present form. Aristotle rejects this approach and everything that smacks of cosmogony. Then, the Pythagorean opposites entail a void outside the universe. Aristotle rejects the notion of a void and of infinite spatial extension. He further rejects the mathematical approach (implicit already in the Pythagorean first principles) to the study of the physical world. So what he has to say of Pythagorean cosmology and physical doctrine consists largely in incidental remarks in other contexts. These, however, fill out the hints given in the discussion of first causes and provide an account which, though far from being as complete as we would wish, is remarkably consistent.

Aristotle's account of Pythagoreanism implies three phases in their description of the physical world: first pre-existing opposites, then the constitution of a cosmos and finally a universe (unlike our own, says Aristotle) in operation. It need not surprise us that these phases appear to occur in time. For Hesiod first of all there was Chaos and then Earth. Throughout antiquity it was disputed whether for Plato in the *Timaeus* the universe had a beginning in time. In the centuries between Hesiod and Plato cosmologies usually attempted to explain the nature of the world by the device of a sequence in time. The Pythagoreans were no exception in this. *Peras* and *apeiron* as their primordial first principles had subsumed under them respectively oddness and evenness, qualities in virtue of which the primary opposites were enabled to produce a number-determined One (986a 18–21). This One the product of the imposition of Limit on the Unlimited, did not use up the Unlimited, some of which remained outside the cosmos as a void, which the One breathed it in to fill the space between things.

It was the third phase that most puzzled Aristotle (and puzzles us). From the One, which is both odd and even, proceed numbers. These numbers are physical existents (987b 28). They are at once cause and substrate, modifications and states in the things that exist (986a 17). There is no other substance nor substrate, and there is no division of sensible and non-sensible existents. Everything is number. There are particulars within our cosmos only because of quantitative differences and because there is a void which separates entities one from another.

It is obvious that this scheme is not congenial, nor even really understandable, to Aristotle. Its features, as known to him, emerge chiefly in his criticisms. In the first book of the *Metaphysics*, having reviewed first principles in Presocratic thought, he proceeds to criticize. He disposes rather summarily of the other Presocratics, and then goes on to say (989b 21–990a 32):

The thinkers I have mentioned [i.e. the physical philosophers] are at home only in discussions of generation, destruction and movement. Their inquiry is directed almost entirely to the causes and first principles of that sort of substance. But such thinkers as extend their inquiry to all existents, both sensibles and nonsensibles, obviously investigate both kinds. So we must consider carefully in their case what contribution they make to the inquiry on which we have embarked and where they are in error.

The first principles and elements of the Pythagoreans are more out-of-the-way than those of the physical philosophers because they took them from nonsensibles, *mathematica* not being in motion except in astronomy. Yet all their discussions and systematic inquiries are about nature (*physis*). They explain the genesis of the universe. They observe its parts, its changes, its events; and to this end they expend their first principles and causes, as if they agreed with the physical philosophers that what *is* is just the sensible and is included within what we call the universe. Their causes and first principles, as we remarked already, would permit of them going on to the investigation of the higher kind of existent and are better fitted for that than for the discussion of nature.

They fail to explain to us how, if they assume only Limit/Unlimited and Odd/Even, motion is to occur, and how, without motion and change, generation and destruction can take place and the movements of the heavenly bodies. Further, even if one were to grant them that spatial magnitude proceeds from these first principles, or if this were proven, how would some bodies be light, others heavy? For to judge by their assumptions and explanations, what they say applies equally to mathematicals and sensibles. The reason why they have nothing to say of fire or earth or such (physical) bodies is, I suppose, that none of their teachings is peculiarly applicable to sensibles.

Further, how are we to understand the thesis that number and the modifications of number are the causes of the things that come to be and are in the universe, both in the beginning and at the present, and yet that there exists no number other than the number out of which the universe was framed? In one part they situate opinion and opportunity, then a little closer to or farther from the centre of the universe injustice and decision or mixture. They allege as a proof that each of these is a number, but it so happens that there are already in this place many composite magnitudes, because such modifications of number occur in each and every region. Are we to take it that this self-same number which constitutes things in the physical universe also constitutes the things mentioned? Or is it not this but some other number? Plato says it is another number. He too considers physical magnitudes and their causes to be numbers, but he considers the magnitudes to be perceptible, and the intelligible numbers to be causes.[1]

In this resumptive passage Aristotle makes the following criticisms of Pythagoreanism:

(1) the Pythagoreans generate sensibles from non-sensible first principles. If at the time their theory was evolved a distinction had already been drawn between sensibles and non-sensibles it is evident that the Pythagoreans could not have maintained that from Limit/Unlimited proceed numbers that are things. Their theory would have had to be modified. In its primitive form it must be early.

(2) the Pythagoreans give no explanation of motion and change. Here again we must assume the theory to be an early one. Early thinkers assume that the world is living and of itself a cause of motion and change.

(3) Pythagorean para-mathematical theories are unsound. Plato and Platonists distinguish between *mathematica* (whether idea-numbers or intermediates between ideas and sensibles) and sensibles. But the simpler Pythagorean thesis which makes no such distinction, leads to

impossible consequences. Physical bodies, if their components are numbers, cannot differ in mass. Concepts, which are numbers and so things, must occupy the same space as physical objects, and so two things must be in the same place at the same time.[2] These conclusions amount to a *reductio ad absurdum* of Pythagorean theories. If the Pythagoreans attempted to face these problems we have no knowledge of their solutions. But that these problems arose in the Early Academy is shown by the theory of Idea-numbers and its modifications by Speusippus and Xenocrates. It would seem highly probable that the Pythagorean theory is earlier.

In this passage Aristotle is not as sharply critical as he later becomes of Platonic number theories and of the Pythagorean theories which he holds to be allied to them. He has failed to appreciate the possibilities of mathematical physics, which we may consider to have been intuited by the Pythagoreans and adumbrated by the Plato of the *Timaeus*,[3] but the criticisms he makes are justified. Before we turn to the consideration of the other full-length criticism of M and N, both later in time than A, let us first consider Aristotle's other remarks on physical theory.

He insists that Pythagorean doctrine is an impossible basis for any sound theory of motion which he defines as "the actualization of the potential *qua* potential" (1065b 34). He goes on to say (1066a 7–16 = *Phys.* 201b 16–26):

That this is a sound definition is clear from what other thinkers have to say about motion, and from the fact that it is difficult to define it otherwise. One cannot put it in another genus than that in which we have put it, as is clear if it is considered how some define it when they say that motion is otherness, or inequality, or non-being. None of these is necessarily in motion. The process of change does not originate nor terminate in them, any more than it does from their opposites. Motion is thus defined because it appears to be an Unlimited, and the first principles in the one column of the table of opposites are all unlimiteds because they are privatives.

Here the Pythagoreans are not mentioned by name, but the "table of opposites" is held by commentators, both ancient and modern, to refer to that mentioned earlier (986a 25) or to some similar Pythagorean table, where the primary opposition is Limit/Unlimited, and where under Unlimited are subsumed terms that in Aristotle's terminology are privatives, matter, form, and privation being the factors involved in his theory of motion and change. But though At Rest/In Motion appear in the table Same/Other, Equal/Unequal, Being/Non-Being do not. These pairs are more reminiscent of Plato in the *Sophist*.

The inadequacy of the Pythagorean theory of motion is reiterated by Aristotle at 1075b 16–31, when he argues that numbers, like Ideas, cannot be the cause of anything, "or in any case not of motion." It is quite probable that early Pythagoreans evolved no theory of motion but that, like other earlier thinkers, and like Plato in the *Phaedrus*, they assumed that being animate implied the capacity to initiate motion.

In Pythagorean cosmology the *apeiron* has a central role as one of the two primordial opposites, and as the void surrounding the universe (*supra* 50). This latter role is mentioned in the *Physics* (203a 1–10):

All physical philosophers of repute have discussed the *apeiron*, and all have treated it as a first principle. Some, as for example the Pythagoreans and Plato, regard it as a first principle *per se* and itself a substance, not an attribute of some other thing. But the Pythagoreans regard it as present in sensibles (for them number is not a separate substance) and hold that what is outside the universe is infinite. Plato on the other hand holds that there is neither body nor ideas outside the universe (ideas are not in place) but that the *apeiron* is present in sensibles and ideas.

In the above passage the three roles of the *apeiron* are distinguished; in two subsequent passages its function is more clearly described (*Phys.* 213b 22–27):

The Pythagoreans too asserted the existence of a void, and that it enters the universe as it were breathed in from the infinite breath. This void delimits existents [*physeis*], it being a sort of separation and delimiting of things adjacent to one another. It is also primary in the case of numbers, the void delimiting their nature.

(*Fr. Sel.* p. 137): In the first book of his monograph on Pythagorean philosophy [Aristotle] writes that the universe is one, and that it draws in to itself from the infinite [*apeiron*] time and breath and the void, which has the function of delimiting the space occupied by individual existents.[4]

In his long discussion of the term "apeiron" in the *Physics*, Aristotle first points out the difficulties inherent in the concept "infinity." If there existed an infinite substance "infinite" would be predicable of it as an attribute, and it would have to be indivisible, which a quantum cannot be. On both these counts he rejects "doctrines like those of the Pythagoreans" (204a 32). But, he continues, in our present inquiry we are not immediately interested in the concept "infinity" but in "whether there exists among sensible things a body infinite in extension." There ensues an exhaustive treatment of the "apeiron" as a physical problem. Anaxagoras is the only thinker singled out for attention; but all theories, including the more primitive ones of the Pythagoreans, are covered. The conclusion is that there is no actually existent infinite physical body.

Pythagorean teachings are described more prosaically in these passages of the *Physics* than in the more fanciful account of the *Metaphysics*, but the basic doctrines are the same. The *apeiron* is a first principle physically conceived as infinite body. (The *Physics* passes over *peras* in silence, as involving a contradiction in terms). Its primary attribute is "even" and it is therefore divisible. It becomes identical with the One (205a 5). Aristotle apparently does not consider appropriate to physical science a discussion of the other two roles of the *apeiron* in Pythagorean theories: as the void outside the universe, and as the source on which the One draws, by breathing, to provide void between number-things (*Fr. Sel.* 137). We conclude that the account given of Pythagorean cosmology in the *Physics* is somewhat more sober than that of *Metaphysics A*, but that in substance the two accounts exhibit no conflicts.

Both cosmology and first principles are again subjected to an exhaustive critique at the end of the *Metaphysics*, and there Aristotle again allows his theme to dictate his approach. Pythagorean theories interest him chiefly because he considers them to have been an important source for Platonic theory, and it is Plato's theory of idea-numbers that is here as elsewhere the principal butt of his attack. But he devotes more effort than heretofore to rebutting the modifications of that theory made by Speusippus and Xenocrates, and distinguishes clearly four principal number theories, in formulae that are probably the product of years of debate in the Academy and elsewhere. To this discussion we now turn. Ross (2.147), following Jaeger, believes it to be attributable to Aristotle's stay at Assos (348–345 B.B.) and therefore to a period when he was critical of, but not yet hostile to, theories of idea-numbers. This critical attitude extended not only to the theory of idea-numbers of Plato and (with a difference) of Xenocrates, but also to Speusippus' separately existing *mathematica* and the numbers as things of the Pythagoreans. In beginning his discussion of these theories Aristotle says (1090a 30–35) that the Pythagoreans are not open to the objections that can be made against those who posit ideas or *mathematica* having separate existence, but, "in that they construct physical bodies of numbers, things having mass from things having no mass, in this respect they seem to be discussing some other universe than ours and bodies other than sensible bodies." This faint praise, however, is conceded them only so long as they are being played off against Plato and Speusippus and their independently existing number. When he turns his attention to them at 1091a 12–22,[5] he says:

It is absurd and indeed impossible to erect a theory ascribing coming-to-be (genesis) to eternal existents. Yet without a doubt the Pythagoreans do so. They say that when the one had been constituted—by being put together from plane surfaces or surface limits or seeds or some other unexplained constituent—at once the nearest part of the *apeiron* began to be drawn in and to be limited by Limit/*peras*. Here they are discussing the generation of the universe and intend their theories in a physical sense. So it is proper to exclude these theories from our present inquiry and relegate the criticism of them to physics. We are seeking the first principles of things exempt from movement and change, and must inquire into the coming-to-be of numbers answering that description.[6]

If Aristotle had adhered strictly to the rule he here establishes he would have had little or nothing more to say of the Pythagoreans in the *Metaphysics*. His purpose however in Books *M* and *N* is to wrestle with and refute the Platonic Theory of Ideas, and theories related to it. Since his criticism is largely devoted to the number aspects of these theories, reference is frequently made to the Pythagoreans. As these references are to their number doctrines or arithmology rather than to cosmology I shall discuss them separately under that heading. The One, however, has a principal cosmological role and it will be well to review what Aristotle has to say of it.

In enumerating the problems of metaphysics (1001a 4–12) he declares unity to be a principal one:

The most difficult problem of all, and the most crucial one for real knowledge, is whether being and unity, each of them having its own identity, are substances of existing things, and if being and unity are both of them substances and neither attributes; or, in seeking to define unity and being, must we assume that they have a substrate. Both views of their nature are held. Plato and the Pythagoreans maintain that unity and being are not attributes but that these terms correspond to natures, the essence of each being unity itself and being itself. The physical philosophers, on the other hand, [specify what the One is].

In his extended discussion of unity in Book I (1053b 9–15), Aristotle refers back to the problem raised here:

In our statement of problems we raised the question, to which we must now seek an answer in respect of *physis* and being—what is unity? Must we assume that the One itself is a substance, as did the Pythagoreans first and Plato later on? Or is it rather the case that some nature underlies it, and that it should be described in more familiar terms as by the natural philosophers?

The solution that Aristotle offers for this problem is that being and unity are universal predicates and no universal can be a primary substance; and that they cannot be substances as genera because genera are not separately existing substances. In this summary fashion he dismisses both the Platonic and the Pythagorean One. However, in earlier discussions in the *Metaphysics* and in the *Physics* he has shown himself aware that the Pythagorean One is not merely the unity predicable of a collective. It is also the cosmos that is product of *peras* and *apeiron*, and the One that is a first principle of number. Against their cosmos theory he here protests again. In his account he does not tell us what physical state preceded the generation of the cosmos, nor how the cosmos was generated, presumably because Pythagorean sources were vague. If he could have discovered in their teaching the embryo of efficient or final cause, it would have merited mention in his discussion of causes. But we are told only that the One was generated "from (geometrical) plane surfaces or from surface limits or from seeds or from some other unexplained constituent."

This list of candidates for physical constituents of the Pythagorean *apeiron* is Aristotle's. He suggests them as possible constituents because a cosmos cannot be made out of first principles—*peras* and *apeiron*—that are attributes. If the Pythagoreans maintain such a position their *apeiron* must imply some other physical bodies or entities. But the Pythagoreans probably found their idea of *apeiron*, not otherwise specified, an entirely adequate one.

Aristotle's further criticism, that the Pythagorean universe is generated, is appropriate only in the context of his own thought. All the Presocratics explained the coming-to-be of the universe as an occurrence in time, or used a temporal sequence as a device of exposition. Aristotle tells us that the Pythagorean *apeiron* pre-existed the constitution of the One, our universe, as did the *apeiron* of Anaximander. (We shall consider later whether theirs *was* the *apeiron* of Anaximander.) It was not altogether inchoate and indeterminate, because it had a companion first principle and opposite, *peras*, and the interaction of these two produced the cosmos. How Limit could co-exist as coeval with the Limitless and yet become operative in time to produce a cosmos, they will have felt no need to explain,[7] as Anaximander felt no need to explain how his *apeiron* began to "separate out." If it was divine and instinct with life it would originate its own processes, and there would be no need of "plane surfaces, or surfaces, or seeds." What Aristotle does tell us of the phase preceding the generation of the cosmos is that it was not merely by the operation of Limit on the Unlimited, but by the operation of Limit *qua* Odd on Unlimited *qua* Even that the One was constituted in the beginning. The first principles were mathematically conditioned. Their product, the One, was surrounded by an *apeiron* that was Even. And after the One had come to be, the principles continued to operate in constituting the sensibles of our world, themselves numbers (990a 9–22). So from the first the Pythagorean *peras* and *apeiron* were mathematically conditioned or coloured. Not only were Odd and Even subsumed under Limit and Unlimited. They were in some functions, identical with them. The first *peperasmenon*, the One, which is "even-odd", is a product of both pairs.

It is remarkable that (always according to the account of Aristotle) the *apeiron* is not restricted to a generative function. When the universe is constituted it is physically bounded by the *apeiron*, as void or infinite breath; and "at once the nearest part of the *apeiron* begins to be drawn and limited by Limit" (1091a 17–18).[8] This secondary operation, of Limit as One on the Unlimited as void, brings into being the sensibles of our world. These sensibles in conformity with their origin, are numbers and nothing but numbers. So the Pythagorean cosmos is a product of their primary contrariety Limit/Odd and Unlimited/Even; Limit, in the language of Aristotle, operating as a formal cause on Unlimited, as a material cause, to produce a number-conditioned universe. These causes continue to operate within the universe after its constitution producing its number-sensibles.

This account of Aristotle's is remarkable in several respects. He obviously considers the manner in which the Pythagoreans generate their world impossible and indeed absurd, but it is equally obvious that he concedes its simplicity and consistency. He even concedes that their notions have metaphysical possibilities (990a 5–8) though, as to physics, the world they describe is some world other than our own. He gives an account of their theories without hesitation or qualification, and though the references are scattered throughout the corpus of his writings, the account is remarkably consistent. He compares and contrasts their theories with those of Plato and the Platonists, to which he feels them to be closely allied, and does so without involving himself in contradictions. It is surprising that though he can dispose of them all quickly and easily by the use of his chosen weapons of the categories and the doctrine of substance, nevertheless he gives a full, and in his own terms, fair account of their theories.

What more general conclusion does Aristotle's discussion of Pythagorean cosmology permit? We cannot suppose that he is seriously misrepresenting or distorting Pythagorean doctrines for his own dialectical purposes. His contemporary hearers and readers were too well informed for him to permit himself such licence, even if he himself were capable of imputing to other thinkers, without qualms of conscience, things they never said. If we assume that his account is generally correct, then we must assume further that it is (1) a least common denominator of contemporary Pythagoreanism or (2) an account valid for two centuries of Pythagoreanism or (3) an account applicable to some earlier, unspecified period of Pythagoreanism.

His account is unlikely to be applicable to contemporary Pythagoreanism which may be assumed to have reacted in some fashion to the theories of Plato in his later years and to those of Speusippus and Xenocrates.[9] So the doctrines must be ascribed either to the beginnings of Pythagoreanism, that is to Pythagoras himself, or to some intermediate but definitive stage in the evolution of their thought. Now, between the time of Pythagoras and that of Archytas, we know of few Pythagoreans of intellectual eminence, and what we know of their thought does not fit well into the scheme Aristotle describes.[10] So it would appear desirable to consider whether there exists ground for ascribing to Pythagoras himself, the theories which Aristotle ascribes to "the Pythagoreans." It is easy to understand why Aristotle himself hesitated to do so, though in almost all other cases he ascribes doctrines to persons rather than schools. As the fragments of his Pythagorean monographs show, his inquiries had led him to the discovery not of an historical person but of a full-fledged legend. It is understandable that he should hesitate to ascribe philosophical doctrines to a person such as the legend presents, and that he should take refuge in the anonymous "Pythagoreans".

The key role in Pythagorean thought that Aristotle ascribes to the *apeiron* is in itself remarkable. For the *apeiron* is central only in the thought of Anaximander, and in that of no other Presocratic thinker.[11] Pythagoras was a younger contemporary of Anaximander, by whose thought he was probably influenced during his formative years and his maturity in Samos. Its two features most likely to have acted as stimuli are the notion of *apeiron* and that of structure capable of numerical expression. Both of these doctrines are reflected in Aristotle's report.

A further argument for an early dating of the theory is the extreme simplicity of the scheme Aristotle describes. It has no place for physical elements, nor for processes such as condensation and rarefaction. It ignores the problems of Parmenides and of Heraclitus.[12] It seems unlikely that it would be untouched by the controversy of the fifth century if it were a doctrine attributable to the end of that century or to the early fourth. And if it is argued that Pythagorean thinking would have evolved how ever early its origins, it may be replied that the very simplicity of this theory suggests that one thinker conceived it. The authority of Pythagoras may have been such as to preserve its character intact. Further, just about the time of the great intellectual ferment in the West—of Epicharmus, Parmenides, Zeno, Empedocles— the towns of Magna Graecia in which the Pythagoreans played an important role underwent an upheaval in which they were either exiled or put to death. What could be more natural than that the survivors should seek to preserve unchanged the thought of their master. Moreover Pythagorean thought, as Aristotle portrays it, would not easily admit of modification or adaptation except towards atomism or as Plato is said to have modified it. Aristotle's account excludes the possibility that such a change in fact occurred.

If we are to deny the possibility that the thought Aristotle reports as Pythagorean is in substance the thought of Pythagoras himself, then we must deny to Pythagoras, as many have done, any status as a thinker. We must deny that he, though an Ionian of the sixth century, can have been deeply influenced by the intellectual tendencies and speculation of his day. And we must explain the long shadow he cast as the shadow of a subsequent construct rather than that of the historical person. But if we concede that Pythagorean thought had its first beginnings with him, and that no later Pythagorean was of the stature to have created such a system of thought, then it would appear probable that what Aristotle describes as Pythagorean doctrine was, in its essentials, the product of the mind of Pythagoras himself.

NOTES

[1]990a 25: I read, with Bonitz, τούτων ἕν which has better MSS authority, and συμβαίνῃ.

[2]Aristotle here suggests, fairly enough, that two things consisting of the same material *stoicheia* cannot occupy the same place at the same time. There is no necessary allusion to the elements and the several regions that are their natural place. The questions of the elements and of how numbers constitute physical

bodies are discussed p. 76 ff. For the relation of the two problems see Eva Sachs *passim*. Alexander 73.12–21 points out that there must be a differentiation between cause and what is caused, and that this is why Plato has eidetic as well as mathematical number. See also his remarks 74.3–75.23, where, however, his equation of dyad and *doxa* is not Pythagorean.

[3]For a discussion, from the point of view of the physicist, of Aristotle's account of Pythagoreanism, and of his failure to see its potentialities see Sambursky 45–48.

[4]These two extracts are cited consecutively by Aëtius (*Dox. Gr.* 316–7), that from the *Physics* only to the end of the first sentence in my translation. The reading of the whole cumbersome sentence in the *Physics* (22–27) is dubious and the meaning uncertain. *KR* fr. 315, p. 252 take issue with the reading of Ross, but the word order of their text is awkward. I should prefer to punctuate (with Aëtius?) after ἀναπνέοντι, τὸ κένον being picked up by καὶ τοῦτο.

This passage has been pressed to yield more detail of Pythagorean doctrine than it can. We have been told that from the One comes number (986a 20–21). The One *qua* universe breathes in from the infinite void that surrounds it, and the void it inhales serves to fill the space by which number things are separated off one from another. But we are not told whether the One takes one deep breath or continues to inhale and exhale. Even if we take it that respiration continues, as seems probable if we are to have life and motion, how are we to envisage the production of numbers? Are we to have recourse to the analogy of animal generation favoured by the Cornford school? But how then can the One function as male principle and the void as female? And what numbers will be generated? The numbers up to ten and then a repetition? How will things be differentiated? There is nothing but the term ἐφεξῆς (which need not have this connotation) to justify the suggestion of *KR* 253 that the discrete quantities arising from inhalation are points, lines, etc. Aristotle gives us no information as to how the further phases in the generation of number things occur. The Pythagoreans may well have contented themselves with establishing principles from which to generate a universe in which things are numbers, and may then have turned to observing, as it were inductively, number relations within that universe. That they did so Aristotle tells us at 985b 26–28.

For the breathing in of time see Burkert 67 and notes. (M. F. Burnyeat *CR.* 12.2. [Nov. 1962] is purely speculative.) Burkert seems to suggest that this notion of time (as breathed in at the constitution of the universe?) is prior to and implied in Plato *Tim.* 37D. But Aëtius has time breathed in with the void, and having apparently the same function of delimiting space. This is so improbable that a doxographical introduction of the time notion is to be suspected. Aristotle makes no reference to any other Pythagorean time doctrine.

[5]Aristotle discusses the same problem on similar lines 1076a 38 ff. There the discussion is oriented rather towards the theory of number than towards cosmology, and therefore will be discussed under the heading of number. Our present passage is analyzed at length by R. P. Saffrey, 24–33.

[6]In the *Physics* Aristotle only incidentally discusses the problem here referred

to that treatise. Ps. Alexander 818.29–820.7 is often quoted in this connection. He paraphrases thus: The Pythagoreans unquestionably maintain
that existents come to be. For they clearly state that when the One has been
constituted, be it of plane surfaces or of colours (this is a mistaken translation
of χροιά) or of seed or of some other thing—for the Pythagoreans are at a loss
to say of what the One is constituted and consequently they sometimes say that
it comes-to-be from colour and surface, sometimes from some other thing—then,
they clearly state, once the One has been constituted, from the parts of the
apeiron, their material cause, the nearest adjacent part is drawn in and limited
and has form imposed on it by the One. For Aristotle says that the One is
(their) Limit." The commentator goes on to explain this intercourse between
the One and the *apeiron*/void as occurring in time and producing physical bodies
or sensibles. His comment neither adds to nor clarifies what Aristotle says. In
the Aristotelian *Problems* $910^{b}23$–$911^{a}4$ it is suggested that from four cubic
numbers the Pythagoreans constructed the universe (Heath, *Aristotle* 258–260).
This probably refers to geometrical progression, and so to a development of the
point–line–plane–solid derivation. It is likely to be posterior to the *Timaeus*
35b-c. See F. M. Cornford, *Plato's Cosmology* 66–72.

[7]Kahn 236 argues (and Guthrie 87 approves) that "For a Milesian they (the
opposites) were no more pre-existent in the *apeiron* than children pre-exist in
the bodies of their parents before conception." But surely a Milesian, even
though he did not distinguish between potential and actual, knew that there was
a potentiality for conception before conception occurred. If our physical world
is generated out of the *apeiron* the term itself would suggest, and indeed imply,
peras. The difficulties, both conceptual and physical, of the pair of opposites
being prior to, coexistent with, or subsequent to a physical *apeiron* he might
feel no need to face. If you have an *apeiron* you have a *peras*.

[8]In his monograph *On the Pythagoreans* (*Fr. Sel.* 137), Aristotle says that their
universe was a unity and "drew in to itself from the *apeiron*-unlimited time and
breath and the void, which delimits the space occupied by all existents." Here
time, breath, and the void are either distinct entities coming from the *apeiron*
and so previously existing as determinate entities in an indeterminate *apeiron*—
which would seem to be a contradiction in terms—or, when the nearest part of
the infinite is breathed in, it has the functions described; that is (1) it is the
breath of the living cosmos, (2) it initiates physical events (and so time, though
this is a later notion), (3) it fills the intervals between bodies and so delimits
them. It is true that, unless there is within the cosmos a previously existing space
or vacuum, it is hard to explain how the "breathing in" should take place, but
this need not have occurred to Pythagoras or early Pythagoreans if they did
not distinguish clearly between air and empty space.

In the *Physics* again (*Phys.* 213b 22–27) Aristotle states that "the Pythagoreans also assert the existence of a void; that from the *apeiron* there enters
the universe itself, as endowed with the capacity of respiration, breath, and the
void that delimits natures—the void being a sort of separation and delimiting
of successive things; and further that this is the case first of all for numbers,

because the void delimits their natures." (I read 1.23 αὐτῷ and 1.24, with Diels πνεῦμά τε.)

Is Aristotle here distinguishing in Pythagorean theory between the *apeiron* and the void? It would seem improbable. Apart from the difficulties already suggested, (1) the concepts of plenum and void do not arise, in all probability and so far as we know, before Parmenides, (2) Aristotle himself does not believe in the existence of a void and might use his terms not precisely. He is well aware (*Phys.* 213a 27–30) that people commonly speak of the absence of perceptible body (and so of what is full of air) as a void. So when he says that, after the One was framed or constituted it began to breath in the *apeiron* at once, we may think of this *apeiron* (once it enters the cosmos) as the "void" delimiting the numbers that are things and so establishing by separation the unit magnitudes existing within the cosmos. The *apeiron* becomes not only the air within our cosmos but also the "void" between successive unit magnitudes. It is "limited" by these magnitudes.

Did the respiration mentioned imply only the inhaling of the *apeiron*, or are we to imagine the rhythmic inhaling and exhaling of a living creature, so accounting for change, process, motion, time? In other words, was one deep breath enough, or are we to imagine breathing as continuously occurring? Aristotle's testimony does not enable us to decide, and his analogical language does not authorize us to assume that an analogy was intended. The language of generation, birth, bodily change is often used by the Presocratics when the *physis* is not thought of after the analogy of a physical body. For these reasons it seems to me dangerous to press these passages too far. They inform us that immediately after the cosmogonical occurrence parts of the *apeiron* were introduced into the cosmos to serve as space between bodies.

It should be noted that this cosmogony cannot be analyzed into phases, as by Cornford (*Plato and Parmenides*). He suggests (5) that there was a One, distinct from the cosmogonical One, which they worshipped. He further suggests that "their cosmogony really consists of two chapters: the first mathematical, terminating in the geometrical solid, and the second physical, beginning with the first sensible body." (16) As I attempt to show there is no indication that early Pythagorean theory is geometrical. The first sensible body is a number.

[9]I would, for instance, take as reflecting the confrontation of Pythagoreanism and Platonism, the famous remark (987b 11–13) that "the Pythagoreans assert that things exist by imitation of the numbers, Plato by participation in them. Plato changed the term." This, though Guthrie 229–231 seeks to explain it away, is, as Cherniss 386 has pointed out, in flat contradiction to the doctrine that things are numbers, at least so long as we understand the term *mimesis* to have its Platonic implications. And even if, with Burkert 40–41, we concede that under μιμεῖσθαι we need understand only that "the one signifies and clarifies the other" we have two non-identical things. But the Pythagoreans must see them as identical if things are numbers. As Ross *ad loc.* remarks, it is surprising that Aristotle should here consider μίμησις and μέθεξις to be terminologically equivalent. He shows himself aware of the important difference between them elsewhere.

See Ross, *Plato's Theory of Ideas* 227–230 for a list of occurrences and discussion.

At 987b 11–3 Aristotle is discussing the relation between things having a common name, and their universal or class or idea. Plato describes the relation as participation. How would the Pythagoreans account for the fact that two horses, both having the same number as substance, are both called "horse"? Would they use the term imitation? and imitation of what? Of the number that *is* their substance? Then the number is an independent existent. I cannot see that the ὁμοιώματα of 985b 27 and 32 offers any escape. There the Pythagoreans observe the occurrence of number patterns in things.

In 987b 11–14 Aristotle says that both Plato and the Pythagoreans recognize ἔιδη as well as particulars, and he reproaches both with not describing the relation between these. There seem to be here only two possible solutions:

1) there were in fact contemporary Pythagoreans who admitted the existence of something like *eidetic* numbers, and described the relation between these numbers and particulars by the term *mimesis*. If this were the case then Aristotle should have qualified and limited his reference as everywhere else he tells us that for the Pythagoreans things *were* numbers.

2) Aristotle is here guilty of using his terms carelessly. He cannot be doing so, as Burkert suggests, to detract from Plato's originality. If he attached any importance to originality he had already denied it to Plato in saying that he derived the substance of his Theory of Ideas from Socrates.

Of these two possibilities the latter seems to me more probable. The problem of the relation between *eidos* and particular cannot have arisen much before the beginning of the fourth century. If any Pythagoreans concerned themselves with it they probably did so in reaction to Socratic-Platonic speculation. No such problem can have arisen for Pythagoreans holding doctrines such as are elsewhere attributed to them by Aristotle.

[10]For a discussion of known Pythagoreans between the end of the sixth century and Archytas see *supra* 24 ff.

[11]As is observed by F. Solmsen "Anaximander's Infinite. Traces and Influences" *Arch. Ges. Phil.* 44.2 (1962) 109–131. Solmsen remarks that already with Anaximenes, ἄπειρον becomes an attribute of ἀήρ, with Melissus, of being, with Empedocles, of σφαῖρα. For the meaning of *apeiron* see Kahn 230–239, and Guthrie 78–89. Guthrie's argument (86) that the sense uppermost in Anaximander's mind was "the notion of internal indeterminacy rather than spatial infinity" seems to me questionable. On Aristotle's account both notions are present in Pythagorean thought. After the One was constituted there remained some infinite stuff outside the cosmos, the nearest part of which was drawn in to play a role in constituting discrete quantities. It seems probable that in Anaximander's cosmology the same sort of thing occurred. Though he had certainly not developed a concept of spatial infinity he must have thought of his *apeiron* as extended in space. *Phys.* 203a 6–7 and 203b 4–15 makes it clear that an *apeiron* such as Anaximander's was a substance and not an attribute, and was thought of as *res extensa*.

[12]The fact that the Pythagoreans described a cosmogony or generation of the

universe need not for them have implied its eventual destruction; and even if they had believed in a final dissolution they need not therefore have believed in a *Magnus Annus* or Great Year, about which three independent but similar notions existed:

1. A cycle of the individual soul, connected with transmigration doctrines that are familiar to us from Empedocles (*Vors.* 31 B 115) and from the *Phaedrus* (248E–249D). See Hackforth, *Plato's Phaedrus* 87–91. In Plato it is usually said to reflect "Orphic"—and so probably Pythagorean—eschatology, and Plotinus (4.8.1) connects the Empedocles passage with the Pythagoreans. No period of years or notion of cycle appears in the account of Pythagoras' metempsychoseis given by Heraclides Ponticus (*D.L.* 8.4 = *Vors.* 14.8 = Wehrli fr. 89) and the much later account of *Theol. Ar.* 52 = *Vors.* 14.8 gives the period as the cube of 6, and connects this period of years with a chronology based on the Trojan War.

2. The Great Year of Heraclitus, a cycle of *ekpyrosis* and cataclysm. This is discussed by Reinhardt, *Parmenides* 183–201, who maintains that the Heraclitean cycle is a soul cycle having no connection with cosmic events. Burnet (156–163) likewise denies that Heraclitus taught *ekpyrosis*, and Kirk, 335, and Guthrie, 454–457, both question the attribution of Stoic *ekpyrosis* to Heraclitus (to whom Pohlenz (*Die Stoa* 2nd ed. [Göttingen 1959] 79–81) does not impute it). Guthrie, however, following Vlastos, *AJP* 1955, 311, believes that Heraclitus's Great Year was connected with a cycle of cosmic events.

3. A cycle in which events recur and history repeats itself. Such a cycle is said to have been taught by Pythagoras (Porph. *VP* 19 = *Vors.* 14.8a 39–40). A cycle of a similar nature is suggested by Eudemus (Wehrli fr. 88) as paraphrased by Simplicius (*Phys.* 732.26). Eudemus is pointing out the ambiguity of the word "identical," as applied to time. "We can say that the same seasons recur, and the same equinoxes, solstices, etc. They are identical in kind. But if we say they recur as to number, as do the Pythagoreans, then at some future time I, pointer in hand, will be again addressing you and you will again be sitting as you do now." Here Eudemus is arguing that there can be a specific identity in certain events in time such as seasons that recur, but that time itself cannot be conceived as it is by the Pythagoreans, in terms of number. Or he is arguing that in terms of Pythagorean number theory, there being no prior and posterior, there can be no sound theory of time. The nature of the theory he is arguing against is not clear, but certainly the conclusion as to the recurrence of a teaching episode is his own and cannot be used to suggest that for Eudemus the Pythagoreans taught recurrence of historical events.

It will be seen that our sources for a Pythagorean Great Year are meagre. In the *Timaeus* 39D Plato speaks of a "perfect year," referring simply and vaguely to recurring coincidence of heavenly bodies in the same positions after a period of years. The 9,000 years since the first founding of Athens, mentioned at Timeus 23E, is not a period between cataclysms. It is probable that the Pythagoreans, like Plato, played with the notion of cycles but we have no more precise information as to these cycles. (Aëtius refers to a Pythagorean Great Year of 59 years, *Dox. Gr.* 363–64).

6

PYTHAGOREAN
NUMBER THEORY

THE number theory of the Pythagoreans derives from their cosmology and, in its principal aspects, *is* cosmology. From number-determined first principles proceeds a One that is the universe. From this One and its surrounding void proceed number-things—stars, elements, creatures—that make up our world. So far, Aristotle's account is unambiguous. However, it leaves important questions regarding origin and internal mechanism unanswered, or answered only indirectly, in hints the interpretation of which is dubious.

Aristotle was little interested in the historical development of thought from its remoter origins, and it was no part of his purpose to discuss those origins. We now assume that early thought is, in great measure, a transposition from the poetic language of religion, that it is influenced by contemporary intellectual and political climate and the stimuli of other cultures, and that it consists as much in a search for a vehicle of expression as it does in the substance of that expression. We are interested in religious, sociological, semantic origins. Aristotle was interested in first principles such that they anticipated the first principles of his own thought. He gives us little help in understanding Pythagorean origins and what reference he makes to them will be discussed later under music and harmonia (pp. 123 ff.).

Regarding the internal mechanism of our world in Pythagorean theory he is prodigal of hints, but the implications of these hints is for ancient as for modern commentators a matter of dispute. One of the recurring themes of the treatises, a theme Aristotle pursued compulsively, was Plato's Theory of Ideas. He never appears to feel that he has refuted it once and for all. In contexts where the theory is relevant he sometimes offers merely an allusive, pro-forma refutation, but often devises a new one appropriate to the question under discussion. He argues, not against a standard version of the Theory of Ideas but against every variation of it, from the early statement in the *Phaedo* to the *agrapha dogmata*, and to the modifications introduced by his own contemporaries in the Academy. In this context he makes frequent reference to the Pythagoreans. He does so in part because to his mind their number theories anticipate the Theory of Ideas but chiefly because he is persuaded (an assertion we still have not succeeded in swallowing) that (987a 29) "On the philosophical systems I have mentioned there followed Plato's school and thought. In most respects Plato followed the Pythagoreans, but some features were peculiar to his own system and non-Pythagorean."

In his treatment of Pythagorean number theory Aristotle is not sympathetic. He has stripped it of any poetic or allusive quality it may have had, and has isolated it from the contexts to which it must have had reference. From his hints we cannot reconstruct a total theory and the problem arises whether we should, at least in the first instance, confine ourselves to his account and seek to understand that, or whether we should supplement his information from our ample sources—the doxography, the commentators, the Neopythagoreans, the Neoplatonists.

The commentators are seeking to explain what Aristotle says. In so far as they confine themselves to exegesis their comments are valuable. But when they give us additional information or views of their own, these are likely to be coloured by subsequent speculation.[1] They possessed one principal and early source to which we no longer have access, Eudemus' *History of the Exact Sciences* (Wehrli, *Eudemos von Rhodos*, Frs. 133–150). But it would appear from the fragments that Eudemus made little reference to the Pythagoreans (Sachs 119–132), and that he did not deal with Pythagorean number theory, as not being part of mathematics proper. The Neopythagoreans and Neoplatonists, however, deal with it at great length. Their views are known to us from the extant mathematical treatises of Nicomachus of Gerasa (2nd cent. A.D.) and Iamblichus (3rd–4th cent. A.D.) and from numerous incidental references, especially in Plutarch and Sextus Empiricus. The picture they present of Pythagorean number theory is, in many respects, remarkably similar to that of Aristotle. They are not concerned with mathematical science proper but with speculations about number itself as a first principle, and about particular numbers as having special significance. But, as is obvious even to the casual reader, the relatively modest structure depicted for us by Aristotle has acquired other proportions and other ornamentation, and the doctrines have been given a Platonic tincture. For these reasons it would seem desirable to confine any discussion to what Aristotle himself tells us, and to study his references in themselves before subsequent comment is used to amplify them.

Aristotle prefaces the *Metaphysics* with a brief review of the opinions of his predecessors regarding first principles. Of the Pythagoreans he says (985b 23–986a 13):

In this tradition and earlier[2] the thinkers known as the Pythagoreans were the first to pursue mathematical studies and to advance them. Having been nurtured in such studies they considered the first principles of mathematics to be the first principles of all things. Now in mathematics numbers are naturally first principles, and they considered that they discerned in number, rather than in fire, earth, and water, many similarities or analogies to existents and things in the process of becoming. They further[3] thought they saw that such and such a modification[4] of number was justice, such and such the soul and *nous*, another opportunity, and so on for most other things. They also saw melodic changes and ratios to be numerical. So, since in these and all other respects they discovered apparent correspondences between all nature and numbers, and numbers were first principles in all nature, they assumed that the elements of number were the elements of all existing things, and that the whole universe was a concord and a number. They made a practice of bringing together the correspondences they found between numbers and concords on the one hand and on the other the parts and attributes of the universe and the whole ordered world. They exhibited an eagerness to complete any gap there might be in their system. For example, since the decad[5] seemed to be a perfect thing and to comprise within itself the whole nature of number, they asserted that the planets too were ten, but as only nine were visible they invented the counter-earth as a tenth. I have discussed all this in more detail elsewhere.

In this introductory survey Aristotle is giving neither a summary nor an historical account of Pythagorean views. He is attempting a rationalization of what seemed to him a curious position. He is seeking to give reasons—his own reasons—for the fundamental notion that things are numbers. He says that the Pythagoreans were the first to pursue and advance mathematical studies. We know that this was not the case for mathematics in the stricter sense. We know that there was, in Ionia, an interest in number and in empirical mathematics before Pythagoras; that such studies were, in the fifth century, pursued and advanced in Ionia rather than in Magna Graecia, and that there is no real evidence for mathematical science among the Pythagoreans before Archytas. Aristotle's statement may be evidence for the existence in the Early Academy of a myth that Greek mathematics was a Pythagorean province, but it does not reflect what we know of the history of mathematics. And it contrasts with what he himself tells us subsequently of Pythagorean thought. His account does not reflect an interest on the part of the Pythagoreans in arithmetic or geometry, the two branches of mathematical science which they are generally supposed to have advanced. It does indicate an interest in number speculation, or arithmology or, if we are disposed to deprecate their pursuits, in number mysticism. An interest in the arcane significance of the cardinal numerals is characteristic of most peoples, and not only in a primitive period of their culture. Such an interest is reflected in the epic (G. Germain), and when mathematical knowledge began to reach the Ionians from Babylon it must have given new life to such speculations. Anaximander explained the relation of our earth to the sun and moon in terms of number relations and mathematical symmetry. Pythagoras went further. He maintained that the cosmos was not only expressible in terms of number, but *was* number. But there were neither means nor methods of quantitative observation. All that could be done was to look for "correspondences." In the physical world this could lead to few correct observations and must lead to much fantasy.

Of more importance was an interest in the nature of number; in unit, dyad, triad, tetrad, each as a self-subsistent entity having a character and properties of its own; in the way numbers can be combined; in square, oblong, prime, amicable numbers; in short, such interests as are reflected in the definitions prefacing Euclid's Seventh Book. This was the only field in which the Pythagoreans could be said to have advanced mathematics. It is precisely the field we find reflected in Plato's mathematical speculations such as the Nuptial Number and the number theory of his later years. It is the field to which Neopythagoreans and Neoplatonists devote most attention in number theory, in their metaphysical speculation and their theology. So we may readily believe Aristotle when he tells us that the Pythagoreans thought numbers to be the elements of sensibles, that they saw a numerical structure in non-sensibles, and that they believed musical concordances to be governed by numerical relations. We can believe him when he suggests that these doctrines, or intuitions, were the result of long application to mathematics only if we understand by "mathematics" the arithmological speculation he proceeds to describe, and which was discussed in chapter 5.[6]

Concerning this arithmology Aristotle had concluded that, although the Pythagoreans maintained a doctrine of the One and of numbers, "How the first One came to be they cannot say" (1080b 20). If it had been possible, Aristotle would undoubtedly have interpreted the

Pythagorean Limit/Odd as "form" and the Unlimited/Even as "matter" or at least would have presented them as active and passive principles interacting, in a substrate, to produce the One. He would have cited any explanations he might have found in Pythagorean writings to explain how their first principles were the basis for the generation of numbers and of the One and Limited—our universe. So we may assume that the Pythagoreans felt no need for such an explanation.[7] But once the One had come to be and was (a living thing) it began to breathe in the Unlimited surrounding it, and the product of that breathing-in was numbers.

What was the role of the *harmonia* or concord that is so frequently mentioned (985b 31; 986a 3, 4, 6)? In this passage it does not necessarily refer to a musical concord. It appears to have no peculiar role but to be simply a name for number in constituted things. The *harmonia* of the One is in the Limited/Unlimited—Odd/Even balance and in the fitting-together that makes the One a unity, and any number-thing the thing it is.

To sum up, in introducing the Pythagoreans in the first book of the *Metaphysics*, Aristotle surveys their doctrines for the first and only time. The account he gives is basically simple. He tells us that from their first principles they generate a One-universe and number-sensibles, and that for them everything is number. But it would appear from Aristotle's account that they did not go on to say *how* the physical world of experience proceeded from their first principles. Instead they looked for similarities, analogies, correspondences, fittings-together in which the operation of their principles could be observed (and which they could regard as "proof").

Elsewhere in the *Metaphysics* and in the other treatises Aristotle makes incidental remarks casting light on Pythagorean number theory, but they do not add up to a coherent doctrine. At the end of the *Metaphysics*, however, there are two major discussions of idea-number theories in which he attempts to demolish once and for all, *all* number theories explaining the physical world quantitatively and having metaphysical implications. That is, he attempts to demolish the metaphysical and physical structures of most contemporary theories and of all the theories of those with whom he had for years been most closely associated. Among his contemporaries the Pythagoreans played a very minor role, but they were considered by Plato and the Early Academy as venerable predecessors. So in the complex structure of Aristotle's critique the Pythagoreans are, as it were, a background theme. For convenience of exposition and because Aristotle's remarks are better understood and evaluated in context, I propose to follow these two discussions in outline, and to observe what he has to say of the Pythagoreans as he develops his theme, and what function is assigned to them in the dialectical process. When constructing his own theories Aristotle lays his predecessors under contribution; in demolishing their constructs he plays them off against one another. It is difficult to infer positive doctrine from his incidental and largely negative references, but what he says contributes to the understanding of his account elsewhere.

In the *Physics* (193b 22–194b 15) Aristotle differentiates between the objects of physical and of mathematical inquiry. Physics studies things that, like snubness, are not independent of matter, while mathematics studies abstractions from sensibles, like the "curved." The objects of mathematics are therefore outside the realm of physics. But this does not necessarily place them within the realm of metaphysics unless they are separately existing substances (*Phys.* 194b 14). And whether mathematical abstractions are such substances is one of the principal questions posed in the last two books of the *Metaphysics*. In the books preceding these, Aristotle develops his own doctrine of substance. In the last two books which are, as we have said (65–66), a later and an earlier treatment of one and the same theme, Aristotle turns to other contemporary and authoritative doctrines of substance which must be rejected if his own is to be accepted. The doctrines against which his arguments are aimed are those of Plato, Speusippus, Xenocrates, the Pythagoreans—doctrines current during Plato's later years and in the first decades after his death. In considering their doctrines Aristotle asks whether, above and beyond sensible substances, there exist eternal and unmoved substances, and in particular whether the Ideas and *mathematica* are such substances.

Aristotle's treatment of his theme differs somewhat in emphasis and perspective in the two versions, that of Book *M* (by which we mean here *M* to 1086a 21) and that of Book *N* (1086a 21 to the end of *N*). Book *M* begins by considering whether mathematical objects can be separate substances, and concludes that they cannot be substances whether as immanent in or as separable from sensibles, but that they do have a qualified or vaguer sort of existence as the quantitative abstractions from sensibles which mathematicians suppose to be separate.

The Pythagoreans, who believe that things are numbers, are not envisaged in this discussion. Nor are they more than glanced at in a refutation of the Theory of Ideas (in its original form in which idea-numbers played no role) that largely reiterates the arguments of the first book. They first appear in a minor role in the discussion of numbers as separate substances having at least in part the role of Ideas. Aristotle classifies such theories according to the nature of the units they pre-suppose (1080a 12–1080b 11): (1) the units may be all comparable to one another and of the same kind; (2) the units may be comparable and of the same kind within one number (as e.g. in dyad or triad), but not as between numbers; i.e. the units composing dyad and triad are not to be thought of as identical; (3) neither the numbers themselves nor the units composing them are comparable and of the same kind.[8] Of these three kinds only the first is such as to permit of the operations of mathematics—of addition, subtraction, multiplication, and division. As Pythagorean number is of this kind (but corporeal) the Pythagoreans are alluded to in the discussion of the complex theme (1080b 16–21):

The Pythagoreans too believe that there is one kind of number, viz. mathematical number. They do not however believe that it exists apart from sensibles, but that sensible substances are constituted of this number. For they construct the whole universe of this number. These numbers however are not monadic (or abstract) numbers. The Pythagoreans assume that the units are extended. But they appear to be at a loss for an explanation of how the first unit or one was constituted as an extended unit.

After a brief review of possible combinations, Aristotle concludes (1080b 30–36):

All who assert that the One is an element and first principle of existents posit mathematical (or abstract) number, with the one exception of the Pythagoreans who, as was said earlier, suppose numbers to have magnitude. It is clear from our discussion in how many ways numbers can be substances and that we have enumerated all possible ways. All such theories are impossible—some, to my mind, more impossible than others.

There follows a discussion of Plato's idea-numbers and, as if in an appendix, of the theories of Speusippus and Xenocrates, after which Aristotle adds: (1083b 8–19)

The Pythagorean view is in some ways less difficult than those previously mentioned, but it has other difficulties of its own. Many impossible consequences are avoided by the position that number is not something existing separately from sensibles. But the position that physical bodies are constituted of numbers, and that this number is mathematical number, is an impossible one. It cannot be maintained that there are indivisible magnitudes. And even if it could be maintained, mathematical units have no magnitude. A magnitude cannot consist of indivisibles, and mathematical number consists of (indivisible) units. The Pythagoreans assert that existing things *are* numbers and apply their theorems to physical bodies, implying that physical bodies consist of numbers.

In this passage we encounter what, for Aristotle, is the rock on which Pythagorean theory founders—indivisible magnitudes. In the *De Generatione* (316b 19–317b 17) he shows that natural process cannot be merely a process in which indivisible magnitudes are associated (*synkrisis*) in the aggregates we know as physical bodies—as is supposed by atomist theories and the minimum plane surfaces of Plato. If they were, there would be no coming-to-be and passing-away. Magnitudes, though they cannot be divided everywhere at once, are everywhere divisible; and points are not atomic magnitudes constituting a line. The *De Lineis Insecabilibus*, though doubtfully authentic and probably somewhat later, shows that such theories were widely held.

In the present passage (1080b 8–19) Aristotle goes on to argue that even if there were indivisible magnitudes, the Pythagorean theory would not be a valid one. (1) Numbers consist of indivisible units; so all magnitudes consisting of a number higher than one, would be an agglomeration of units and divisible into these units. (2) Mathematical (abstract) number consists of units that have no magnitude; and out of units having no magnitude you cannot construct magnitudes. (3) The theory that "things are numbers" implies that numbers have no existence or status apart from things; and so the Pythagoreans proceed to apply to things of the physical world all the theorems and discoveries of mathematics.

Of these summary objections the first and second are (with some qualification) valid. The third, if we are correct in our understanding of it, describes the method of the mathematical physicist, though it does not perhaps describe the relations between numbers and the quanta of the physical world as he would describe them.[9] However, these are objections that imply a much later stage in scientific inquiry than does the original thesis. Aristotle argues that numbers are abstractions from sensibles, and regards as untenable all theories built on indivisible magnitudes (the Atomists), indivisible planes (Plato), indivisible lines (Xenocrates), or indivisible points. The Pythagoreans, whatever their ultimate constituent, would fall under this condemnation.[10]

It is obvious that the arguments Aristotle uses against the theory that "things are numbers" are weapons of argument developed against later and more elaborate forms of number theory, evolved by others than Pythagoreans, or at least other than "the Pythagoreans" of whom he gives us an account. This is not to suggest that the Pythagoreans, under the stimulus of criticism particularly from Zeno and the Atomists, may not have worked out their theory in greater detail. But it is remarkable that in his criticism of the Pythagoreans, particularly in the crucial area of mathematicals, Aristotle appears to argue against their theory in its simplest form.

In the remaining part of Book *M* (1083b 19–1086a 18) Aristotle discusses numbers as ideas, and numbers as separately existing *mathematica*, but not numbers as things, and so the Pythagoreans play no role in his argument. As Bonitz (555) points out, problems do not follow on one another in logical order, and one cannot with any certainty attribute to individual thinkers the opinions Aristotle is citing. It would appear however that they are Platonists and not Pythagoreans, and that the distinction between these two on the basis of *chorismos* is maintained.

In Book *N*, where there is more emphasis on Plato's Theory of Ideas in both its earlier and its later form, the Pythagoreans play a role only when the discussion of self-subsistent numbers begins (1090a 20):

The Pythagoreans observed that many properties of number were predicable of physical bodies. They therefore said that things were numbers; not however separately existing numbers but numbers constituting things. And why? Because musical concordances, the movements of the heavenly bodies and many other things are numerically determined.

After pointing out once again that this position is not open to the objections that can be made against separately-existing *mathematica*, Aristotle continues (1090a 32):

But they construct physical bodies of numbers, of things having no mass, things having mass. In this respect they seem to be discussing some other universe than ours, and bodies other than sensible bodies.[11]

After an allusion to Pythagorean cosmology Aristotle turns to Speusippus and the problem of the relation between first principles and the Good, a problem that we discussed earlier (p. 48; n. 7, cf. 1072b 30). The problem relates primarily to Speusippus and its connection with the Pythagoreans may be only an inference of Aristotle's from the position of the Good in the (late?) Pythagorean Table of Opposites. Then, following on a polemic against Speusippus' number theory, comes a final chapter that is mainly directed against the Pythagoreans (1092b 8–25):

We are not told how numbers are the causes of substances and of being. Are they boundaries in the same sense that points bound magnitudes? (Eurytus (p. 33) used to allot numbers to things, e.g. a number to man and a number to horse, depicting the forms of creatures by means of pebbles, like those who arranged numbers as triangular and quadrilateral figures.) Or are numbers the cause of being because harmony—and also man and every other existent—is a numerical ratio? But how can attributes like white, sweet, hot be numbers? That numbers are not essences nor causes of form [*morphe*] is obvious from the fact that the ratio is essence and the number merely matter. For example, the ratio of flesh or bone—"three parts fire to two parts earth"—is essence in this sense. Any given number, whether of fire or earth or unitary, always denumerates something; but the essence is "so much of this to so much of that" in accordance with the ratios of the compound. This is no longer a number. It is a numerical ratio, of corporeal or non-corporeal numbers. So number is not an efficient (neither number generally nor unit-number) nor a material cause, nor a formal cause, nor indeed a final cause.

Aristotle continues in this vein, piling up arguments against any number theory on Pythagorean lines. Compounds, he says, are an addition of so many parts to so many, not a multiplication. So the Pythagorean formulas are meaningless. Further, if things are numbers can the number of a thing be the cause of its being? And won't all things having the same number be identical? How of "correspondences" like the seven vowels, seven notes in the octave, seven against Thebes? Is seven here a cause? He goes on to inveigh against the theorists of *mousike* who, in the letters of the alphabet, in prosody, and in music, find numerical correspondences of deep significance, as the early critics used to do in Homer (1093b 5–29).

Such correspondences can be found as easily in eternal as they can in corruptible things. When you look at them as we have they seem to elude you—the characteristics of number, their opposites, and generally those mathematical relations which according to some are causes of the natural world. None of them is a cause in any of the senses we have defined concerning first principles. It is, however, in a sense made clear that they (the numbers) may be said to be good and that odd, straight, square, and the powers of some numbers belong in the column of the beautiful in the Table of Opposites. For there is a numerical coincidence with the seasons, and all the other coincidences they collect from mathematical speculations are of this kind. They are not necessary relations. For they are accidental to their subject but all related to one another, and so one by analogy. In each category of being is to be found an analogous predicate; e.g. as the straight is in length, so is the plane in surface and let us say the odd in number and the white in colour.

Moreover it is not idea-numbers that are the causes of musical concordances. For equal idea-numbers differ from one another in *eidos* if, as is the case, the units composing them do. So we need not posit them to explain musical concordance and the like.

Such are the conclusions to be drawn from number theory and further similar conclusions could be drawn. The fact that the genesis of numbers is such a laborious business, incapable of systematic structuring, would seem to be a strong argument against the theories of some thinkers separating *mathematica* from sensibles and making of them first principles.

In these final sections of Book N Aristotle may have the Pythagoreans in mind more than other thinkers (Ross *ad* 1092b 8) but his arguments are directed against theories rather than thinkers, and the paragraph in which he states his conclusion (1093b 21–29) certainly envisages others than Pythagoreans. Therefore we can only cautiously draw conclusions from it concerning Pythagorean number symbolism. But we have ample evidence elsewhere in the *Metaphysics* that they sought numerical "correspondences" and there can be no doubt that Aristotle is condemning their practices as well as other similar ones.

The whole critical review and analysis of number theories in Books M and N is as important for the knowledge of Pythagorean thought as is the more constructive account in Book A. For this reason we have attempted to survey its course and to bring into focus discussions in which Aristotle clearly has the Pythagoreans in mind. We must now attempt to draw what conclusions it justifies, always remembering its nature and purpose. Aristotle is not directing his arguments against any one person or school, but rather against the whole character and trend of thought at Athens in his day—against the mathematization of philosophy, both in physics and in metaphysics.

First let us note that in both books the Pythagoreans play a relatively minor role. The principal objects of Aristotle's attack in their order of importance are: Plato (the Plato of the *agrapha dogmata* in M; of the whole Theory of Ideas in N), Speusippus (especially in N where he appears sometimes to be paired with the Pythagoreans), Xenocrates (assuming more importance in M), and finally, other thinkers holding number theories, chief among whom are the Pythagoreans.

In the second place the Pythagorean number theory as reflected in the two final books of the *Metaphysics* is, wherever comparison is possible, the theory of Book A. The same simple cosmology in its three phases, the same account of the generation of number, the same refusal to specify how numbers proceeded from the One, the same search for correspondences, the same identification of numbers and things, with no doctrine of separate substance. This presentation of Pythagoreanism serves well what we might call Aristotle's dramatic purpose. The theory from which all number theories ultimately derive is shown to be simple, logical in its internal structure, free of the contradictions involved in Platonist versions of it. All that is wrong with it, Aristotle appears to say, is that it is obviously impossible as not answering to the world we know. And the more elaborate Platonist theories, with their new device of separate substance by means of which they create a "real" world other than the sensible one, though they appear to avoid the obvious Pythagorean error, only compound it by more errors of their own contrivance. This is such an obvious device of exposition that we might be inclined to suspect Aristotle's account. However, we must remember that his theme is perhaps the most important theme of philosophical debate during the decades when the *Metaphysics* was written, and that his lectures were delivered to an informed public, brought up on just the problems he is discussing. Even if we could imagine him distorting the truth for rhetorical or polemical effect, we cannot imagine him attempting a distortion that would destroy the effect of his argument on an informed audience. So we may take it that the Pythagoreanism he describes in Books *M* and *N*, corresponding as it does to the account of Book *A*, is the Pythagoreanism known to his hearers and readers.

Let us now turn from number theory proper to what Aristotle, in listing the problems of metaphysics (996a 4), tells us is the thorniest problem of all; namely, whether the One and Being are substances, "as the Pythagoreans and Plato used to maintain," or are attributes. Aristotle's answer—that they are attributes and not substances—transpires only later (1040b 15–24; 1083a 20–1085a 2), but he states the problem, as his 11th *aporia* (1001a 4), thus:[12]

The most difficult problem of all, and the most crucial one for real knowledge, is whether being and unity, each of them having its own identity, are substances of existing things, and if being and unity are both of them substances and neither attributes; or, in seeking to define unity and being, must we assume that they have a substrate. Both views of their nature are held. Plato and the Pythagoreans maintain that unity and being are not attributes but that these terms correspond to natures, the essence of each being unity itself and being itself. The physical philosophers, on the other hand, [specify what the One is].

As arguments for considering the One and Being as substances, Aristotle mentions that (1) if they are not substances no other universal can be a substance, and (2) if the One or unity is not a substance number cannot be a substance nor can any unit. As arguments *contra*, Aristotle suggests: (1) If the One and Being are substances how can there be any other substances, "as Parmenides argued"; (2) If unity is a substance, from what shall another One proceed? From a not-One?; then (3) Aristotle continues (1001b 7-13):

If the One is indivisible then, on Zeno's postulate,[13] it will be nothing. He argues that that which does not make that to which it is added greater nor that from which it is subtracted smaller, is not an existent. He obviously bases his arguments on the grounds that whatever *exists* is a magnitude and so corporeal. For the corporeal is existent in all dimensions; some other (non-corporeal) things will in a sense when added cause increase—e.g. lines and surfaces—yet others, e.g. points and units, never.

In this passage Aristotle ascribes to Plato and the Pythagoreans, to all appearances as a common doctrine, theories that in part belong to both, in part to one or other, and in part to neither. Nowhere else does he impute to the Pythagoreans a doctrine of Being; in this passage he must be thinking of their One as being like the One Being of Parmenides who, surprisingly enough, is alluded to both by name and indirectly, through Zeno. (We shall discuss later if we can infer from this, as some have done, a relation between Pythagorean and Parmenidean theories.) Further, Aristotle nowhere else attributes a number-derivation theory to the Pythagoreans. Here he describes a theory, certainly not Platonic[14] but which might by elimination be thought to be Pythagorean, in which line, surface, and solid proceed from the unit-point. This is precisely the theory that Speusippus (*Theol. Ar.* 84 = fr. 4 Lang) describes as Pythagorean. We remember that when Speusippus was appointed to the headship of the Academy on Plato's death, Aristotle together with Xenocrates left Athens, and that he is elsewhere very critical of Speusippus's interpretation of the Theory of Ideas in a "pythagorizing" sense. In this passage, where he is concerned with theories rather than persons, it seems probable that he has included as a type of objectionable number theory one that, though it is neither that of Plato nor of the Pythagoreans, nevertheless exhibits the features to which he takes exception.

If it were possible in this passage to distinguish clearly between Platonic and Pythagorean doctrine, and to maintain that Aristotle is implying that Zeno's arguments are directed against Pythagorean criticisms of Parmenides' doctrine of his, Zeno's time, (the point of departure of the Pythagoreans being the Pythagoreanism here described) then our knowledge of Pythagoreanism would be substantially increased. But it is not necessary to suppose that Zeno is reacting to contemporary attacks or indeed to any attack. He may simply be defending the position of Parmenides against all other pluralist systems and against "common sense" objections. That is the conclusion to which we might be led by the *aporia* (1001b 26–1002a 12) immediately following on the one we have been discussing. There Aristotle raises the problem of whether numbers, solids, plane surfaces, and points are substances. As argument for their being substances, Aristotle suggests that bodies/solids (there is some play on the ambiguity of the term) are substances because qualities can be predicated of them and they are constant through change. But if bodies/solids are substances then *a fortiori* planes, lines, and points must be substances because they can, it would seem, exist without body, whereas body cannot exist without what bounds and defines it.[15] So, Aristotle continues, most thinkers and (all) earlier thinkers held body, the corporeal, to be substance. Later and more subtle thinkers held numbers to be first principles and substances. He does not identify these earlier thinkers and the later and more subtle thinkers. The first qualification does not necessarily exclude the Pythagoreans, who thought that things were numbers. The second could only include Pythagoreans who believed that number was not corporeal, and, despite the assertion of Alexander (230.11–13) that the Pythagoreans are to be included with Plato in this class we know nothing of Pythagoreans who held that number was not corporeal (Cherniss 41–42).

It seems probable that Aristotle means by "later and more subtle thinkers" the Platonists, and that we must look for the Pythagoreans among the majority, perhaps among earlier thinkers. This does not exclude the possibility that Zeno was addressing a specific contemporary audience, and that there were Pythagoreans among his critics. But there is nothing in our tradition, and no grounds to be gained from analysis of the Zeno fragments (see n. 14), to enable us to say either that there *was* a Pythagorean reaction or of what nature that reaction was.[16]

Our grounds for believing that Parmenides himself reacted to a Pythagorean system of a time earlier than his own are stronger. Here there are two theses, radically differing the one from the other. The first and older of these, that of Tannery, suggested that Parmenides' *Doxa* was a reply to Pythagorean cosmology. This thesis may be said to have been abandoned since Reinhardt's *Parmenides* and its onslaught on a Pythagorean Parmenides (231–249). The second thesis is that the Way of Truth itself is a reaction to Pythagorean cosmology. Raven (*KR* 272–277) argues that "each of his [Parmenides'] affirmations involves a corresponding denial" (273) and that the predicates of the One which he is rejecting are Pythagorean predicates of their One. If we may take it that the Pythagorean cosmology against which

Parmenides was reacting was the cosmology described by Aristotle, and that Parmenides was denying a generation of the cosmos, a surrounding void, and a procession of number from the One, then the thesis that the Way of Truth was a direct reaction to Pythagoreanism seems to me to gain weight. The proem describes a journey to the source of truth, undertaken to discover or learn truth. It seems both probable and credible (though incapable of proof) that what Parmenides describes is a wrestling with the philosophical system that, in his youth, had most authority in Magna Graecia—Pythagoreanism.

Let us now attempt to sum up what Aristotle tells us of number theories. The form of that theory to which he makes most frequent reference is that "things are numbers" and that these number-things come to be in the course of cosmological process, a process occurring in three phases. In the first phase the two first principles interact to produce the One, our universe. In the second phase this One breathes in the surrounding void, and produces the numbers. In the final phase we have the universe as constituted, its existents being bodies consisting of number, with between bodies a void.

Simplicity is the most surprising aspect of this cosmological scheme. From number-determined first principles comes a number that is no number but rather a first principles of number, and from it in turn come the numbers that are things.

The Pythagorean scheme, however, simple and symmetrical though it was, did not satisfy Aristotle. He remarks (1080b 20) that the Pythagoreans "appear to be at a loss for an explanation how the first unit or One was constituted as an extended unit." He would apparently expect to be told not merely that the One came to be from its original constituent causes, but also how it acquired its corporeality. Without a substrate their two first causes could not produce a physical world. (But it would appear that the *apeiron* surrounding the One was corporeal, so we may assume that for the Pythagoreans *peras* was also somehow corporeal, or capable of acting on a corporeal *apeiron*.) Had the One internal constituent parts, such as planes or surfaces or seeds (1091a 15)? If we interpret this question of Aristotle's, he expects them to say that their universe is constituted of geometrical elements (like those of the *Timeaus*), or of body surfaces (as for the Atomists), or of seeds (as for Anaxagoras). In each case he implicitly refers to these preceding thinkers by the term he uses, and he suggests that he finds nothing analogous to these minimum constituent parts in the case of the Pythagoreans. He is arguing that there must be some such constituents in physical existents, and if in existents, then in the One from which these proceed: and if in the One then in its first causes. He tells us elsewhere what their minimum constituent parts were. The Pythagoreans, he says (1080b 16–20), recognizes only mathematical number but for them it is the *res extensa* constituting sensible substances. Nevertheless there remains a real ambiguity. We may accept the theory that first principles which are number-determined and somehow corporeal produce a universe resembling the One Being of Parmenides. But how could the Pythagorean One either already contain within itself a plurality of existents that become discrete quantities as soon as "breathing in" begins; or if, on the contrary, it is a unity, how could it breathe in and in this manner create a plurality? Aristotle asks of the Pythagoreans that they explain just when and how a plurality of existents and of corporeal existents came to be, in what is the equivalent of a material substrate. He repeatedly alludes to this defect in their system and this suggests that the system was an early one and that in it derivation went unexplained.

That these were his principal grounds for criticism is apparent from a comparison he makes between Pythagorean and Platonic theory (987b 19–988a 1):

Plato considered the elements of the Ideas, as causes, to be the elements of all existing things, that "the great and the small" was their material principle and the One their essential form. For from "the great and the small" by participation in the One come numbers. [See Bonitz *Aristotle's Metaphysica* 93–94] He maintained, in approximate agreement with the Pythagoreans, that the One is a substance and not a predicate of some other existent; and like them he held that numbers are causes of the real existence of other things. But Plato introduced as a characteristic doctrine the dyad instead of the Pythagorean unitary *apeiron*, and his *apeiron* consisted of a "great-and-small." For him numbers existed apart from sensibles, whereas for the Pythagoreans things are numbers and there are no intermediate *mathematica*. These two innovations—unlike the Pythagoreans he made the One and numbers separate substances and he introduced Ideas— arose from dialectical inquiries not pursued by earlier thinkers. Plato, further, introduced the dyad as the other of his pair of first principles because numbers other than prime numbers could be produced from it as from a mould (*ekmageion*).

We may neglect the difficult problems regarding Plato's later Theory of Ideas that are involved in this passage. For our purposes the important statement is that whereas Plato had a theory of the derivation of numbers from first principles, the Pythagoreans had none, contenting themselves with the statement that things are numbers. This is one of the two characteristics that for Aristotle mark the difference between Platonists and Pythagoreans. Here he adds an illuminating explanation of their difference. Plato, he says, introduced the *chorismos* of things and numbers because it was demanded by his logical procedures. Further, while keeping the One as a first principle, he changed the other Pythagorean opposite from *apeiron* into "great-and-small" in order to generate number. That is, Plato modified Pythagorean number theory in such a way as to permit of the construction of a logically viable theory of the derivation of number from first principles.

Now we need not believe that Plato in fact took over Pythagorean number theory and subjected it to the modifications necessary to adapt it to his own Theory of Ideas. But clearly Aristotle considers it to be a principal difference between Plato and the Pythagoreans that the one has a theory of derivation, the others have not. It would also seem clear that though, for Aristotle, the Pythagoreans escape many difficulties by propounding no such theory, its absence is a serious defect in their thought. They should not "be at a loss for an explanation of how the first unit or One was constituted as an extended unit." (1080b 19–21).

It is worthy of note that for Aristotle a Pythagorean derivation, if there were one, would be after the manner of Plato's and not simply the point–line–surface–solid scheme so often attributed to them by later tradition. Such a derivation proceeds not from the One but from the unit. It does not, at least immediately, explain derivation from first principles or causes. It fails to account for the origin of the unit. And it moves toward the solid of geometry. What Aristotle is looking for (and rightly) in the case of the Pythagoreans is a derivation from first principles. Plato has a unity like that of the Pythagoreans but paired with it is a duality having the capacity to produce two's. Unity and duality together generate number. The Pythagoreans' unity on the other hand is the product of *peras* and *apeiron*, there being no substrate. This unity when constituted ("how they cannot say"), in its turn generates number-things by breathing the void. Why should the products of its generation be either numbers or things.

If, as I have suggested, the doctrine set forth by Aristotle is an early one, problems of separate substance, of substrate and of derivation had not yet arisen at that time; and it is not surprising that, as Aristotle repeatedly asserts, the Pythagoreans took refuge in "correspondences." In some cases, as in astronomy and harmonics, the practice of looking for "correspondences" could lead to important observations of phenomena. It was unlikely to lead to advances in arithmetic or geometry. Even within the mathematical disciplines, once they were established, it led towards further observations of "correspondences" or the behaviour of numbers such as we find reflected in Euclid's Seventh Book. This sort of theorizing is also expressed in the "elegant little treatise" of Speusippus and, in a much profounder way, in Plato's number speculation.

What degree of credence must we give to Aristotle's account of Pythagorean number theory? It has the merit of internal consistency and credibility. In his many references to this and other aspects of Pythagoreanism, Aristotle neither contradicts himself (except in the one questionable instance (73–74) of a mimesis doctrine), nor offers as Pythagorean doctrine his own explanations of theories that are to him otherwise unexplainable. His report is not contradicted by other earlier or contemporary reports. In short, if we make due allowance for Aristotle's method and purpose, his account of Pythagoreanism is the only one in which we can put faith. If Pythagoreanism was something other than what he reports, then we can have no real knowledge of it.

However, we cannot deny that his report is a biased one. He was not endowed with a mathematical imagination, and so failed to appreciate the possibilities, and the validity, of number-related theories such as those of the Pythagoreans and of the Platonists (Heath, *Maths* 2). In him they awakened only hostility as logical and physical aberrations. He was also blind to the philosophical, and especially the ethical, implications of Pythagorean religious (or para-religious) beliefs and practices. Though "all men by nature have a desire for knowledge," what he considers to be possible objects of knowledge are not those of the Pythagoreans. He would not concede that knowledge can have direct consequences for conduct. So his report, though fair and conscientious as far as it goes, is not sympathetic and cannot be more than partial.

One of the most peculiar and striking characteristics of Aristotle's report is that it gives us no inkling who "the Pythagoreans" were, nor to what epoch the report is to be referred. I have suggested that it should be referred to an early period of Pythagoreanism and probably in its essentials to Pythagoras himself. The reasons for such attribution have already been discussed and will be merely recapitulated here.

1. The notion of *apeiron* is Anaximander's.[17] Pythagoras is the only succeeding thinker who adopts it in the sense in which it was propounded (74. n.12), and it seems more likely that Pythagoras should have adopted it before his departure from Ionia than that some

subsequent western thinker should have revived it. If we try to impute
the paternity of the idea to a successor of Pythagoras in the first half
of the 5th century we are forced to postulate an X (Hippasus will
not do), living in the year "Pythagoras-minus-30," as the father of
Pythagorean doctrine. On the other hand, we suppose that this X lived
in the second half of the century (and Philolaus will not do) he is
curiously untouched by post-Parmenidean speculation and the critique
of Zeno.

2. The fact that the doctrine is a simple one, showing little sign of
modification or erosion by later criticism, might be taken to indicate
that it cannot be early. But apart from the fact that it is difficult to
imagine this sort of synoptic simplicity in a later thinker, it seems
what we should expect in terms of what we suppose the historical
development to have been. We may assume that the authority of
Pythagoras, to which the Pythagoreans continued to appeal through
the centuries, will have been felt strongly in the generation immediately
following his death, and that this authority would tend to preserve
his teachings, especially if they were simple in outline. Their authority
would probably not be shaken by the frontal attack of Parmenides,
some forty years after Pythagoras' death, for that attack came when we
assume the Pythagoreans to have been under political pressure
inclining them to conservatism; and in the *débâcle* that followed,
surviving Pythagoreans would tend to cling to their traditions. In the
next half century the only Pythagorean of whom we have real knowledge is Philolaus, and his thinking, in so far as we can judge of it,
seems to rest on assumptions similar to these.

3. The doctrine of number-things is a simple one, and is often described as "primitive." This description is reasonable if by it we mean
a doctrine earlier, and therefore simpler, than would be possible after
the time of Parmenides and Zeno, when other problems had arisen. If
Pythagoras was a thinker at all we must imagine him as a thinker after
the manner of Anaximander, his question being "What is the nature
of our world?" and his answer, an hypothesis as to the nature of *things*.
That his hypothesis remained unchanged in substance may be due in
part to the conservatism of the Pythagoreans, but chiefly to the fact
that it was useful and fruitful.

If the Pythagoreanism of Aristotle's report is to be attributed to
Pythagoras himself, how can he have arrived at those theories? We
may assume that Pythagoras either "heard" Anaximander or read
his writings, and that the companion notions of a Boundless and of
mathematical determination will have made particular impression on

him. Further, Babylonian mathematics, when they became familiar to the Ionians of the sixth century, may have provided the stimulus and excitement that the opening up of a new world of ideas often gives to its epoch.[18] As, a century earlier, Ionia had come under orientalizing influences in art, so in the sixth century Thales, Anaximander, and Pythagoras may have come under the influence of Babylonian mathematics as a revelation of a new idiom in which the mind could express its thought.

For Anaximander the symmetry of his cosmos was exhibited in mathematical relations. Problems remained however. Why, from an indeterminate *apeiron* that is in motion probably as chaotic as that of Plato's Receptacle, an *apeiron* from which qualitative and not quantitative opposites are separated off, is there generated an orderly cosmos the parts of which stand in a number relation to one another? Why are some of the numbers expressing these relations even, with affinity to the boundless, and others odd, having the characteristics of limit? Does *apeiron* imply *peras* and if so what is its role? The cosmology reported by Aristotle is an answer to questions such as these, but has, as a characteristic of its own, a physical imagination such as is postulated by Max Planck (*Wege zur physikalischen Erkenntnis* [Leipzig 1944] 181): "Besides these two worlds—the real world and the world of sense perception—there is a third world which we must distinguish from them, the world of physical science or the world picture of physics. . . . The function of this world picture is, in respect of the real world, to make it as nearly understandable as possible, and in respect of the world of sense perception, to describe it as simply as possible." In so far as the knowledge and the means of the times permitted this is what the Pythagorean system achieves.[19]

NOTES

[1]Burkert 47–73 discusses the post-Aristotelian tradition re Pythagoreanism, for which he sees two sources; the first being Aristotle, the second and more important being the Early Academy and in particular Speusippus, Xenocrates, and Heraclides Ponticus. He sees as the principal characteristic of Pythagoreanism, as presented in the Aristotelian tradition, Limit/Unlimited; as presented in the Academic tradition, monad/indefinite dyad and *chorismos*. In an attempt to distinguish between these two traditions as sources for Aëtius's doxography he

suggests that references to "Pythagoras" are to be referred to the Academic, those to "the Pythagoreans" for the most part to the Aristotelian tradition. The expression οἱ ἀπὸ Πυθαγόρου is declared secondary and ambivalent. But *Dox.Gr.* 313.4, 13 shows that it was considered merely a variation for "Pythagoreans," and 307.22 and 312.11 certainly do not derive from Aristotle. A glance at the *Index nominum* of Sextus Empiricus, where we have some fifteen ways of expressing "Pythagoreans," suggests that the change may often be made for variety. Burkert's is not a criterion that can be applied as a sure means of making the important distinction.

The fact is that the doxography, in so far as it deals with first principles and numbers, reflects, not Aristotle, but the Pythagoreanism of the Early Academy. The reason may be, as Burkert (55) suggests, that Theophrastus (*Metaph.* 11a 27) so reports it. It seems likely that, even assuming that the doxographers referred to the Aristotelian account, it made no sense to them, whereas the alternative account was on the lines of later Platonic doctrine and so more familiar.

If Aristotle's account was not reflected in the doxography, no more were the modifications of Platonic doctrine of Speusippus and Xenocrates. Speusippus, in particular, had ample opportunity to familiarize himself with Pythagorean thought in Italy. P. Merlan (*Philologus* 103 [1959] 183–214) has suggested that he accompanied Plato to Sicily not only in 361–360 B.C. but also in 366. His interest in Pythagorean numbers is well attested, but he abandoned the Platonic One and Indefinite Dyad. Yet it is the indefinite dyad that the doxography consistently reports as Pythagorean.

Burkert 349.5 argues, as against Tannery, that musical theory cannot have given rise to a mathematical treatment of the problem of irrationals and (412) that the problem can have arisen only in the course of geometrical inquiry.

[2]I have translated this phrase ambiguously because it is ambiguous in the Greek. Alexander 37, 6–16 offers three different interpretations. Asclepius 35.29 treats it as temporal. Ross' suggestion that Aristotle is associating later Pythagoreans with the Atomists seems improbable. More probably the phrase is meant to suggest that there were Pythagoreans active through the whole development just sketched.

[3]Ross treats the subordinate clause following ὅτι (29–31 ὅτι-ὁμοίως) as explaining what precedes, i.e. that justice, soul, etc. are the things resembling the existents referred to in l. 28. But the explanatory phrase "rather than in fire, earth, and water" excludes this interpretation, and the meaning must be as it is summarized 986a 1–2,—that the elements of number (rather than fire, water, earth) are the elements of things.

The long and complex sentence 985b 26–986a 6 has an initial part alleging the several reasons why the Pythagoreans thought number to be a first principle. This part is marked off by a resumptive ἐπεὶ δή l. 32, and the reasons are then summarized: (1) numbers are prior, (2) nature reflects number. The subordinate clauses 26–32 specify how nature reflects number: (1) it is the element *in* things, rather than fire, etc., (2) things like justice and soul are modifications of number, (3) musical consonances are governed by number. These are three principal fields in which the Pythagoreans held everything to be an expression of number, and I can see no way of subordinating (2) to (1). If we are to understand the sentence thus we must suppose either that Aristotle has lost track of his rather breathless periods, or that an early copyist has omitted a connective, possibly ὅτι δέ l. 29. Bonitz, *ad loc.*, suggests that there was a corruption of the text.

[4]Ross, following Bonitz, would translate πάθος by "property." It is difficult to see what property of number justice could be. At 1004b 10 Aristotle uses πάθος of numbers in the sense of property, but the properties he mentions are such as evenness/oddness. The meaning here seems to be "modification" in the sense that justice is a square number $= 2^2$. See Aristotle, *Magna Moralia* 1182a 14 and *E. N.* 1132b 22 where justice is said to be a reciprocal relation between crime and punishment, and also a square number. Though not all correspondences are such modifications, Iamblichus (*Theol. Ar. passim*) lists many.

πάθος recurs at 986a 17 together with ἕξεις, with obvious reference to the categories, in the sense of modifications. Alexander 41.18–24 suggests that the phrase alludes to numbers as efficient cause. He also cites Aspasius' impossible suggestion that we are to understand number as matter, even as modification, and "odd," as state. But the phrase need not refer to Aristotle's doctrine of causes nor of matter–form–privation. He has already alluded to aspects of Pythagorean theory where number was not a material cause.

[5]We note here that reference is to the decad and not to the *tetractys*, which is neither tetrad nor decad. The *tetractys* does not designate any one number, but is a summation of numbers, being $1 + 2 + 3 + 4 = 10$. It gets its name from τέτραχα (Plato *Gorgias* 464c) formed on the analogy of δίχα τρίχα, and so has as its basic meaning "in four parts or ways." According to the Commentary of Hierocles (*FPG* 1, 408) on the *Carmen Aureum* (48), this is the meaning implied in the Pythagorean oath—"by him who brought our kind the *tetractys*, in which is the source and root of everlasting nature." The oath is often regarded as a document of early Pythagoreanism attesting the *tetractys* as a central doctrine. But it has been pointed out that the oath cannot be earlier than Empedocles whose term *rhizoma*—root is used, and if by γενέα we are to understand "Pythagorean sect" rather than "human kind" then it is likely to be much later. Delatte (*Études* 249–268) has collected and discussed (sometimes uncritically) the references to the *tetractys*. He cites variant readings for the oath (250). The originally negative form of the oath, altered in the *Carmen Aureum*, is as yet unexplained.

In sources subsequent to the 1st cent. B.C. we find the *tetractys* doctrine presented as a central one. Sextus Empiricus (*M.*7.94) has it in its "fourfold" significance and connects it with musical *harmonia*. He refers to the basic ratio of 2:1 (chord), 3:2 (fifth), and 4:3 (fourth), all expressible in terms of the four numbers of the *tetractys*. For Nicomachus (*mus. script. gr.* Jan 279.9) and Plutarch (*de Iside* 381F–382A) the fourfold aspect remains constant but the sum changes with change in intervals. Theon of Smyrna (97.14 ff.) knows several interpretations.

It seems unlikely that the *tetractys* doctrine with its connotations was known to Aristotle. In the present passage he speaks of the *decad* as a perfection embracing the whole nature of number. Though he says earlier (985b 31) that the Pythagoreans consider musical harmonies to be numerical and (986a 2) the universe to be a fitting-together (*harmonia*) and a number, he connects neither of these two kinds of "harmonies" with the decad. (The commentators however—Alexander 39. 19–22 and Asclepius 36. 28–30—introduce the *tetractys* of the first four numbers and connect it with the musical scale.) In 1073a 20 he tells us that for some Platonists numbers do not proceed to infinity but are limited to the decad, and this theory is referred to again (1084a 12, 32) without reference to persons. But in *Phys.* 206b 32 it is explicitly referred to Plato himself. See also *Prob.* 910b 32–38 where we have the decad as a perfect number and as Pythagorean.

In 1078b 23 Aristotle tells us that the Pythagoreans defined numerically, but he does not include *tetractys* nor *harmonia* among his examples, as would have been natural if the developed doctrines had been known to him. He knows that the decad has a special status in Pythagorean speculation. (He will have known Speusippus' essay on the decad *Theol. Ar.* 79–85) He knows that for them *harmonia* is numerically expressible. But neither he nor Speusippus knows the term *tetractys* nor its special significance. This may be another case in which a Platonic doctrine has been subsequently declared Pythagorean and given a "mystical" significance. For the importance later assumed by the tetrad see S. K. Heninger, jr., "Some Renaissance Versions of the Pythagorean Tetrad," *Studies in the Renaissance* 8 (New York 1961) 7–35, where a bibliography to 1700 is given (34–35).

[6]In 985b 23–986a 13 Aristotle suggests that the Pythagoreans observe similarities and deduce identity, and from this we infer that they had no theory of the derivation of number-sensibles from the One. If Aristotle had had warrant for imputing to them what is usually said to be the pythagorizing solution of the Early Academy, that from the monad or point comes the line, from the line, plane surface, from plane surface, the solid and physical magnitudes (or any of the current variations on that theme which he reports), he would surely have compared and contrasted Pythagorean theory with Academic versions of it and would have noted the aspects in which the former differed from Plato, Speusippus, and Xenocrates. But he nowhere does so. It is possible that some Pythagoreans, contemporaries of Aristotle, had evolved or adopted a theory of derivation. For them, the point, as a unit having position and corporeal, would be an indivisible magnitude and so monadic. In the *Physics* (227a 27) Aristotle points out that points and monads differ. There can be something (viz. a line) between two points but not between two monads nor between monad and dyad. At the beginning of the *De Caelo* 268a 11, Aristotle appears to be attributing to the Pythagoreans the line–plane–solid derivation usually attributed to Plato. But it then appears that he is citing a Pythagorean dictum on the triad.

Cornford in *Plato and Parmenides* (London 1939) 11–13, principally on the basis of *De Anima* 409a 4 (where, however, the reference is rather to Plato than to the Pythagoreans) argues for a fluxion theory from points, taking the fluxion from Sextus Empiricus. Previously, Taylor had propounded a similar thesis in his *Commentary on Plato's Timaeus*. Ross (*Physics ad* 203a 10–11) pointed out, as against Taylor, that though a related thesis explains some late doxographical comment it does not explain the arguments of Zeno, which may be directed against the Pythagoreans. Cherniss' attack is more basic. He argues (224–225) that the notion that the Pythagoreans generated the number series from the unit is a mistaken notion of Aristotle's; but Mondolfo (*ZM* 354–355) has argued, it seems to me effectively, against this thesis. Aristotle does not in fact speak of the generation of the *unit*, nor of the number series.

Plutarch (*de E ap. Delph.* 387F–388E) has a curious account of the generative capacities of male and female numbers, but nothing authorizes the supposition that such a theory had an early origin or that the pattern of animal generation served as prototype in cosmology/arithmology.

For further discussion of derivation theories pp. 101–104, and my article *Phoenix* Vol. xx (1966), pp. 32*ff*.

⁷We have no explanation for many important aspects of the theory. Why, for instance, did the Pythagoreans subsume Odd under Limit, Even under Unlimited? We can understand why, in Limit, they should see a principle of arithmetical determination, in Unlimited an indeterminacy. But this is not given in early linguistic usage: for the epic, ἄρτιος is perfect, good, or fitting; the prepositional prefix of περισσος implies that ἴσος was primary and the norm. Why with the Pythagoreans are normal connotations reversed? Why, at least for some of them, was Limit/Odd good, Unlimited/Even evil? We can only assume that, for the Pythagoreans, Limit/Unlimited was the primary pair, determining the nature of what was subsumed under them; they produced the One, and a One that was limited, thus Odd must be subsumed under Limit.

This One, however, was not said simply to be odd. It was *artioperissos* or even/odd as the product of both first principles. Theon of Smyrna tells us that according to Aristotle in his Pythagorean monograph (*Fr. Sel.* 137) the One partakes of both natures, even and odd, because if it is added to an even number it makes it odd, if added to an odd number it makes it even. This is obviously later sophistication that may have been alleged as "proof."

Of what complexities a similar scheme is capable we see in the *Timaeus*. There Plato invokes a Demiurge to fashion a world soul of a stuff the ingredients of which are Identity, Difference, and Being, and he imposes on it both numerical ratios and musical consonances. Nothing authorizes us to suppose that the Pythagorean scheme exhibited similar complexities, and, indeed, we may argue from the silence of our tradition that the coming-to-be of the cosmos was probably not described in much greater detail.

Cherniss has suggested (225–226) that "the identification of even and odd with limit and unlimited represents a later development." The grounds given in chap. 3 and again here, and Aristotle's repeated statements, seem to me strong arguments against this.

Guthrie (276–279), on the strength of a casual use of σπέρμα "seed" in 1091a 15 and 1092a 32 and with the aid of a questionable γόνιμον from Anaximander

(Kahn 57) can write "the first unit consisted of a seed, the seed of the world, like the γόνιμον attributed to Anaximander." This seed, he asserts is "both a number and the nucleus of the physical world (278)." Nothing suggesting this is to be found in Aristotle. The σπέρμα is only one of Aristotle's suggested constituents. In *Orpheus and Greek Religion* 223, Guthrie suggested that the γόνιμον of Anaximander was to be interpreted as a world-egg. Aristotle rarely reports theories with an obviously primitive background in the *Metaphysics*.

⁸For comparable and non-comparable numbers see J. Stenzel, 45–48, where Stenzel refers to the discussion in Aristotle and the commentators.

In 1080a 12 ff. Aristotle would appear to believe that there is only one kind of number, namely additive number; and that it is arrived at by adding a unit (always a similar unit) to the preceding number in the number series. 1 + 1 = 2, 2 + 1 = 3. (And so only the numbers of class 2 would be numbers properly speaking.) He then goes on to add a further complexity. In all three classes the numbers may be (a) separate substances, (b) immanent in particulars, (c) some separate substances, some immanent. He adds that all combinations of these possibilities have been propounded—except the view that all units are incomparable—and argues that three types of solution have been offered (1080b 11–20):

1. Besides the "Ideal" or natural numbers there were also mathematical numbers, both being separate substances. (This may be the Platonic solution.)

2. Only mathematical numbers exist, and they exist as separate substances. (This is probably the solution of Speusippus.)

3. Only mathematical numbers exist. They exist not as separate substances but as monads having magnitude. All sensibles, and the whole universe, are composed of such numbers. (This is expressly said to be the Pythagorean view.)

In thus classifying the Pythagoreans Aristotle is undoubtedly mistaken. They did not believe only in additive numbers, whether corporeal or non-corporeal. The role of unity, dyad, triad, tetrad in their scheme is undeniable; and the importance of the *tetractys* is well attested. But they did believe in comparable units in that their monads lent themselves to ordinary arithmetical operations.

Eva Sachs (145–146) quotes the scholiast to Euclid: "The Pythagoreans first inquired into incommensurability, approaching it from considerations of number. In all number there was a common measure, the unit (monad). But they could find no such measure for magnitudes, because in every number—of whatever kind—there remains a minimum part that cannot be further divided. But every magnitude is infinitely divisible and no part remains which as minimum does not admit of further division. . . . As the unit of measurement must be smaller than what is measured, and every number is measureable, there must be a unit of measurement smaller than all numbers. Likewise with magnitudes, if they are to be commensurable, there must be a smaller unit of measurement. For numbers there is such a smallest unit, for magnitudes there is not."

Here the scholiast is concerned with the passage from arithmetic to geometry. His argument would suggest that if the Pythagorean unit is substantial, it must be the unit of both arithmetic and geometry. How Xenocrates could arrive at such a position is explained by Pines, "A new fragment of Xenocrates," *TAPS* 51.2 (Philadelphia 1961) 17. It is a problem that could arise only after the problem of the irrational and of commensurability had been formulated, and cannot have reference to fifth-century Pythagoreanism.

⁹*Ad* 1083b 8 [Alexander] 767.9–21 describes their operations as being very simple. They say, for instance, that water is the number nine. Nine is the square of a prime number which, being odd, lies between (and so limits) two even numbers. These characteristics of nine are the characteristics they seek in water. The particular operations Alexander describes may be Neopythagorean, but similar procedures characterized Pythagorean arithmology in all periods.

¹⁰It is commonly stated that the Pythagoreans derive number-things from the One by the mediation of point–line–surface–solid or some variation of that theory. Diels (*Vors.* 58 B 23-25) cites three passages regarding the theory in which, as his inclusion of them suggests, the anonymous thinkers (τίνες) are to be regarded as Pythagoreans. Raven (*KR* 252–256) describes the cosmological process by which in the one act the units of arithmetic and the points of geometry both come to be. Raven concedes (253) that "Aristotle himself nowhere in his extant works tells us anything at all of the first consequence of this 'inhalation' of the void by the first unit," but, on the authority of Ross, he cites Alexander (*KR* fr. 317) "to fill the gap."

Ross (*ad* 1036b 8) imputes the derivation theory to the Pythagoreans. In this passage Aristotle is discussing theorists who will not accept the usual definition of a line, in abstraction from the material in which it is described. They maintain that e.g. a circle is to the bronze as a human person is to his flesh and bones, and that any sound definition must cover both aspects, as does the Platonic definition of the line as a dyad. But then the dyad turns out to be many differing things, just like the numbers of the Pythagoreans. Aristotle elsewhere (987a 26–27) complains that Pythagorean numbers turn out to be differing things. It is not suggested here that Pythagorean numbers are lines.

Ross (*ad* 1028b 16) with the support of Asclepius (379.3–8) and again later (*ad* 1090b 5) identifies some anonymous thinkers who hold the line derivation theory as Pythagoreans. The latter passage has been analyzed in detail by Saffrey (27–28) and his arguments need not be repeated. In 1002a 4 Aristotle points out that, for persons holding the line theory, the monad or point is more truly substance than line, and so on. But he goes on to say that "subsequent thinkers, more subtle than they" hold number to be substance. Here Ross, and the commentators, suggest that both Platonists and Pythagoreans may be referred to. But how could "the Pythagoreans" be subsequent thinkers? Would they have evolved a number theory from a point-line theory? Are we to impute to them a doctrine of substance?

It need not surprise us that every time Aristotle refers to a point-line derivation theory the commentators name the Pythagoreans. By their time, the doxography recognized the Pythagoreans as the authors of that theory, and the Neopythagoreans were elaborating on it.

It has been suggested by P. Kucharski that *de An.* 404b 19–27 refers to the

Pythagorean *tetractys* and to the point-line theory. (This has been refuted, Saffrey x–xi.) All of the ancient commentators ascribe it to Plato, with the one exception of Themistius in his *Paraphrasis* (ed. Heinze, 11.20–12.1) who attributes it to Xenocrates (see Pines [14–15] for comment).

In *De An.* 403b 20 ff. Aristotle is outlining his predecessors' theories of soul. He divides these into two classes, those in which the soul is the cause of motion and those in which it is the source of knowledge and perception. These latter, on the principle that like is known by like, in some fashion situate their first principles in the soul in order that, being present there, they may *know* their like in the sensible world. So the *autozoon* is formed from unity and primary length, breadth, and height or, to express it in another way, *nous* is the one, *episteme* is the two (being the one extended), the number of plane surface is opinion, and that of the solid, perception.

That the theory here described may have Pythagorean origins, as Kucharski suggests, is possible. But it is not possible to deny that Aristotle is here ascribing it to Plato, that it describes the *autozoon* and that it can be understood of the *Timaeus* in the sense in which Ross in his comment suggests. (See also Theiler, *Aristoteles* note *ad* 404b 21.) Burkert (23–25) argues convincingly that the derivation theory is Platonic, not Pythagorean.

In conclusion, Aristotle's account of the Pythagoreans represents them as having para-arithmetical and not geometrical interests. The point-line theory suggests a background of geometry. It is unlikely to be early Pythagorean, and even if later Pythagoreans adopted it, nevertheless, its origin would be Academic. But in fact Aristotle nowhere says that the Pythagoreans held this theory. The commentators cite the Pythagoreans for it only because it was an established feature of their tradition.

We find the theory full-fledged in Speusippus' treatise (Iambl. *Theol. Ar.* 85.21–23), in the sequence point–line–surface–solid and this becomes the traditional "Pythagorean" form. Nicomachus (*Eisagoge* Hoche 86, 9–87.6) develops this form. Sextus Empiricus deals with it in some detail and variously. (*Math.* 3.19–91; 7.99–100; 4.3 and 10.248–309). He introduces the fluxion theory on which Cornford, *Plato and Parmenides*, built. Burkert (60) with ref. *de An.* 409a 1–4 has suggested that we may have the origin of this fluxion theory with Xenocrates.

Aristotle (*Anal. Post.* 87a 36), without ascribing it to any school cites the definition: "A monad is an entity (οὐσία) not having position, a point is an entity having position." This second definition, in which the term οὐσία is used (and we may assume that Aristotle would not have used it unless it were in the original) though it may be Pythagorean, can only belong to a Pythagoreanism that knew a doctrine of being. If the definition is contemporary with the term it is probably ascribable to the fourth century. It may be merely a rephrasing of the first definition quoted. And the first implies a critical examination of the notion "unit" in which (1) the ordinal function of number is apprehended and (2) a distinction is drawn between units in the abstract as serially occurring and a unit having position. (If we except the highly suspect fragment of Philolaus 44 B 11, οὐσία as a philosophical term does not occur before Plato.)

It is commonly suggested that the Pythagoreans derived their notion of monad, unit, point empirically from the practice of *psephoi*-arithmetic, as by Burnet (99–105) and among others Becker (40–44). K. von Fritz in a review of Becker (*Gnomon* [1958] 81–87) suggests that, though *psephoi*-arithmetic cannot go back to the sixth century, it must be early. In the epic ψῆφος does not occur and ψῆφις only once (*Il.* 21.260); ψάμαθος, ψάμμος and ψάω from which they all derive, are frequent. With voting procedures (which involve counting but not calculation) ψῆφος and its cognates achieve wide currency in the fifth century. Herodotus speaks of λογίζεσθαι ψήφοις as common to Greeks and Egyptians (*Hdt.* 2.36) but he clearly implies abacus-reckoning (whereas the *abax*—see *LSJ*—is a sand-table). The other fifth-century references all imply counting procedures such as would occur in voting. The exception is Epicharmus (*Vors.* 23 B 2.1–3) where by the addition or removal of a ψῆφος an even number becomes odd, an odd even. This has an arithmological background (and hence Gigon, *Untersuchungen zu Heraklit* [Leipzig 1935] 140 concludes for Pythagorean influence) and does not allude to reckoning.

What we know of the pebble-procedures of Eurytus (*fl. ca.* 400 B.C.) (*Vors.* 45.2–3) if it is typical of so-called *psephoi*-arithmetic, also suggests caution. Whatever it may be it is not a reckoning procedure, but probably again arithmological. I am not suggesting that pebbles—with or without sand tables—were not used at an early stage for reckoning and for visualizing arithmological number patterns such as the *tetractys* (though Callimachus [191.59] seems to have been the first to suggest that Pythagoras so used them). We must however be cautious in inferring from a supposed use of *psephoi* conclusions as to number theory that seem obvious to us. It seems clear that the primary interest of early Pythagoreanism, up to the end of the fifth century, was in cardinal numbers and their properties, "mystical" or other, an interest that continues to characterize Pythagoreanism throughout the ten centuries of their history. For the early Pythagoreans, Greek notation of number was such that it did not facilitate the step from number speculation to arithmetic. The Pythagoreans of course were familiar with, and doubtless used, methods of calculation current in the fifth century, perhaps also *psephoi*-arithmetic. But inferences from a hypothetical *psephoi*-arithmetic to theories involving units, monads, and points, with their much more complex background of speculation, seem hardly justified.

[11]1090b 5—"Because the point is the *peras* and extreme end of the line, the line of the plane, the plane of the solid, some think there must be substances (φύσεις) of this kind." Ross, following Bonitz, suggests that the Pythagoreans are here referred to. Alexander 815.5–19 and Syrianus 179.5–10 in their comments name no persons.

The derivation theory Aristotle here refers to is the most usual one (point–line–surface–solid) with the difference that its elements are said to be substances because they are limits. It seems probable that some thinker simply inferred that the point was a substance because it was a *peras*, etc. In this form the theory must refer to a geometrical development, the line being conceived as extending between two *perata* or extremities, and not as a series of monads or atomic magnitudes. If we have no sufficient grounds for attributing the usual derivation theory to the Pythagoreans then *a fortiori* there is no reason for attributing this development of it to them. Burkert 39. n. 148 with reference to this passage, points out that the *chorista* of b 13 should suffice to eliminate the Pythagoreans. In no other place than 1090b 5 does Aristotle impute a doctrine of Being to the Pythagoreans and we must take it here that he is thinking of their one as an existent, perhaps having in mind the one Being of Parmenides.

¹²The ancient commentators accept without comment the pairing of Plato and the Pythagoreans in this passage, showing their awareness that the real question is not one of persons but whether the One and numbers can be substances. Few modern commentators have attempted to distinguish between Platonic and Pythagorean doctrine, and Frank (244) is the only one known to me who has used the passage to support the contention that Pythagoreans and Plato both derived solids/body from point, line, and surface. However, it is impossible either to treat the doctrine expounded as common (there is no simple Platonic derivation theory) or to distinguish, unless we do so on the basis of separate substance, and then it is hard to understand why the Pythagoreans are mentioned.

Nor can we be sure why the Parmenidean One is introduced and why the later reference to Zeno. Burnet (317) cites the passage and remarks "it seems impossible to draw any other conclusion than that the 'one' against which Zeno argued was the 'one' of which a number constitute a 'many,' and that is just the Pythagorean unit." Ross cites it with approval (*ad* 1001b 7), agreeing with Burnet that Zeno's reference cannot be to the Parmenidean One and must be to the Pythagorean unit. If we could be certain of this it would be strong grounds for believing that the Pythagorean doctrine reported by Aristotle was earlier than Parmenides.

¹³For Zeno's thesis see Simplicius *Phys.* 97.13 quoted *Vors.* 29 A 21; Wehrli, *Eudemos* fr. 37a; H. Fränkel, *Wege und Formen* 198–236, and especially 215–222; Cherniss 40–42; J. E. Raven, 71–77. These are a sample of the literature only. Burnet (314–317) makes a case for considering that Zeno is arguing against a Pythagorean indivisible unit, one of the unit substances that go to make up bodies and the physical world. But his translation of αὐτὸ τὸ ἕν as "unit" is hardly possible. However, Ross *ad loc.* points out that Aristotle is attributing to Zeno only the postulate, and that what he is criticizing Zeno for is the notion that being is corporeal. However the passage is evaluated, it will not bear the weight of the hypothetical structure erected, in part on such hints as these, by Cornford *Plato and Parmenides* (53–62) and others, who believe that the pluralists against whom Zeno was arguing were Pythagorean "atomists."

¹⁴For Plato and unit-points see Ross, *Analytics* 14–15. The grounds for believing that unit-points were any part of Plato's scheme are tenuous. See Aristotle *Metaph.* 992a 19–24 and Ross's comment on 992a 20, in which Ross seeks to make a case for Plato's believing in the existence of indivisible lines but not of points. (Heath *Maths.* 199–200, concurs.) This is the only passage in which such a position is imputed to Plato. There appears to be nothing in the *Timaeus* to bear it out, as there the minimum element is the plane surface. Alexander in his

comment (119.14–120.17) simply cites Aristotle for a belief in indivisible lines by Plato, "and not only Xenocrates," as he adds. He then proceeds to justify by subsuming under the great-and-small. See Stenzel 74–75.

The Pythagorean definition of the point is given by Proclus *in Euc. El.* 95.21: "The Pythagoreans define the point as a unit (μονάς) having position." *Phys.* 203a 1–15 is often quoted in connection with *psephoi*-arithmetic. (And to this passage reference is made, if we accept Bywater's emendation to 1091a 19, in the important passage of obvious relevance where Aristotle tells us that the Pythagoreans do not explain how the One is constituted, but they do say that the One then inhales *apeiron*.) At *Phys.* 203a 10–15 Aristotle writes: "[The Pythagoreans] assert that the *apeiron* is the even. For the even, being divided off and limited by the odd, imparts to existents their unlimitedness. This may be illustrated by what occurs in the case of numbers; when gnomons are placed around the one and separately, in the one case the resultant geometrical figures, as gnomons are added, always change, whereas in the other case the figure remains one and the same."

Precisely what is meant in this difficult passage, and in particular by χωρίς "separately," "will probably never be solved with certainty" (Guthrie 243). Ross *ad* 203a 13–15 summarizes the solutions offered by the ancient commentators and by some of the moderns, opting for that of Milhaud which has been adopted also by Burnet (103). Heath (*Maths.* 101–102) also discusses it.

For some reason commentators assume that Aristotle must be using a Pythagorean procedure to illustrate a Pythagorean doctrine. But his words suggest only that he is offering an illustration (immediately comprehensible to his hearers) of a process difficult to explain. How does it illustrate? What we are led to expect is a parallel such as: as in the field of number, even is taken up and limited by the odd, so in the physical world *apeiron* is taken up and limited by limit. But this will not do. Aristotle presents us with two cases produced by his gnomons, constant figures with an increase in scale only, and changing figures. I can see only two possibilities. Either Aristotle has unnecessarily complicated his illustration or he is suggesting that if a gnomon (or limiter) is placed around what is already limited the product is limited, but if the gnomon is placed around an unlimited (as is the case in the Pythagorean generation of number things from One and *apeiron*) then an unlimited factor is "built in" to the thing limited. So only the second case would provide the illustration Aristotle wishes, the first serving merely for contrast.

However that may be, the illustration is Aristotle's and we have no justification for assuming that this is a case of *psephoi*-arithmetic as practised by the Pythagoreans.

Burkert (30–35 and especially 31, n. 99) discusses the passage with a wealth of reference. He interprets it according to his basic tendency, that old cosmological myths are being translated into a number mysticism.

[15]Aristotle's discussion of the substantiality of solids, lines, points (1001b 26–1002b 11) is an attempt, and an exceedingly acute one, to state the case for all candidates to the status of substance; and—barring his own solution—it

would almost appear that he considers the best contenders to be solids, lines, and points. In his definition of the term "substance" (1017b 10–26) he again mentions as one sense "the limits present in bodies," i.e. surface, line and, in general, number. Again (1028b 16–18) "some think that the limits of body—surface, line, point, and unit—are substance, and more so than body or solid." This has been considered an obvious reference to the Pythagoreans, but it is odd that Aristotle does not name them when he names Plato and Speusippus immediately thereafter. It is unlikely that he is citing canonical Pythagorean doctrine because (1) for the Pythagoreans the unit is not the last member of a series of abstractions from the limits of body, and (2) the unit here referred to is arrived at geometrically, whereas the Pythagorean unit must have proceeded from the One as an arithmetical abstraction.

The question of substance and number is raised again (1036a 26–b20) in the context of a discussion of essence and definition. Since a definition defines the universal and the form, before defining we must know which parts are parts of the form and which of the concrete whole only, as e.g. you may have a circle in bronze, but bronze does not enter into the definition of a circle. There are cases in which it is difficult to abstract the form from the matter, as in the case of man and his bones and flesh. It has been suggested (by the Pythagoreans?) that the circle and the triangle should not be defined in terms of lines and surface; but that as flesh and bones are to a man, and bronze or stone to a statue, so is the line to a circle, the surface to a triangle. They reduce everything to number, and maintain that the definition of the line is that of two.

In the doctrine I have paraphrased, two is the essence of the line and what defines it, and that "two" stands in the same relation to line as man does to flesh, or statue to bronze. We note that mention is made of "the two" and not of the one or unit. It seems reasonable here to suggest that the dyad, in becoming two and a line, invests itself in some quantitative stuff in a way comparable to man in flesh and bone. Alexander (512.23–24) suggests (and Ross concurs) that the Pythagoreans are being referred to. It seems more probable that this is an inference of Aristotle's—if he is indeed referring to the Pythagoreans—and that he is arguing that they must have derived their ordinal numbers, which are things, from their cardinal numbers in a manner similar to that in which Plato generated numbers from the dyad as from some plastic material (977b 33–35). It is also possible that he is referring to some platonizing Pythagoreans, but as to the earlier Pythagoreans, he has told us that he does not know how, from the One, the things that are numbers came to be (1091a 12).

Alexander (512.23), in identifying the "some" as Pythagoreans, says that they argued that a circle should not be defined as a plane figure enclosed by one line, nor a triangle as a plane figure enclosed by three lines, nor a line as continuous length extended in one direction. In all these instances the definitions cite the ὕλη or matter. Instead they should be reduced to non-material number. The definition of the line should be that of the dyad, i.e. the first extension of the monad. Ross suggests that Alexander derives his information from Aristotle's lost work *On the Pythagoreans*, but there is nothing similar in our fragments, and the theories expounded suggest Neopythagoreanism, say Nicomachus of Gerasa. Ross further cites *Theol. Ar.* 82. 10–15, but we can have no confidence in Iamblichus' statement that Speusippus excerpted Philolaus and so composed a statement of Pythagorean doctrine having historical value.

In attempting to evaluate what Aristotle says of number under the aspect of substance we note the importance that the theory of number-substance assumes in his discussions. He cannot regard it with sympathy because it disregards the fundamentals of his own thought; but its affinity with Platonic number theory demands careful scrutiny for it. What we miss in his discussion is some point of historical reference. Pythagoreans earlier than Parmenides cannot have faced the problem of Being. Pythagoreans after Parmenides must have reacted to his revolutionary thesis as did Empedocles and Melissus, even if the Pythagoreans were not the principal butts of Zeno's polemic. There are hints in Aristotle's accounts that some Pythagoreans had modified the earlier theories attributed to "the thinkers known as Pythagoreans." These hints however (hints in which the thinkers are referred to as "some" or "others") suggest that Aristotle is there referring to contemporary Pythagoreans who had modified their doctrines in reaction to later Platonism. But that some Pythagoreans may still, in Plato's time, have adhered to earlier theories and have focussed their interest rather on observed phenomena of the physical world is suggested by the famous remarks of Plato (*Rep.* 529A–531c). It is true that the Pythagoreans are there mentioned only in connection with harmonics (530D), but the whole discussion is referred to them or their like by 531B.

The persons to whom Plato refers are concerned with the visible heavens and with audible harmonics. Plato reproaches them with indifference to the metaphysical presuppositions of their sciences, i.e. that they content themselves with mathematical inquiry into the physical world. If they are Pythagoreans they may well have pursued those inquiries without abandoning their traditional position that "things are numbers." Neither Eleatics nor Platonists nor Atomists had evolved a satisfactory solution to the metaphysical problems involved. It may well be that the Pythagoreans' interest was in fact directed towards the sort of inquiry modern scientists (whose metaphysical interests are also usually negligible) would have wished them to pursue. For a moderate statement of the scientist's position vis-à-vis Plato and the Pythagoreans, see Sambursky *The Physical World of the Greeks* 42–45.

[16]J. E. Raven, 21–42, discusses critically Cornford's hypothesis in *CQ* 16 (1922) 137–150 and 17 (1923) 1–12 and in *Plato and Parmenides*. Though many would maintain that Pythagoreanism had a shaping influence on atomism, few now agree with Cornford. Raven's own thesis as described in *Pythagoreans and Eleatics* is modified in *KR* 236–262. Burkert, 256–267, has a useful review of the discussion but concludes for his own shamanistic thesis, and describes Parmenides' proem as reflecting a shaman journey to the other world.

[17]In the *Physics* (203b 15–30) Aristotle lists five reasons why an *apeiron* may be held to exist: (1) because time is infinite, (2) because magnitudes are infinitely divisible, (3) because generation and corruption must have an infinite source on

which to draw, (4) because what is limited is always limited in relation to something other than itself, and so on *ad infinitum*, (5) because in thinking of number, mathematical magnitudes, and what is outside the heavens we reach no end.

Though he does not here profess to be giving an account of the opinions of any or all of his predecessors, in fact the first two grounds may be called mathematical and the last two logical, and none of the four is such as we would expect Anaximander to use. The third and remaining reason is that γένεσις and φθορά must have an infinite source on which to draw if their process is to continue ad infinitum. This opinion is elsewhere (*Dox. Gr.* 277) ascribed to Anaximander who, according to the excerptor, held that "the *apeiron* is cause of the coming-to-be and passing-away of the universe." Of the context Diels (*Dox. Gr.* 158) remarks that "Sucus et sanguis est Theophrasteus." In attempting to understand the nature of Anaximander's *apeiron* we may therefore give special consideration to this notion of an infinite reservoir of matter, external to our universe, that can be—and is—drawn on to maintain physical process. We have already encountered a similar idea in the breathing in of the *apeiron* which Aristotle (*Fr. Sel.* 137) ascribes to the Pythagoreans. This *apeiron* we must imagine as either identical with, or as some modification of, that of Anaximander if it is conceded, as I suggest, that Pythagoras himself adopted from Anaximander the *apeiron* notion.

Aristotle has other quarrels with the *apeiron* concept. With reference probably to Anaximander he remarks (*De Gen.* 332a 24–25) that you cannot have privation (un-limited) without state, nor only one of a pair of opposites as cause. This would suggest that Anaximander had, as his first cause, only the *apeiron* (and this we have other reasons for believing), whereas the Pythagoreans certainly had as their primordial substance, principle, or cause, the two terms of the contrariety *apeiron-peras*. Nevertheless their *apeiron* was both a substance, like that of Anaximander, and infinitely divisible. (Aristotle makes this a reproach against them. *Phys.* 204a 32–34.)

The Anaximandrean conception of the *apeiron* differs from the Pythagorean in that it is the *sole* first principle, containing and governing all things: "as all maintain for whom there is no other cause, such as νοῦς or φιλία, in addition to the *apeiron*. They assert that it is the Divine, for it is immortal and imperishable, as Anaximander says, and so do most of the natural philosophers." (*Phys.* 203b 11–15). Diels [*Vors.* 12 B 3] cites the epithets as Anaximander's own words.) For Pythagoras it cannot have this unique status when *peras* and *apeiron* are equally first principles, and it is unlikely to have had divine status or to have carried that epithet when the principal function of *peras/apeiton* is to produce the One and discrete quantity, and to aliment the universe.

The problem of the relation between the Anaximandrean and the Pythagorean *apeiron* arises also in *Phys.* 187a 20–21. There Aristotle is drawing a distinction between those who believe in some one elemental substance from which, by condensation and rarefaction, come sensibles, and those who believe in some indeterminate, but corporeal, substance from which sensible substances are separated out. Of the second class he says: "Others hold that the contraries, being present in the One, are separated out." This is a surprising statement. For Anaximander things proceed not from the One but from the *apeiron*, and his *apeiron* is nowhere else referred to as the One. For the Pythagoreans the product of *apeiron/peras* is the One, our cosmos; and what is separated off (Kahn 41)—if that term may be used in a Pythagorean context—is not contrarieties (which have a cosmogonical role), but numbers. I can see no solution but to suggest that Aristotle, by the One, here refers (loosely) to the *apeiron* of Anaximander, in which the contraries do not inhere, despite what his language would appear to suggest.

For a detailed discussion of the problem of Anaximander's *apeiron* see R. Mondolfo, *L'infinito* and his note ZM 2.187–205; and Kahn's appendix 231–239. Kahn argues that, for Anaximander, the primary sense of *apeiron* is that which we find in the *Physics* 204a 2–7, "what cannot be traversed," and that this *apeiron* is an infinite material principle (Kahn 33), whereas that of the Pythagoreans is also essential form.

[18]We may imagine this to have occurred much as the ideas of Darwinism, Freudian psychology, relativity, however much garbled and watered down, took possession of imaginations for a few decades. See van der Waerden 82–87: his account of Egyptian and Babylonian science is informative; but he is uncritical of the sources he uses for the history of science in Greece and he is wedded to the Neoplatonist account of Pythagoras and early Pythagoreans as mathematicians. Neugebauer (146–152) is much more sceptical. He is willing to attribute to the early period "a comparatively large amount of mathematical knowledge" but without any formal method or proof, such as was developed by the mathematicians of the fourth century. For mathematics in Anaximander see Kahn 91–98.

[19]See appendix 2 for a discussion of irrationals and incommensurability.

7

ASTRONOMY AND HARMONIA

IN the case of both cosmology and number theory Aristotle describes one coherent doctrine. Though contemporary Pythagoreans may have been its depositaries and exponents we have seen reason to believe that this doctrine must have been a traditional one. In astronomy, however, the picture we are given is composite. Some of its elements display the imagination of the early physical thinkers, or are half-mythical; some are a product of observation, whether Greek or Babylonian; some are mathematical, deriving from a period which had developed notions of space, and mathematical techniques. These elements are not in themselves an indication of period of origin, but are sometimes found all present in the doctrine of one thinker.

The nature of our tradition creates further major difficulties. Here, as in mathematics, we find all astronomical thinkers whose allegiance is at all doubtful being dubbed Pythagoreans. This myth of Pythagorean science is generally accepted by the later doxography and the commentators, who can be used to supplement or to verify Aristotle's account only with caution. Aristotle himself speaks consistently of "the Pythagoreans," and even Philolaus is only mentioned once by him and in another context. But his account is haphazard. In the *De Caelo* he is concerned to recommend his own astronomical solutions and what doxographical information he gives is occasional; and even if his information is eked out from other reliable sources, we gain no satisfactory picture of Pythagorean astronomy.

Our object, however, is not to give an account of Pythagorean astronomy in the context of the history of Greek astronomy,[1] but to consider what may be learned, from Aristotle's account, of the phenomenon of Pythagoreanism in the fifth century B.C.

In the second book of the *De Caelo* Aristotle discusses at some length a Pythagorean application of the terms "right" and "left" to the universe. In the course of disagreeing with them, he develops his own theory of the three pairs of translatory motions, up and down, right and left, forward and backward (*De Caelo* 284b 6–30).

There are some who assert that there is a left and a right in the universe, as do the Pythagoreans—(for this thesis is theirs). Let us inquire whether there is a right and left as they describe them or if some other description would be more appropriate if we are going to apply these terms at all to the physical universe. In the first place, if left and right can be predicated of it then we must assume as predicable the predicates prior to these. We have discussed these in our treatise *De incessu animalium* as being pertinent to zoology. For in animals obviously there are such parts as right and left—in some all of them, in some only some— whereas in plants there is only an "up" and "down." If any such term is to be applied to the universe, obviously the primary characteristic present in animals should be present there too. There are three such pairs, each of them being a sort of first principle, namely up/down, back/forward, right/left. These dimensions are obviously all present in all entire physical bodies. Upwards is a principle of length, right of width, forward of depth. The situation differs in respect of motion. There I call principles those from which the motions of those so endowed first begin. Growth is upward, locomotion is from the right, the motions of sense perception are from in front. (By in front I mean that towards which our perception is directed.)

So, Aristotle goes on to say (285a 1–13, 25–27), we quarrel with the Pythagoreans because they recognize only one of the three pairs of translatory motions and that not the most important pair, and because they think that that pair, right/left, applies to all existents equally. It is true that we may properly apply right/left as well as the prior pair up/down to the universe because it is a living creature. But the "up" part of the living creature must be the southern hemisphere because only so will the heavenly bodies rise from its right. This is the opposite of what the Pythagoreans assert (285b 25–28). For them we are in the upper part of the universe and the heavenly bodies rise on our right. (That is, the Pythagoreans imagined themselves in the position assumed by soothsayers and diviners, facing north.)

In this long excursus on the translatory motions Aristotle is seeking to give them an absolute rather than a relative sense. What puzzles us is why the Pythagoreans are made the object of his attack, when Plato also appears to regard the three pairs as accepted doctrine. In the *Timaeus* (34A) he denies all three to the *autozoon*, endowing it with axial rotation only and describing this motion as occurring from the right or the east, as did the Pythagoreans.[2] The pair right/left appears in the Table of Opposites in the *Metaphysics* (986a 24). Simplicius (386.9), referring to that or to some similar table, tells us that that pair of opposites were those of spatial extension, and that they were considered good and bad respectively. He adds (386.19–23 = Ross *Fr. Sel.* 137): "According to them the other spatial opposites proceeded from these. They used to call 'right,' 'up,' and 'forward' good; 'left,' 'down,' and 'backward' bad, according to the account of Aristotle himself in his collection of Pythagorean opinions." When in the *Timaeus* (43B) Plato specifies the three pairs, he mentions them in the following order: backwards/forwards, right/left, up/down, but the order need not be specially significant for him. As Aristotle must have known the *Timaeus* but refers the three pairs of opposites to the Pythagoreans we can only conclude that the opposites must have been Pythagorean, and must have had some application in Pythagorean astronomy.

Let us now turn to the *De Caelo*, the major account in Aristotle of Pythagorean astronomy. He refers consistently to "the Pythagoreans," but the doxography refers the same doctrines to Philolaus, and there can be little doubt that in the passage we are about to consider it is "Philolaic" astronomy that is presented.[3] Why Aristotle should not have attributed it to Philolaus we do not know. He may have felt, or Philolaus may have said, that his astronomical doctrines were in substantial part traditional. Or he may have felt it the part of caution to adhere to his general practice of ascribing everything Pythagorean to "the Pythagoreans" as an anonymous body. (*De Caelo* 293a 15–293b 1)

It remains for us to discuss the earth—its position, its form, and whether it is at rest or in motion. Regarding position not all thinkers are of the same opinion. Most of those who assert the universe to be limited in extension hold that the earth lies in the middle of their universe. But the Pythagoreans assert the contrary. They maintain that at the centre of the universe is fire; and that Earth, which is one of the stars, by revolving about this centre causes day and night. They introduce another earth opposite to our own that they call the Counter-earth. In these theories they are not seeking for reasons and causes based on phenomena, but rather are twisting and seeking to accommodate the phenomena to arguments and opinions of their own. If we were to accept as a basis for our theories *a priori* arguments rather than observed fact, many others might agree that the central position should not be assigned to Earth. The Pythagoreans consider that the most honorable place should go to the most honorable thing, and that fire is more honorable or of greater worth than Earth, extremities or ultimate boundaries than what lies between them (and centre and circumference are boundaries). On the basis of these arguments the Pythagoreans maintain that fire and not Earth lies at the centre of the sphere of the universe.[4]

In the *Metaphysics* (986a 8–12) Aristotle tells us that the Pythagoreans invented their Counter-earth to bring the number of the
heavenly bodies up to the perfect number ten. Later, in the *De Caelo*
(293b 20–25), he suggests that they used it to explain eclipses. Neither
of these passages contradicts his present statement, that the hypothesis
of a counter-earth had no basis in observed phenomena but was a
consequence of the notion of the centre of the universe as the noblest,
worthiest, most honorable place to which to assign what was noblest
in their cosmos. In this vein Aristotle continues (*De Caelo* 293b 1–11):

Further, the Pythagoreans, because they feel it peculiarly important that a
watch should be kept over the most important part of the universe, that being
its centre, call the fire occupying it the "keep of Zeus"; as if centre were an
unambiguous term and the centre of a physical magnitude were the centre of a
thing and of its nature. That is why they ought to make no confident assertions
about the universe, introducing a keep in its centre. They should rather ask what
sort of centre and where it is naturally situated.

The structure Aristotle describes here is a relatively modest one.
His report is amplified in some detail by the commentators. Alexander
(38.8–39.19 = Ross, *Fr. Sel.* 138–139), commenting on the passage
in the *Metaphysics* (985b 27) where things are said to be numbers,
remarks: "As the sun is the cause of seasons they assert that it has its
place where the seventh number (which they call 'due season') is
located. For the sun occupies the seventh place from the periphery
among the ten heavenly bodies moving around the hearth at the centre.
Its orbit comes after the fixed stars and the five planets. After the sun
comes the moon as eighth, next the earth as ninth, and then the
counter-earth." Later (39.24–40.9), citing Aristotle as a source, he
gives us some information as to interplanetary distances or rather ratios
but as these are adjusted to musical harmonies they will be discussed
in that connection.

Simplicius (*in De Caelo* 511.25 = *Fr. Sel.* 141) who quotes both
De Caelo and *On the Pythagoreans*, gives us a similar order among the
heavenly bodies but no interplanetary distances or ratios. He points
out, however, that the planets are not said to be carried around on
spheres, but move in their paths of their own motion (470.15 ff.).

The commentators base their account on Aristotle as a principal
source, and what they add is in the same vein. The doxography, though
it cannot be said to contradict Aristotle's report, differs in character,
as may be seen from one principal extract (*Vors* 44 A 16 = *Dox. Gr.*
336–337):

Philolaus maintained that there was fire in the middle of the universe round about its centre. He calls this Hearth of the World, House of Zeus, Mother of the gods, Altar, Meeting-place, Goal of Nature (*physis*). And again he maintains that the periphery is another fire at the highest point of the universe. The middle is by nature first in rank. Around it move in choral dance ten divine bodies; the sphere of the fixed stars, the five planets, after them the sun and beneath it the moon; beneath the moon the earth and beneath that the counter-earth; after all these the fire that fills the role of hearth in the area of the centre. He calls Olympus the uppermost part of the periphery where are present the elements in their purity. The part under the revolution of Olympus, where are the five planets, sun, and moon he calls *Cosmos*. The sublunary, circumterrestrial part, where are the things subject to birth and change, he calls the heavens. Wisdom appertains to the order of the heavenly bodies, virtue to the lack of order of things that come to be; the former being perfect, the latter imperfect.[5]

The doxography adds other details regarding single aspects of this astronomical picture, each detail having its own history of comment. We need discuss only the central problems. Is the so-called Philolaic system a statement of Pythagorean astronomical doctrine common to Pythagoreans of some determinate epoch? Is it the theorizing of Philolaus himself? Or has the book of Philolaus been so modified in the Early Academy that it has become simply an answer to the demands of the period for a Pythagorean document? This problem has been under discussion for so long, and has been discussed with such subtlety, that perhaps new insights are more to be feared than hoped. I shall attempt the naïve approach of listing the salient features of the reports without assuming, as is usually assumed, that behind these reports there lies a long history of Pythagorean speculation and research in mathematics and in astronomy and that, therefore it must make some sort of scientific sense.

1. The criterion determining the character of the system appears to be a value rather than a scientific one. God is assigned a throne in the centre of the universe, and has his stronghold there; the number of the heavenly bodies is the perfect number ten; the serial position of the planets is associated with significant numbers.

2. The most honourable place is said to be in the centre, the "keep of Zeus," and to be occupied by fire. But fire also surrounds the sphere of the fixed stars and this fire is said to be called Olympus. Why is this not the most honourable place? And if the highest sphere is called Olympus, the intermediate sphere cosmos, and the sphere of things subject to change the heavens, why is the most honourable place in the lowest sphere? If there is no confusion of thought in the doctrine itself, then the doxography has introduced confusion.[5]

3. The system is not mathematical. The comparative size of the

heavenly bodies is not discussed, and their distances from one another are given only as ratios of the musical chord in connection with the harmony of the spheres. Yet the problem of sizes and distances had been one of the problems of astronomy since the time of Anaximander.

4. We are told that the counter-earth was introduced, among other reasons, to explain eclipses. (Was the author unaware of Anaxagoras' explanation *Vors.* 59 A 42.9 = *Dox. Gr.* 562?) But there is no suggestion that intervals were stated between centre, counter-earth, and earth, and it is only *Vors.* 44 A 21 that suggests the distinction between celestial equator and ecliptic. It is difficult to imagine that there can have been a model, however primitive, or even that the author of the system had a lively astronomical imagination enabling him to see his system in motion.

5. This theory moves the divinities to astral locations as Empedocles' does; but the religious background is more conventional than his and the poetical imagery (*Fr. Sel.* 135,141 = *Vors.* 44 A 14) is unscientific rather than para-scientific as in Empedocles. This is true also of the explanations given of the Milky Way (Aristotle *Meteor.* 345a 14) and in a lesser measure of comets (*Meteor.* 342b 30).

6. If the earth and its accompanying counter-earth move in orbit around the central fire, thus causing day and night, and one face of the earth is always turned away from the central fire, then the sun must stand still to cause day and night of constant length and it is difficult to see how the seasons can be produced.

7. The face of the earth we inhabit must be at a considerable distance from the central fire. The author of the system cannot have faced the problem of parallax and the great change in our perspectives that the daily orbit of the earth would entail. (Frank [20–21] has shown that this problem arises about the middle of the fifth century.) Aristotle (*De Caelo* 293b 25–30) reports only an unconvincing reply to a criticism along these lines.

8. We are told that *all* the heavenly bodies are in motion. Whether the sphere of the fixed stars is in motion or stationary, it has so far proved impossible to devise a convincing explanation of the operation of the whole system, and Heath (*Aristarch.* 104) concludes that "it is to be feared that a convincing solution of the puzzle will never be found."

The characteristics of this system are such that reconstruction would appear impossible without the assumption that the theory is a scientific and a coherent one. As there seem to be no compelling reasons for making such an assumption when Aristotle, with a better knowledge of his sources, certainly did not make it, I shall attempt a hypothesis to explain the features known to us.

Philolaus must have been a youth or a very young man when he went into exile at the time of the Pythagorean *débâcle*, about the middle of the fifth century. He found refuge in Thebes, a city which, at that time, was not a great centre of intellectual or scientific life but which appears to have had a musical tradition. Judging by Philolaus' fragments and by the statement (*Vors.* 44 A 7) that he himself practised *auletike*, one of his major interests may have been music. He appears to have done some teaching in Thebes, but produced nothing philosophically distinguished.

Philolaus wrote a book, probably a short one, that treated of most aspects of Pythagorean doctrine including first principles, cosmology, numbers, astronomy, music. Its emphasis may have been on music. This book was perhaps a product of Pythagorean piety, an effort to state the doctrines of Pythagoras because they seemed to be threatened by oblivion, but what Philolaus can have recollected from instruction in his youth or have learned from hearsay in the course of his years in exile would have been scanty and vague, its tendency being towards ethical *paideia*.

What knowledge of this book can be derived from the fragments[6] or inferred from Aristotle suggests that it was unscientific and without real philosophical understanding of the doctrines it reports. It was, however, the earliest written document of Pythagoreanism. Though Plato, Speusippus, and Aristotle will have known, from their contacts with the circle of Archytas, that it could not have any canonical status and that its doctrines had a larger background, nevertheless, it existed as written word. So it served as a basis for the interpretation of Pythagoreanism, the first generation of the Academy either using it cautiously or reinterpreting it, the doxography using it as an authoritative source. So Philolaus' vague, airy, poetical speculation on Pythagorean themes, neither philosophy nor astronomy, probably furnished a background for the ethical *paideia* of Pythagoreans in mainland Greece during the last half of the fifth century. It was for this ethical *paideia* that they were held in singular respect and esteem.

Our conclusion then must be that the Aristotelian report yields us little information regarding Pythagorean contributions to astronomical science. It is probable that, if Pythagoras himself is to be conceived of as also a physical thinker, astronomical or, in the Greek sense meteorological speculation will have been an aspect of his system as it was of all early Ionian systems. But of any such speculation Aristotle

preserves no tradition. Nor is there any echo of Pythagorean astronomical theory, with the one exception of Philolaus, earlier than the fourth
century.[7] There remains however one astronomical/musical tradition
preserved for us by Aristotle that in all ages has been regarded as
typical of Pythagorean thought, the music of the spheres. To that we
must now turn.

NOTES

[1]For a general discussion of Pythagorean astronomy with bibliography
ZM 2.520–551, Burnet 110–112, 276–309. Heath, *Aristarch.* 46–51 has a brief
reference to Pythagoras and a fuller account of Pythagorean astronomy (94–120)
where he makes no distinction of persons and does not attempt to isolate a
Philolaic system. Frank (19–46, 184–218) gives an account of the development of
Greek astronomy that is in part illuminating but in part misleading. He attributes
"Pythagorean" astronomical theory in large part to Archytas and his circle. He
discusses Philolaus in an appendix (263–335) that is in large part devoted to
discrediting the fragments printed in the *Vorsokratiker*. (See Cardini 2, 82–109
for a defence on the lines of Mondolfo.) Van der Waerden, *Die Astronomie der
Pythagoreer* is an ambitious attempt at reconstruction in which the use of sources
is rather uncritical. Burkert 278–347 discusses the whole tradition and history of
Greek astronomy, in general a convincing account. He dismisses the Philolaic
system as non-scientific, assigning it to the second half of the fifth century (and
so probably to Philolaus). Burkert tends to relegate non-scientific speculation,
and in particular Pythagorean theories before Archytas, to the realm of
shamanism, the *deus ex machina* of his thesis.

The general reader is surprised to find how small the area of agreement is,
how important the differences, and how flimsy the basis of some reconstructions.
In what follows I have sought to use only the most obvious and unmistakable
landmarks and to confine myself to non-specialist clarification, in particular of
the role astronomical doctrines played in the total structure.

[2]It is not clear why Plato establishes right for the *autozoon* where he does.
Heath (*Aristarch.* 160–163), who refers to the discussion the passage has generated, suggests that "east" must almost by definition be right, and that Plato,
who recognizes motions and their direction as relative rather than absolute,
could, as it were by his fiat, declare the east to be on the right of the *autozoon*.
This however does not seem a very satisfactory solution. It may be that Plato
simply assumed the east to be on the right hand, right being associated with
good omens and rising sun.

It is worthy of note that at *Timaeus* 43ʙ the human creature is endowed with all three pairs of motions. Frank's suggestion (259) that the Table and the three pairs of motions derive from Speusippus, is without foundation.

That Aristotle had thoroughly confused his commentators is shown by Simplicius (*in De Caelo* 392.16–23 = *Fr. Sel.* 141–142) who cites Alexander as suspecting corruption.

³Cardini (2.110–249) prints the Philolaus fragments of Aristotle, the commentators (with exception of *Fr. Sel.* 141 = Rose³ 205), and the doxography together. These fragments are scattered in Diels, some being assigned to anonymous Pythagoreans (*Vors.* 58). Burkert (218 n. 91), like Cardini but for different reasons, argues for the attribution of all the fragments to Philolaus. There can be little doubt that Aristotle's report is to be referred, in whole or in part, to Philolaus as its proximate source. Our decision on how much of it is Philolaic will depend largely on what we consider the nature of Philolaus' book to have been. We may take it as certain that Philolaus wrote and published a book. If it was known to Speusippus, it is highly probable that Aristotle knew it. What its contents may have been is another matter. Even if it contained the matter of Aristotle's report *plus* the doxography, we are not justified in assuming that the system it reflects is original to Philolaus rather than being Pythagorean. Like the fragments (and irrespective of our judgment as to their authenticity) it may have been simply a "rehash" of Pythagorean speculation. See Cherniss (393–396) for comment and refutation of the Philolaic system as reconstructed by Frank.

Nor is there justification for Burkert's general statement (221) that: "It is not the case that the subsequent picture of Pythagoreanism is in substance determined by Aristotle's account. It is determined by Platonic interpretation. Aristotle's report is ignored, reinterpreted, or rejected in discussion." In some respects Theophrastus' *Opinions* differed from the Aristotelian report. In some respects the compilers of compendia modified and amplified the *Opinions*. But that Aristotle's treatises and monographs were a principal basis of the *Opinions* we cannot doubt.

⁴This argument, or a very similar one, is (*pace* Cherniss 394) by Theophrastus attributed to Speusippus (*Metaph.* 11a 22–26 = fr. 41 Lang). It is to be connected with the theory attributed to him by Aristotle (*Supra* p. 48; n. 8, chap. 4) that the Good is not prior to other first principles but posterior. How does it happen that a doctrine which Aristotle attributes to the Pythagoreans, but which the doxography, by implication, attributes to Philolaus (*Dox. Gr.* 332b 19; 336b 20) is attributed to Speusippus by Theophrastus?

In the catalogue of Speusippus' writings (*D.L.* 4.1.5) no mention is made of *On Pythagorean Numbers* and none of the extant titles could have covered that work (Lang 28). Yet it was still available to Iamblichus who excerpts it. It may have been variously interpreted; by Aristotle as an account of Pythagorean speculation in which he placed no great trust, by Theophrastus as a fictional cloak for Speusippus himself, by the doxographers as reproducing in substance the thought of Philolaus. Apparently Philip of Opus, like Aristotle, attributed the Counter-earth theories to "the Pythagoreans" (*Dox. Gr.* 360b 1).

⁵Burkert (227) rejects the second part beginning τὸ μὲν οὖν. This is an arbitrary

simplification where there is so much confusion. The author of the fragment
was concerned with *ethical* values.

⁶Burkert (222–256) has sought to show that *Vors.* 44 B 1–7, 13, 17 are genuine
fragments of Philolaus' book, and that it "contained that philosophy of limit
and unlimited, of number and harmony on which Plato builds in the *Philebus*
and which Aristotle attributes to the Pythagoreans" (256). That Philolaus published a book needs no proof since the discovery of the Menon fragments (*Vors.*
A 27, 28 = *Supp. Arist.* 3.1.31). That the book was known to Aristotle, if it
was known to Menon, seems probable. In the absence of internal evidence to
suggest that it was inspired by the *Philebus*, it is safe to assume that Plato also
knew it. Our judgment in that question will not be affected by the preposterous
fables of the biographical tradition suggesting that Plato bought this book or
caused it or some other books to be bought for a sum variously reported as
40 or 100 minas (when at the trial of Socrates he and his friends offered to stand
good for 30 minas, and Anaxagoras' book could be bought in the *agora* for a
drachma). The monstrous price is meant to suggest that the book or books
were unique and were used as a source for Plato's pythagorizing plagiarism.
These tales, for which we have no source earlier than Timon (*Vors.* 44 A 8)
cannot even be used to substantiate the existence of the book apart from other
evidence.

The criteria by which Burkert proposes to decide what fragments are genuine
are these. If they derive from a post-Aristotelian forgery then a complete and
relatively easy interpretation should be possible in terms of Platonic, Aristotelian,
and post-Aristotelian concepts. If the fragments are Presocratic then the formulae
and concepts of later philosophy will fail us, but an approach will be possible by
means of the modes of Presocratic thought (233). Burkert's defence of the language and the concepts of the fragments, is convincing, and his rebuttal of
previous critique is generally effective. But in the welter of controversy (Boeckh,
with whose elegant little treatise the controversy began, would have deplored its
consequences) no clear appreciation of the substance of the fragments emerges.

Before we attempt to establish what Philolaus in fact says, let us consider the
contention of Burkert (222) that it was the only original document of early
Pythagorean thought. Burkert assumes that the book was written in Thebes
"not too long before 400 B.C." (247). Philolaus *may* have returned to Tarentum
after that time, though the suggestion in *Vors.* 44 A 5 that he did not has the
authority of Hermodorus. So Archytas in his youth may have encountered him.
But even if he did not meet him in the flesh he must have known his book.
If he and other Pythagoreans of Magna Graecia derived their knowledge of early
Pythagoreanism chiefly from Philolaus' book, surely that fact would have been
communicated to Plato and Speusippus (and through them to Aristotle) and
we would somehow have had hints of the major role Philolaus played.

Further, it is surprising that no one from Thebes or from the Phlius groups
(neither reflected in Plato nor reported by Aristoxenus who was so anxious to
discredit Plato and the pythagorizing of the Academy) says anything of such
an important book. If it treated of first principles, world order, elements, it should

be reflected in the doxography. But in fact we find (*Dox. Gr.* 283 = *Vors.* 44 A 9) only one fragment making the bald statement that for Philolaus the first principles were *peras* and *apeiron*, and even this statement is not quite correct if 44 B 2 is a genuine fragment. The other doxographical references are to his astronomical theories. If Theophrastus used the book it seems probable that it discussed only astronomy as a principal theme (and perhaps also physiology, a theme which Theophrastus would have passed over), and that if first principles were alluded to, it was in a preamble which Threophastus felt he could neglect. In fact, the fragments Burkert defends suggest prolegomena, leading, by means of the *harmonia* notion, to astronomy.

Was Philolaus' the *only* book on Pythagoreanism? Apart from a problematical book written in the early fourth century by Anaximander the younger (*Vors.* 58 C 6 = FGrH 9 T1) it was the only book of which we know. But the Aristotelian monograph *On the Pythagoreans*, and in particular the report on the *Acusmata*, has all the appearance of deriving from some written source or sources. On their visits to Tarentum Plato and Speusippus must have looked about them for written material such as they possessed for most of the other Presocratics. They may have made—or have had made—memoranda. The Tarentine production of pseudepigrapha began soon after their time and must have arisen from demands made by persons having a genuine desire to know.

We must also reckon with an oral tradition (and perhaps a written one as well) the existence of which must be assumed because the book of Philolaus alone, or even as a principal document, does not suffice to explain Pythagoreanism as it is reflected in Plato and Aristotle. Let us consider first of all how Philolaus presents his first principles (*Vors.* 44 B 6; see Burkert 233–235): "Nature and *harmonia* are to be explained thus. The being of things, which is eternal, and nature itself, admit of divine and not of human knowledge, with this proviso, however, that it would be impossible, for us at least, to know any of the existent things if it were not for the existence of this Being of the things from which the world is constituted, both limiting and unlimited things."

Here we have a Being that is humanly unknowable and that yet, as underlying the things we know, makes them knowable. It is the Being not of a One or cosmos but of those limiting and unlimited things of which our world is made. This may be a superficial allusion to fifth century problems. Philolaus may imply that there exists a Being such as that of Parmenides. But it is difficult not to see in this formulation both use and repudiation of the Aristotelian notion of ὕλη in which the opposites inhere (cf. Burkert p. 237. n. 93). The things constituting the phenomenal world arise from this Being of Things (not apparently identical things, though *pragmata* is used in both cases) of which some are limiting and some unlimited. We cannot simply equate them with Limit and Unlimited as principles. They cannot be numbers as in the Aristotelian account because number things are limited. Whatever they are, they are apparently held together by Being until *harmonia* supervenes to create and constitute an order. This passage might be made intelligible by subtleties of interpretation, but the notions with which it is operating are vague. Burkert (236), recording the puzzlement of

others, seems himself puzzled. Rothenbucher (68–70), after analysis, declares the
fragment "absurd und nicht pythagoreisch." The fragment continues (*Vors.*
44 B 6) : "But as these first principles [Diels suggests these are the numbers 1 and 2,
but from the context they appear to be the things mentioned earlier] are neither
the same as one another nor homogeneous, clearly it would have been impossible
to create from them a world order if *harmonia* had not in some way or other
supervened. Now things that are the same and homogeneous have no need of
harmonia, but the unlike, non-homogeneous, not similarly-structured had need
of *harmonia* to bring them into line, by means of which they are to be held in the
order of the world."

Here an ordering principle supervenes, as an officer might on a phalanx. This
principle need not concern itself with like things which are always in their place.
But it must constrain unlike things to assume their proper place in an ordered
world. These "things" are called *archai*, but it is not clear what they are. They
cannot be the same as the things that Being underlies, which may or may not
be the things of the phenomenal world because they seem to be cosmogonical.
Harmonia finds before it a confusion of same and different (and not limited and
unlimited). Things that are the same are already in their place. *Harmonia*
constrains things that are different to take their place.

This passage may be somewhat clarified, though not explained, by B 2.6: "So
it is obvious that the universe and everything in it has been constituted in a
harmonia of limiting and unlimited things. The facts illustrate this. For things
made of limiting things limit, things made of limiting and unlimited both limit
and are unlimited, and unlimited things show themselves unlimited." The meaning of this little exercise in logic is difficult to grasp (Burkert 236 does what can
be done, and cites preceding interpretation) but the entities of the physical world
belonging to Philolaus' three categories *may* be what *harmonia* has to bring
into line.

The fragments B 1–6 suggest an author who has attempted to write a brief
introduction to a treatise on musical, and perhaps by extension astronomical,
theory, and who has used rather carelessly, but gracefully, some current philosophical notions, giving them a vague Pythagorean colouring by the use of the
terms "limiting" and "unlimited." These fragments certainly are not a basis
for suggesting that Aristotle derived from Philolaus the knowledge of Pythagorean doctrine displayed in the treatises.

(1) For Aristotle first principles are Limit and Unlimited. For Philolaus there
is an eternal being/substance from which proceed limiting and unlimited things,
whatever these may be, and the entities of the physical world are themselves
limited, unlimited, or a combination of the two.

(2) For Aristotle Pythagorean *harmonia* refers especially to numerical relations
in the musical chord (985b 31) and in the heavens (986a 2). For Philolaus it has
an ordering function in the cosmos.

(3) For Aristotle, Pythagorean numbers are things. For Philolaus things are
limited, unlimited, or a mixture, and number makes them knowable (B 4).

Boeckh, who has done as much for his author as any subsequent commentator, writes (57): "Zum Schluss dieser Untersuchung bemerke ich noch dreierlei: dass dieser Anfang des philolaischen Werkes mit einer gewissen Dialektik abgefasst war, die aber freilich nicht grösser gewesen zu sein scheint als sie in jeder dogmatischen Darstellung nöthig ist: dann, dass nach dem bisherigen die philolaischen Sätze mit dem, was wir als pythagoreisch nennen, ziemlich überein-stimmen, ohne gerade die später gebräuchliche philosophische Sprache zu enthalten." Finally, Philolaus' Limit/Unlimited [Boeckh translates thus] are identical with the Limit/Unlimited of the *Philebus*. This seems almost tanta-mount to saying that if the fragments are treated gently but firmly they can be made to yield sense. Rothenbücher (66–73), in his polemic against Boeckh, argues that the fragments are a pale and misunderstood reflection of the *Philebus*.

I would therefore conclude that the analysis of the fragments does not encourage us to look on Philolaus as a principal source of the Pythagorean tradition. This does not diminish the value of Burkert's discussion of Philolaic astronomical and musical theory. In a long discussion (278–347) of the history of Greek astronomy, on the merits of which only a historian of astronomy can pronounce, but which I find generally convincing, he attempts (315–335) to situate the astronomical theses of Philolaus. He ascribes to him (318–323) a rather primitive and unscientific astronomical scheme, with a hearth of central fire as its only fixed point and a counter-earth as its most original feature. This scheme, and a belief in celestial harmony to which Philolaus also subscribed (335), Burkert would refer to prescientific reflection with a background of shamanistic ecstasy. Regarding Philolaus' musical theory he points out (377) gross errors, but ascribes these errors to the fact that before Archytas, Pytha-goreanism aimed not at mathematical nor at natural science but at a theory of the universe as number.

Burkert's chapters on mathematics and astronomy are a valuable discussion in a field where for some time there have been murmurs among philologists that the specialists were romancing. (As for example, G. E. L. Owen 199–222.) His conclusions reflect his basic tendency to interpret prescientific Greek thought as shamanistic.

[7]Hicetas, Ecphantus, and Heraclides Ponticus are fourth-century thinkers and so outside the scope of this study. See Guthrie 323–329, Heath, *Aristarch* (249–283), Wehrli, *Herakleides Pontikos* frs. 104–117 and comment. Unsuccessful attempts have been made to depict them as exponents of a Pythagorean astro-nomical tradition.

8

THE HARMONY
OF THE SPHERES

T HE theory of "the harmony of the spheres" which, throughout
antiquity and ever since, has been considered typically Pythagorean, presents difficulty in both astronomical and musical
theory. The word *harmonia* itself is an ambiguous one.[1] Its primary
meaning is not musical concord but a "fitting together" produced by
a craftsman such as to result in a unified object, or "perfect fit."
Typical are the joints produced by a carpenter-joiner. It is in this
sense (Bonitz, *compages*) that the word is often used in other than
Pythagorean contexts. Even in discussions of Pythagorean *harmonia*
it is not always the early four notes and intervals of the chord, the
heptachord, or any system of ten notes that is implied, but simply a
concord (rather than a discord) of musical sound. Thus the primary
sense is that of a principle producing a unified complex, and, deriving
from this sense, that of a complex in musical sound and, finally, such
a complex as a succession of sounds, a type of scale or mode expressible
in numerical ratios which state how the sounds "fit together."

In his discussion (985b 23–986a 13) Aristotle implies all these meanings. The Pythagoreans, he says, saw that concordant musical sounds
could be represented as ratios and, as their universe was number, they
concluded that these ratios must also be present in the relations one to
another of the heavenly bodies. He suggests that they increased the
number of those bodies to ten for numerical rather than for musical
reasons, but refers us for a description of the theory to another, more
detailed treatment. Alexander (41.1/2) tells us that the reference is
to the monograph *On the Pythagoreans* (but there is no mention in our
fragments) and to the *De Caelo*, probably the following passage
(290b 12–291a 13):

It follows that to assert there is a *harmonia* or concordant sound produced by
the heavenly bodies in their motion, the sounds they produce being in accord, is

a clever and unusual theory but does not correspond to fact. There are some [the Pythagoreans] who believe that when bodies of such a size are in motion they must produce sound, as occurs in the world of our experience with bodies of lesser mass moving at lower speeds. When sun and moon and stars in such numbers and of such magnitude move as they do, with the speed they do, it is impossible that they should not produce a sound of tremendous volume. On this assumption, and further assuming that their relative speeds, as determined by the intervals between them, stand to one another as do the ratios of the musical chord, they assert that the sound emitted by the stars in their revolutions is a musical accord; and since it seems improbable that we should not hear that sound, they allege as reason for this that the sound is present from our birth on, so that we never become aware of it by contrast with its opposite, silence; sound being recognized by contrast with its opposite and *vice versa*. All mankind (they say) is in about the same case as bronze-smiths who become so accustomed to the noise of their forge that they grow oblivious of it.

Now this, as I said earlier, is an appealing and an intelligent thesis, but it cannot correspond to the facts. It is improbable not only that we should hear nothing—they attempt to explain this—but also that perception by ear should be the only consequence. For excessive noises break up the substance of even inanimate things. Thunder splits asunder stones and the solidest of bodies. When so many bodies are in motion, if a sound reached us in proportion to the size of each, it would reach us many times multiplied and in incredible strength. So, obviously, we hear no sound, and bodies are not subjected to any violent consequence, because there is no sound. The reason for this is clear and a proof of the soundness of our own thesis, as is shown if we consider what was the problem the Pythagoreans posed themselves and why they maintained that there is a concord produced by the heavenly bodies in motion.[2] Everything that has a motion of its own produces sound and impact. But things present in or located in a moving body—e.g. parts in a ship—emit no sound (nor does a ship in movement on a river).[3]

An exposition of Aristotle's own theory of the motion of the heavenly bodies precedes this passage. He explains that they do not move of their own motion but are carried on spheres, they themselves being at rest. The fixed stars are carried around the earth, the centre of the universe, by the uniform daily rotation of their sphere. The sun, moon, and planets are moved in their paths by a complex mechanism of concentric spheres. No star nor planet has a movement of its own, neither rotation on its axis nor revolution in its orbit. If they had any such motion then, as animate creatures, they would have been provided with the means or instruments of locomotion. So, Aristotle concludes (290b 8–11):

"Since the first heaven must rotate about its own axis, and since the other stars cannot move of their own motion, it is as we should expect that both are spherical, spherical shape furthering the motion of the first heaven, excluding self-movement for the other heavenly bodies."

He then digresses to discuss Pythagorean music of the spheres, and to extract from it a confirmation of his own theories (pp. 286–288).

From Aristotle's reference it is clear that for the Pythagoreans their universe was an ordered one in which the heavenly bodies moved of their own motion (and not on spheres) at determined velocities and intervals. It would appear that anterior to their astronomical theory was a knowledge of the mathematical ratios obtaining in the musical scale and that they argued from this knowledge (rather than *vice versa*) that the intervals between the heavenly bodies produced sounds corresponding to the notes of the musical scale, the more distant bodies producing higher notes, the bodies nearer to the earth producing lower notes because their velocity was less. It is not suggested nor implied that the theory took into account the "wandering" of the planets. It may simply have assumed that the angular velocity of all bodies was identical.

To us, as to the theorists of later antiquity, it seems impossible that the theory should not specify the musical scale to which it had reference nor the order of the heavenly bodies to which it applied. As it is by a combination of these two independent elements, musical theory and astronomical theory, that the doctrine of the music of the spheres is constructed, and as each of these two theories has an independent history of development, they may best be considered separately. If we can form some idea of their development in the fifth century, we can then better hazard a guess when they could have been combined to yield a doctrine such as "the music of the spheres."

There is no real evidence for the statement often made that Pythagoras "discovered" the numerical relations obtaining in the musical scale,[4] or at least octave, fifth, and fourth (though why he should have discovered only these when Terpander had long since invented the seven-stringed lyre, remains unexplained). The Pythagorean tradition annexed for itself all scientific discoveries of a mathematical character, and systematically attributed them to their founder, obscuring both the time and the nature of the discoveries. In music, as in mathematics and astronomy, our best hope is to consider the tradition that is not dependent on Pythagorean or pythagorizing sources.

By the end of the sixth century and the time of Pythagoras the craft of the musician and the craft of the instrument-maker had a long history and had reached a high level of proficiency. This does not necessarily imply the development of any musical theory, but we have some evidence for an interest in theory. Lasos of Hermione is said by Theon of Smyrna (59.4 = *Vors*. 18.13), to have discovered the musical intervals. Agathocles, Pindar's instructor in music, was also the teacher of Damon (Plato, *Laches* 180D = *Vors*. 37 A 2) who was undoubtedly a theorist, probably not only in prosody.[5] This Agathocles is said to have been the pupil of Pythoclides, a Pythagorean (?), and according to both Plato (*Alcib*. 1.118c) and Aristotle (Plut. *Peric* 4 = *Vors*. 37 A 4), Pythoclides taught music to Pericles. There are difficulties of chronology here, though we need not think of the pupil-teacher relation as implying the difference of a generation. But, because of association with the names of Pericles and Pindar, we learn of a teaching activity in music that had aspects of theory. From Pindar (*Nem* 4.45) we learn that the principal modes were not only established, as we would expect from the historical development, but that they were so familiar as to permit casual allusion.[6] Where there is a high degree of musical culture and an interest in theory, can we assume that the mathematical relations between notes would be known?

If we take it that a knowledge of musical ratios is possible only when mathematics and harmonics have developed to the point that a mathematical theory is possible, then this could have occurred only after the middle of the fifth century. But if we consider that the ratios could be arrived at empirically, in the course of the development of music as a *technê*, then there is no reason why they should not be known as early as the last half of the sixth century, and our problem becomes not one of musical scale, but of the history of astronomy. At what date could the Pythagoreans, or others, have associated musical ratios and orderly movement of the heavenly bodies and, by combining the two, have evolved a doctrine of the music of the spheres?

We cannot answer, as does Burnet (110) that "it is extremely probable that Pythagoras identified the intervals between these (Anaximander's wheels) with the three musical intervals he had discovered, the fourth, the fifth, and the octave." There are no good grounds for believing that Pythagoras discovered these three intervals and no grounds at all for thinking that he identified them with Anaximander's three wheels. It is more likely that the theory arose in connection with seven notes and seven planets, but a scale can be constructed based on seven planets plus the sphere of the fixed stars or, as in the "Philolaic" system, with ten heavenly bodies.[7]

In Plato's Myth of Er (*Rep*. 617A–B) we have, for the first time, an exposition of the "music of the spheres," and musical and astronomical components are full-fledged. Eight Sirens are seated on the eight whorls of the spindle of Necessity. They represent the sphere of the fixed stars, sun, moon, and the five planets. Each of the Sirens sings one note, and the succession of notes corresponds to the musical scale (Heath, *Aristarch.* 108–110). We are not told why these notes sounded together should produce a *harmonia* and there is no need to speculate, for the Platonic theory arises not in music but in astronomy. We believe that Plato had an earlier source for his myth. What was that source?

Here we encounter an obstacle to progress in our inquiry. The obvious answer would be Philolaus. For to Philolaus are attributed both astronomical and musical theories. If the music of the spheres is Pythagorean, we would expect him to have expounded some version of it, but neither in the fragments nor in the doxography is there any suggestion that he did so. Zeller (ZM 2.540, n. 2 = ZN 2.540, n. 2) suggests that Philolaus may not have referred to it because it was related to a theory of seven planets and the seven-stringed lyre, and not to the ten planets of his own system. But a scale could be constructed on the basis of ten planets, and the consideration that Sun, Moon, and Venus appear to move together, could serve as the point of departure. If the music of the spheres was a central doctrine of Pythagoras' it seems strange that a Pythagorean whose speculation embraced both music and astronomy (in however crude a form) should altogether neglect it. But we cannot conclude from Philolaus' silence that there was, at his time, no Pythagorean doctrine of a music of the spheres. As we suggested earlier (*supra* 116) he may be representing Pythagorean thought on the basis of little more than recollections from his youth. If he had any knowledge of a doctrine of the music of the spheres it may have seemed to him of marginal importance.

So we have the Platonic whorls, we have an earlier Philolaic system in which, so far as we know, there was no reference to music of the spheres, and we have a pre-Platonic system reported by Aristotle (Alex. Aphr. 41.1–6) in which, as in the system of Philolaus, there were ten heavenly bodies separated from one another by "harmonic" ratios and moving at velocities that produced the musical sounds of the scale. As all these theories have some astronomical and musical background, and as the Myth of Er seems not much more advanced, although Plato's theories in the *Timaeus* do, it seems probable that they should all be referred to some time about the end of the fifth century.

These three theories have a scientific character or colouring. But the notion of a music of the spheres need not have had such a character in origin. All that it demands is a knowledge of the seven notes, probably to be connected with the seven-stringed lyre, and of the seven planets. The number seven itself would serve to provoke a search for "correspondences." By a simple leap, the inference would be drawn that as the seven-stringed lyre produced music, the seven planets must also by their regular motions produce music. Mathematical elaborations of this simple correspondence can come later.

So we conclude that as an astronomical-mathematical theory we can have a music of the spheres only in the last decades of the fifth century; but that, as a poetical notion comparable to the lyre of the Muses or the hounds of Persephone, (*Fr. Sel.* 135) it may be attributed, if we will, even to Pythagoras himself. Any such attribution however is merely a guess. The theory, in so far as it is a "correspondence," is not necessarily the product of an original imagination. We may find some confirmation for the suggestion that it was a poetic insight in the fact that it long outlived the musical and astronomical theories on which it was based.

NOTES

[1]Only in secondary and occasional instances does ἁρμονία mean concord, the musical attunement which we observe as present in musical sounds. In origin and usually it is a "fitting together," primarily of things, that is imposed by a craftsman or maker. In the *Iliad* (5.60) Phereclus, the builder of the ships in which Paris carried off Helen, and a favourite of the artisans' patron Athene, is the son of *Tekton* (or carpenter-builder) who in his turn is the son of *Harmon* (or joiner). Odysseus (*Od.* 5.248) fits together his raft with ἁρμονίῃσιν (joints) and dowels. Anything apparently that is fashioned with joints such that they make the original pieces part of a unified structure is a ἁρμονία.

In the Presocratics (*Vors.* vol. 3—*Wortindex*) we find the word used first by Heraclitus largely in a musical sense of an accord or fitting-together of sounds in a melody, each note "fitting" that which precedes it (and not as what we call harmony, part-singing or polyphonic music). But Heraclitus also refers to the ἁρμονία of the bow and the lyre. In Empedocles we encounter the word, personified and deified, as a fitting-together or union. Sphairos is established in the secret place of *Harmonia* (B 27). Bones are fitted together by the strong glues of *Harmonia* (B 96).

Though we find that the Pythagorean usage is predominantly musical—either as a concord or as a concordant musical scale—the earlier sense of a fitting-together-into-one imposed by a craftsman is often also present.

[2]Aristotle refers again to the music of the spheres (1093b 4) where he uses the curious Ionic term οὐλομέλεια (see Ross *ad loc.*). The same term recurs *Theol. Ar.* 48.7 where it is said that the Pythagoreans, following Orpheus, applied it to the hexad and one of the "correspondences" given for the hexad is the music of the spheres. (Cited *Vors.* 1.458, where n. line 12 gives references to uses.) The normal meaning of the word appears to be that of Parmenides' use (*Vors.* 28 B 8.4). Aristotle, by using the word in its Ionic form, may perhaps suggest that it is a Pythagorean term. For occasional intrusions of Ionic in Pythagorean writings Thesleff 90, n. 1.

[3]The commentators do not aid us greatly in understanding this passage (Alexander 39.22–40.9; *Fr. Sel.* 138–141; Simplicius, *in De Caelo* 463.16–465.6; Themistius, *in De Caelo* 116–117). Alexander explains that, according to the theory, the moving bodies in the heavens were separated by proportionate intervals; that some move faster, producing high notes, others slower, producing low notes; that these sounds occur according to distance ratios; and that they produce a concord. Let us say, he continues, that the distance of the sun from the earth is twice that of the moon, the distance of Venus three times, and that of Mercury four times. It was the belief of the Pythagoreans that all other relevant ratios could be expressed numerically, and that the motions of the heavens were harmonious. Those farthest removed from earth had the greatest velocity, those nearest the least, and the intermediate bodies in proportion to the size of their orbit. In recapitulating (41.1–11), Alexander adds that there were ten bodies and that the intervals separating them were *harmonic* intervals. He goes on to say that we do not hear the music because we have been accustomed to it from childhood up.

This sounds as if the angular velocity of all bodies were the same, and the intervals separating them the same. The size of the several bodies is not taken into account. See Heath, *Aristarch.* 111, n. 2. It may be possible to devise a musical scale on the basis of Alexander's information. None of the comments I have seen attempt it.

Themistius (116) quotes Alexander (not of Aphrodisias, see Heath, *Aristarch.* 112) for another argument against the Pythagoreans, in addition to those of Aristotle. If we do not perceive the sound produced by the stars then we would not hear the sounds produced by the motion of any lesser bodies.

[4]For a review of the evidence see Guthrie (220–229) who disagrees with what seems to me a reasonable suggestion of Frank (11–12) that even the early instrument-makers must have had an empirical knowledge of the musical intervals. Guthrie refers to *Metaph.* 1093b 2–4 where the αὐλός is said to have 24 notes. But there existed then as now, much simpler pipes with fixed intervals between stops. Early pipes had three or four holes, but more were added before the sixth century (C. Sachs, *The History of Musical Instruments* (New York 1940), 139). According to Sachs (131) lyres are depicted with three to four strings from the ninth century, with five strings from the eighth, and with six or seven from the seventh. It seems probable that later writers suggested that Pythagoreans used what was for them the most primitive form of the instrument.

Sometimes the monochord was suggested, though it was not a musical instrument properly speaking.

Zeller (*ZM* 2.537–541) argues that the music of the spheres assumes the heptachord and seven heavenly bodies and Heath, *Aristarch.* 107 agrees. Burnet 110 is willing to credit the beginning of the doctrine to Pythagoras, suggesting that he based it on the three "wheels" of Anaximander and the three musical intervals he had discovered. Pythagoras is later credited with every variation, both astronomical and musical. It is worthy of note, though it probably has no great significance, that Nicomachus, *Encheiridion* chap. 5 credits him with a modification rather than with the discovery of the scale.

⁵If the fragment of Philolaus (*Vors.* 44 B 6; see Burkert 365–378) in which he describes his musical scale may be assumed to be genuine then, whatever the defects of that scale may be, there is a *terminus ante quem*, approx. 424 B.C. Some support for this assumption is afforded by what Plato (*Rep.* 400A) tells us of Damon's prosodical theory, alluding to a complex doctrine in which different forms of verse are analyzed in terms of long and short sounds. We are meant to understand from Socrates' casual reference that he is well aware of Damon's system, but that polite conversation does not lend itself to its explanation. Any such system must assume a preceding musical scale which need not be but, given the fragment of Philolaus, probably is numerical. If Pericles died in 429 B.C. Damon's activity may reasonably be placed at about that time, whatever the problems of his chronology (A. E. Raubitschek, *Class. et Med.* 16.78–83). Somewhat earlier in the history of mathematics Hippocrates attacked the Delian problem by means of proportionals (*Vors.* 42.4) about the middle of the fifth century. If a theory of proportionals was given at his time it is likely that the much simpler ratios of the musical chord were also known then.

How much earlier can those ratios have been known? Nicomachus (Iambl. *in Nicom.* 118.19) says that Pythagoras introduced from Babylon the theory of proportionals and the knowledge of the arithmetic and harmonic ratios which are those of the musical scale. We will hesitate to ascribe to Pythagoras or anyone else before the middle of the fifth century, knowledge in terms of theorem and proof. But there seems no reason why, empirically and in terms of "correspondences," Pythagoras or early Pythagoreans should not have "discovered, the ratios obtaining in the musical scale. Whether the original discovery was octave, fifth, and fourth or corresponded to the seven-stringed lyre, becomes of real importance only in connection with astronomy.

A. E. Taylor, *A Commentary* 155–173 bases his discussion on the assumption that Timaeus is expounding Pythagorean doctrine.

⁶The Pythagoreans are said to be not musicians nor teachers of music, but musical theorists (ἀρμονικοί). At what period may we suppose this differentiation to arise within the craft? The early poets were usually themselves musicians, and composed the melodies to which their verse was sung. But there were also teachers of music who were apparently recognized practitioners of the *technê*. And though we find *mousikos* used with a professional connotation only in later sources, the fact that Athenian youth were trained in μουσική implies, as well

as a general education in letters, some specialized training in music (H. I. Marrou, *Histoire de l'Éducation dans l'Antiquité*[4] [Paris 1958] 188–199). We find, for example (Plato, *Laches* 180D), Socrates recommending Damon as a teacher of *mousike* for the son of Nicias. From the *Republic* (400A) we know that this teaching was, in part, theory.

This Damon was eminent in his profession. He is known to us not only because he is deferred to by Plato, but also because he was the teacher of Pericles. (Wilamowitz, *Gr. Verskunst* 59 ff.; von H. Koller, *Die Mimesis in der Antike* [Bern 1954] 21–25; Raubitschek *supra*). But we learn of other outstanding teachers, such as Agathocles and Pythoclides (214). Aristoxenus in his *Peri Mousikes* (Wehrli, *Aristoxenus* 76, 82) cites yet other eminent names. But among them all only one is said to have been a Pythagorean, and that claim is made by a scholiast (*Vors.* 37 A 2 = Schol. Plato *Alcib.* 1. 118c) writing at a time when all possible candidates were being rebaptized Pythagoreans.

It might be suggested that all these were teachers, and not theorists with a mathematical preparation. But if we look for theorists between Pythagoras himself and Philolaus, we find only that Hippasus into whose story we have already inquired (26 ff). There we found that he was little more than a name used to fill a gap in the history of mathematics. Now we find Aristoxenus attributing to Hippasus an experiment (*Vors.* 18.12 = Schol. Plato *Phaedo* 108D; see Burnet, *Plato's Phaedo* [Oxford 1911] 150; Wehrli, *Aristoxenus* fr. 90 and comment) in which he makes four disks of equal diameter but differing thickness, the thicknesses being such that when the disks are struck they emit the four basic or "stationary" notes of the octave (Burnet, *Greek Philosophy* I. 46). Von Fritz has made much of this experiment in the article on the discovery of incommensurability. The tale, however, is supposed to illustrate the craft of Glaucus and not of Hippasus, and in fact Eusebius (*Vors.* 18.12) attributes the experiment to Glaucus. To complicate matters further Theon of Smyrna (59.4 = *Vors.* 18.13) tells us that "Hippasus and his school" performed a similar experiment intended to prove the same mathematical relations in the notes of the chord, with four vessels that he filled with liquid to appropriate levels. But before this experiment is attributed to Hippasus it is attributed to Lasus of Hermione (*ibid.*), whom we must suppose to have been of mature years when he caught Onomacritus in the act of forging oracles, some time before 514 B.C. (*Hdt.* 8.5). Lasus is never said to be a Pythagorean, and it would appear that the experiment (if it is not, as seems likely, merely an aetiological fiction) might with more justice be claimed for Lasus, a contemporary of Pythagoras.

The whole later tradition ascribes to Pythagoras himself the discovery of the four basic ratios of the musical scale. (*Theo. Smyr.* 56.9–12; *Timaeus a Calcidio Tr. Comm. Instr.* ed. Waszink [Leiden 1962] 93–94). Porphyry and Iamblichus give us circumstantial accounts of the discovery. It would appear that Aristoxenus, in attributing the experiment (of Glaucus?) to Hippasus, was here, as elsewhere, shaping the Pythagorean myth. What fact is behind the tradition we cannot say.

[7]*ZM* 2.454–455 discusses Pythagorean *harmonia*; 537–541, the music of the

spheres, with reference to the literature. Guthrie 295–301, with reference to subsequent discussion, argues reasonably for only three intervals and so four tones. Sambursky 38–45 has an interesting discussion of the scientific background.

It is obvious that Aristotle cannot entertain the theory seriously. Our only hope of penetrating further into the details known to him is to examine the arguments he uses against it (*De Caelo* 290b 12–291a 28). He argues that though the theory of the Pythagoreans is a brilliant and original one it cannot be true that the heavenly bodies, in their motion, emit a musical sound, for it is absurd to think that we should not hear the sound which would reach us in tremendous volume, and would have disastrous consequences, as in the case of the thunderbolt. The Pythagoreans suppose the sound to be caused by the proper motion of the heavenly bodies but in fact there is no sound because these bodies do not themselves move (291a 23); they are carried around by their spheres and no more emit sound than do the parts of a ship under sail.

In commenting on the earlier reference to the celestial harmony, Alexander (39.20–22) mentions, as the basic harmony, the octave having three intervals, and says that the ratios of these intervals are the same as the ratios of the heavenly bodies' distances. But he does not apparently imagine those bodies as moving in three circles because he goes on to add (40.3–6): "Let us say that the distance from earth to sun is twice that from earth to moon, three times that to Venus, four times that to Mercury" and so on. Later he adds (41.3) that the ten heavenly bodies are at intervals identical with those of musical attunement.

Simplicius (*in De Caelo* 463–470) discusses the theory at length. He recapitulates Aristotle's arguments and adds some of his own: (1) By attending to accustomed sounds we hear them. In any case the illustration of the coppersmith's shop is a poor one. The smith may not hear the noise of his shop, but neither does he hear the buzz of a gnat—and we do. (2) He quarrels with the assertion that Pythagoras could hear the music of the spheres, whereas the rest of us cannot. (Dogs have a keener sense of smell than we do.) Only another philosophy than a human one can explain how, by purifications or a good life or religious practices, one can perceive sights and sounds not otherwise accessible to mortal eyes and ears. Pythagoras must have meant simply that he perceived the *numerical ratios* of the celestial harmony.

Simplicius' interest in the music of the spheres, like Aristotle's, is in its negative aspect as confirming Aristotle's theories. If there is no sound, then the heavenly bodies cannot themselves be in motion. But so much is clear: (1) that the theory known to Aristotle has an astronomical background, assuming numerically determined intervals between whatever bodies or spheres moved in however many circles; (2) that there was a correspondence between these intervals and the intervals of the chord; (3) that the sound supposed to be emitted was not a loud one; (4) that the sound emitted is perceived by us, though not consciously. (The heavenly bodies may have been said to be animate.) If we hear them (but do not attend to them) we must hear them as we do other attunements because the musical ratios are identical and for us consonant.

Raven suggests (*KR* 259) that "it may perhaps be surmised to have originated early in the fifth century B.C." We must then attribute "the music of the spheres" either to Hippasus (and then why not to Pythagoras, as Hippasus appears to be his younger contemporary) or to that anonymous research group of early Pythagoreans who seem to me such a gratuitous hypothesis.

The date is uncertain at which we may assume a knowledge in the Greek world of the Babylonian seven planets which, as Neugebauer remarks (169) "has nothing to do with the arrangements in space." The doxography (*Dox. Gr.* 345) attributes to Alcmaeon a knowledge of the fact that the planets have a retrograde motion and Heath (*Aristarch.* 50) would attribute this to Pythagoras himself. If retrograde motion is recognized there must already be a clear differentiation of planets from fixed stars. Eudemus in the astronomical chapter of his history of the sciences says that Anaximander was the first to discuss distance and order of the planets (Wehrli, *Eudemus* fr. 146 = Simpl. *in De Caelo* 471) but it appears probable (Kahn 61) that he was discussing only some of the planets.

Burkert (294–295) argues that about 430 B.C. Meton introduced Babylonian astronomical theories describing τάξις. If by this is meant that Meton, on the basis of Babylonian observation, offered a theory of the order of the planets this seems a reasonable thesis. We need not, however, assume, as Burkert seems to do, that all contacts were interrupted between Greece and Persia 500–449 B.C. If we had no other evidence, the Themistocles episode would suffice to show that contacts were not difficult. Nor must we assume that a knowledge of the fact that seven was the number of the planets could not have reached Greece before 500 B.C.

9

THE PYTHAGOREAN SYMBOLA

ARISTOTLE'S account of Pythagoreanism falls into two distinct parts. In the treatises he reports and discusses Pythagorean theories having a scientific or para-scientific character. In his monograph *On the Pythagoreans* he transmits a collection of material relating to Pythagorean religious practice and to legend. He makes little or no attempt to relate these two aspects of Pythagoreanism. We would expect him to find common ground in a discussion of the soul, or in a theory of the music of the spheres in which the soul as number or ratio plays a part. But we have seen (123–128) that the soul plays no part in his account of the music of the spheres, and we shall see (151*ff*.) that in his discussions of the soul he refers to Pythagorean notions only incidentally.

In our attempts to reconstruct the modes of Presocratic thought we use both philosophical and legendary or mythological material, and we seek to create a composite picture. We must remember that Aristotle had evolved no historical method, that he did not see philosophical development in an historical perspective, and that the investigations made in our times by the social sciences, investigations which enable us in a measure to understand his report, were as yet undreamed of. It must be accounted a merit that he reports legends and practices he had no means of understanding, and which were untractable for his purposes. The absurdity of the interpretations of his contemporaries and of later antiquity make it apparent how laudable was his restraint. The fragments of his collection, if they are used with caution, permit us to infer something of the background of the legend they report.

The Pythagorean *Symbola* or *Acusmata* exercised the same sort of fascination on the Greek mind that they do on our own. They were felt to be curious and somehow significant, but to be altogether incongruous with the scientific character of Pythagoreanism. So we find them allegorically interpreted, explained away, sometimes repudiated. Our task is not to consider them singly, as anthropological documents, but to interpret them as a complex capable of throwing light on the character of early Pythagoreanism.[1]

The names *Symbola* and *Acusmata* by which we designate the somewhat heterogeneous material do not reflect two distinct classes of precepts and, as Guthrie (183) observes, distinctions made between them are arbitrary. The term *acusma* in the sense of a precept to be learned is a purely Pythagorean usage that first occurs in Porphyry and Iamblichus. It must be connected with Iamblichus' division of Pythagoreans into the two classes of *mathematici* and *acusmatici*. However, he draws no clear distinction between *symbola* and *acusmata*, both being imparted to the acusmatic members of the sect or brotherhood which Iamblichus imagines to have been founded by Pythagoras. As their arcane rather than their catechistic character is of importance to us, and as allegorical interpretation appears to have attached to them from the time of their collection, it will be convenient to call them *symbola* and to understand that name as covering all the data of our tradition.

The first question that arises for us concerning the *symbola* is how the Aristotelian collection was formed. We have in Iamblichus (*VP* 82–86) an attempt—probably not original—at classification in which each *symbolon* is the answer to a question of one of three kinds:

1. What are the Isles of the Blest? Moon and Sun. What is the oracle in Delphi? The *tetractys*, which is the harmony in which the Sirens are.

2. What is *most* just? To sacrifice. What is *most* wise? Number, and then to give names to things. (Iamblichus points out that apophthegmata of this class are patterned after those of the Seven Sages, who were earlier than Pythagoras.)

3. What must we do or refrain from doing? We must put on the right shoe first, avoid the public road, shun public baths, etc.

There follows a list of what we would call superstitious rules and observances. All are short and imperative. Most of them have following them a brief statement of the reason for the injunction or veto. Iamblichus (*VP* 86) denies that these explanations are Pythagorean, and in some cases he is certainly right. He is obviously troubled by the ridiculous nature of some of the *symbola* (*VP* 105) and insists (*VP* 227) on the value of their arcane significations.

Iamblichus has cast his net very widely for *symbola*—some of those cited in the *Protrepticus* (21) look like inventions of his own, and the Neoplatonic character of some is apparent. But many are common to Iamblichus and Aristotle.[2] Iamblichus apparently found in his sources a classification of the *symbola*. Aristotle, too, found in his tradition a classification according to kinds. "There was," he says (Porph. *VP* 42; *supra* 23), "*another* class of *symbola* such as the following." And in Diogenes Laertius (8.34–35) he is cited as a source for a list of dietary vetoes that is clearly a product of classification.[3] Now it is possible that Aristotle, or some younger Peripatetic on his behalf, by a process of field-work collected current Pythagorean *symbola* and classified them, and that if his classification did not become canonical at least the practice of classification persisted. But it seems more probable that in the fourth century there existed collections of Pythagorean *symbola* and that they were characterized by classification according to kinds. We know that by the sixth century Onomacritus was engaged in the collection and editing of oracles. We know from Euripides (*Alc.* 967–68, *Hippol.* 954) that in his time Orphic writings were widely current. Plato (*Rep.* 364E) can speak of a mountain of Orphic writings. It seems highly probable that in Orphic or in Pythagorean circles a record would be made of the Pythagorean *symbola*, particularly as they may have been, at least in part, common to the Orphics.

We know of one such collection, made by Anaximander of Miletus (*Vors.* 58 C 6) who wrote an "exegesis of Pythagorean *symbola*" in the reign of Artaxerxes Memnon (405–359 B.C.). His work is therefore earlier than Aristotle's monograph if Aristotle entered the Academy in 368–67 at the age of seventeen. If at least one collection of *symbola* existed before the time of Aristotle, there may have been others. Certainly the tradition was still vigorous enough in the time of Aristoxenus for him to combat it (Wehrli, *Aristoxenos* fr. 25), and apparently it retained its vigour because we have knowledge of two further collections, that of Alexander Polyhistor and that of "Androkydes," before the beginning of the Christian era. We may therefore assume that Aristotle had adequate sources for his account, and that it reflects the tradition of about the end of the fifth century. We may not suppose it to be much earlier, because of the explanations and justifications accompanying each *symbolon*.

What are we to make of this tradition? Are we to say that Pythagoras formulated a rule for his disciples or brotherhood, or sect, and that this rule consisted in whole or in part of the *symbola*? Boehm's discussion (*De symbolis Pythagoreis*) renders any such simple solution impossible. Most of the *symbola* are ancient usages or superstitions that long antedate the sixth century and many of them have an almost world-wide diffusion. As has been frequently pointed out, there are parallels for them not only in primitive practice but also in Homer, Hesiod, Delphic precept, and the practices of the mysteries (Nilsson

705). The conclusion is inescapable that the *symbola* are not Pythagorean in origin but were adopted and systematized by them as congenial and appropriate to their way of life. The question then arises whether they were common to Orphics and Pythagoreans—a question to which, as there are no Orphic documents of the period, no positive answer can be given.[4]

We can, however, with some confidence describe the salient characteristics of the Orphics. Jaeger (*Theology* 61–63) has effectively pointed out what they were not—they were not a Church teaching a revealed religion, and their theogonies and other teachings were not a dogmatic theology. Nilsson (698) has described them more positively:

Orphism has its roots in traditional belief, and is related to contemporary religious tendencies, (among them Pythagoreanism), with which it shares a belief in transmigration and in rewards and punishments in the underworld. It took up the notion of retributive justice, that had a powerful influence in a period full of social need and injustice. There is also elsewhere, e.g. in Eleusis, a demand for moral as well as religious purity. . . . One of its ideas, namely that the body is the tomb of the soul, appears to be of great originality, even though certain preliminary conditions were present; and it produced a revaluation of the relations existing between body and soul, between this life and the next. The second great idea of Orphism is that it connected the creation of mankind with the fate of the soul, even though there is no complete logical correspondence between the two ideas. The act of the Titans against the child Dionysus, and the creation of mankind out of the soot that arose from the combustion of their bodies, is something new.

Of the two principal Orphic ideas to which allusion is here made we find the first, in as far as it concerns ritual purity, reflected in our *symbola*; and the idea of transmigration, with its related notion of rewards and punishments and its inversion of the values of body and soul is in part implied in the *symbola*, in part reflected in the legend. Of the second principal idea, the anthropogony connected with the birth of Dionysus, there is no echo in our legend (and not everyone would agree that it is as early as the sixth century). What precisely were the relations between Orphism and Pythagoreanism in the sixth century we have no means of determining, but we may assume that they had much common ground in doctrine of the soul, demand for ritual purity, and allied notions. For our purposes however it is more important to know what their differences were, and we may infer something of these differences from the direction their respective adherents took. Plato, in a famous passage of the *Republic* (364B–365A), depicts the Orphics of his day as hawkers of pardons from door to door, and all his references to them are contemptuous (*Vors.* 1 B 1–8) as are those of other contemporaries. However revolutionary their religious innovations may have been in an earlier age, by the fourth century they had degenerated into practitioners of formal rites of purification, and their writings were a chaotic mythology.

Of Pythagoras on the other hand, Plato speaks (*Rep.* 600A) as of the founder of an ascetic way of life that procured for his followers, even in Plato's own day, singular consideration. That they did in fact enjoy such consideration, even though their discipline made them a butt for the New Comedy, is shown by the way in which not only Plato but also Isocrates (*Vors.* 14.4) speaks of them; and Aristotle could present Pythagorean thought as a cornerstone of Plato's.

Is the reason for this vast difference in the development of Pythagoreanism and of Orphism to be sought in the fact that Pythagoras himself established a brotherhood, and gave it a rigid rule and discipline of which the *symbola* are a part? Before we attempt to answer that question we must ask ourselves whether there was a Pythagorean brotherhood, and if so what its nature was. It is generally assumed, and often unhesitatingly affirmed, that there was such a brotherhood, and that it was something like the community described by Iamblichus, with a superior, postulants, a novitiate, and at least two orders of adepts, the *mathematici* and the *acusmatici*. Any such institution would be unique in the Greek world before the Christian era. The *hetaireiai* and the *thiasoi* were familiar institutions, but they never had the characteristics of a brotherhood with a rule. They were closely linked to the religious structure of the state and its rites. Their members lived as citizens of their communities. Even when at a later date we have philosopher communities like the Academy or the Garden, they are small and are not governed hierarchically, by a rule. The Academy and the Stoa both admit wide differences of opinion. Further, none of the early philosophers founded anything having even a similarity to a brotherhood. They were either solitaries, like Heraclitus, or had one disciple, as Parmenides/Zeno or Empedocles/Pausanias. Even when they collected more persons around them, as did Socrates, Plato, and Aristotle, they never attempted to govern them by rule or to establish an *ipse dixit* orthodoxy. So, in approaching the question of a brotherhood, we should rather anticipate that no such institution existed than confidently assume the existence of what would have been an anomaly and an anachronism.

Let us then review the accounts of the founding and organization of a Pythagorean brotherhood, and seek to evaluate the sources.

Iamblichus (*VP* 37–57) gives us a stirring account of Pythagoras' arrival in Croton. The Sage arrives preceded by the news of a miracle just performed, and first addresses the youth of Croton in their gymnasium-school, exhorting them to respect and obedience towards their elders. The elders, constituting the magistracy or senate, are favourably impressed when the tenor of the speech is reported to them. They invite Pythagoras to address them too, and he does so, on the theme of justice and concord. This is his first step towards achieving moral and political sway over all Magna Graecia.

Festugière has shown (*La révélation* 2.33–47) that Iamblichus' picture reflects patterns of the third and fourth centuries of our era. Missionary enterprise, conversion, the establishment of ascetic communities—no unusual occurrences especially among Syrian Christians (Vööbus, *History of Asceticism in the Syrian Orient* I, iv–ix and 136–150) —will have been familiar to Iamblichus, himself a Syrian. Eunapius (*V. Soph. Iambl.* 458–460; Loeb ed. 362–372) tells us that Iamblichus gathered around him a large number of disciples, that he performed miracles, and that while in prayer he was seen to be lifted from the ground, a halo about his head. If he himself was surrounded by this atmosphere it need not surprise us that he credits Pythagoras with success on a yet grander scale in Croton, and we would probably dismiss his account (cf. *ZM* 2.403, n.1) if it were not that Porphyry gives us an account in substance very similar, alleging the authority of Dicaearchus (Porph. *VP* 18 = Wehrli, *Dikaiarchos* 33). As this account of the arrival in Croton is the primary source for all accounts of the Pythagorean "brotherhood" I give a translation *in extenso*:[5]

Pythagoras, when he disembarked in Italy and reached Croton, was a much-travelled and an exceptional man, endowed by fortune with great natural gifts. He was tall and of noble aspect, having grace and beauty of voice, of manner, and of every other kind. On his arrival the effect he produced in Croton was immense. With a long and eloquent discourse he so moved the magistracy of elders that they bade him pronounce an exhortation suitable to that age to the young men, and then to all the boys assembled from their schools. Then an assembly of women was arranged for him.

Here Wehrli, *Dikaiarchos* fr. 33, terminates the fragment of Dicaearchus because there follows a reference to the immortality of the soul and, as we know, Dicaearchus did not believe in immortality. Diels, however, (*Vors.* 14.8a) without ascribing it all to Dicaearchus, terminates it only later.

As a result of these meetings his reputation rapidly grew, and he gained many disciples in that city, men and women as well—the name of one of the women,

Theano, has come down to us—and many princes and rulers from the neighbouring non-Greek country. There is no certain account of what he used to say to those frequenting him, for they preserved an extraordinary secrecy. But it became known, and is commonly known, that he declared the soul to be immortal, that it transmigrates into creatures of other species, and furthermore that there are cycles in which events recur and nothing is absolutely new, and again that we must consider all animate creatures to be of one genus or kind. Pythagoras is said to have been the first to bring these beliefs to Greece. [end of Diels' quotation] He so converted everyone to his way of thinking, as Nicomachus asserts, that with one single lesson which he gave on disembarking in Magna Graecia he gained two thousand adherents by his discourse. They did not return to their homes, but together with their wives and children set up a great school [or lecture-hall] and created the state generally called Magna Graecia. They received laws and regulations from him, and respected them as if they were divine covenants. These disciples pooled their goods and counted Pythagoras to the gods.

Wehrli is undoubtedly right in suggesting that the first part of this passage is inspired by Dicaearchus, and reflects his portrait of Pythagoras as a hero of the "active life." But his implication that Porphyry is quoting verbatim (and that his *Life* is a composite of such quotations) is questionable. There is no reason why Porphyry should not continue his paraphrase, as he often does, with material from an unnamed source (perhaps Apollonius) or simply with an account the matter of which was supplied by his own imagination, aided by his observation of the contemporary scene.

For our purposes, however, what is really important is to observe that Nicomachus, and not Dicaearchus, is alleged as his source for the founding of a community. It is *prima facie* unlikely that Dicaearchus (born *ca.* 360–340) should be the source for such a notion. We know of political and other associations (*hetaireiai*) in the fourth century, but none of them are religious communities of the kind here described, having their goods in common and living a communal life. Such communities however are common in the time of Nicomachus (c. 100 A.D.), and when Apollonius of Tyana (Iambl. *VP* 254) describes a brotherhood of 300 members as the foundation of Pythagoras, he is speaking of an institution with which he is familiar.

Porphyry (*VP* 21) continues his account of the initial period in Magna Graecia with another tale, at least in part ascribed to Aristoxenus, to whom Wehrli (*Aristoxenus* fr. 17 and comment) ascribes the whole context. In this account we learn that on coming to Italy and Sicily he stirred up the spirit of freedom and procured the liberation of subject states, that he legislated for them by the agency of Zaleucas and Charondas, and that he persuaded the tyrant of Centuripe to abdicate and distribute his patrimony. His influence extended to the nearby non-Greek tribes and to the Romans. Aristoxenus' prophet of freedom and concord who travels through Italy and Sicily preaching his gospel, is very different from the philosopher-statesman of Dicaearchus who settles in Croton and establishes an ascendency there.

We need not seek to reconcile the two pictures. The Peripatetic *Bios*-biography is a tract in which an ethical, political, or philosophical ideal is outlined under the name of a person, in this case Pythagoras. The events of the actual life are interpreted according to the tendency of the author, and suitable events are freely invented. Dicaearchus is depicting a hero of the "active life," in protest against the Aristotelian ideal of the contemplative life. Aristoxenus is depicting the Pythagorean Sage, as distinct from the philosopher of Academy or Lyceum.

Is it not possible that Aristoxenus and Dicaearchus had in mind an idealized Academy,[6] and perhaps also the institutions of Plato's Republic? Such a solution is excluded by the fact that the guardians of Plato's *Republic* were all philosophers with a lifelong training, and that they were equals among themselves, governing by consent. Their community of property is not ascetic in intention but is a political device. And as for Plato's role in the Academy, he neither played nor aspired to that of a master speaking inspired truth. So, in the fourth century, the notion of a community or brotherhood could not have been the casual product of Peripatetic imagination, suggested by contemporary institutions. We must conclude that there is no evidence for the idea, nor any likelihood that it arose before Nicomachus of Gerasa and Apollonius.

It has been suggested that a parallel to Pythagoras' arrival in Croton is to be found in Empedocles' boast of the honours paid him by all men (*Vors.* 31 B 112). Crowned and wearing the fillets he visits their cities, and they follow him in their thousands to ask for oracular utterance or a word to heal all manner of illnesses. But Empedocles was not winning adherents; he had been preceded by his repute as *iatromantis* and his divine status was acknowledged. He dispensed prophecy and healing as he moved from city to city, and his mission, an end in itself, did not aim at the establishment of "brotherhoods" or any political organization.

There are obvious similarities between Pythagoras and Empedocles, a kinship that Empedocles appears to recognize (*Vors.* 31 B 129), The parallels have been brought out forcibly by Rohde (378 ff.). and by Dodds (144–147) regarding common "shamanistic aspects.'

But the analogy can be misleading. It is not for nothing that Aristotle calls Empedocles the father of rhetoric (*DL* 8.57) and we can readily imagine him as a wandering poet-philosopher addressing throngs. As for Pythagoras, there is nothing but the suppositious Croton discourses to suggest that he gained adherents by preaching. The whole Pythagorean tradition is non-rhetorical until we come down to Apollonius of Tyana, who himself was an itinerant preaching prophet. Earlier Pythagoreans seem to have been sparing of their words and to have sought disciples rather by instruction than by emotional conversion. About a century after Apollonius we find Justin Martyr discouraged from adhering to Pythagoreanism because of the indispensable propaedeutic in geometry, astronomy, and music which, as Porphyry remarks (*VP* 46–47) prepare the eyes of the soul for the contemplation of true being.

It may be added that Empedocles' surprising insights appear to be the result of acute observation and intuition. His tendency is not mathematical, and quantitative abstraction is quite foreign to the character of his thought, which is if anything biological.

A further argument for the existence of a Pythagorean community or brotherhood hinges on the saying κοινὰ τὰ φίλων or κοινὰ τὰ τῶν φίλων. The critical passage (Schol. T Plat. Phaedr. 279c = Jacoby *FGrH* 566 F. 13a) reads:

κοινὰ τὰ τῶν φίλων: Applied to things shared well. They say the proverb first became current in Magna Graecia, in the period in which Pythagoras persuaded the inhabitants to have all goods in common. Timaeus in Book 9 says: "When the young men approached him, desiring to join his community, he did not accede to the request at once but replied that they must have property in common." And subsequently Timaeus continues: "It was through them that the saying spread in Magna Graecia κοινὰ τὰ τῶν φίλων."

Diogenes Laertius (8.10 cf. Porph. *VP* 33) on the same authority, expands this somewhat:

Timaeus asserts that Pythagoras was the first to say κοινὰ τὰ φίλων and "friendship is equality." His disciples paid their substance into a common pool and observed silence for five years, never seeing Pythagoras, but only hearing his discourses, until they passed the test. Then they became members of his household and shared in (the privilege of) seeing him.

Here we must note first that the proverb is not necessarily of Pythagorean origin. The scholiast goes on to give another account of how it arose, and it is often used in contexts where its meaning is quite un-Pythagorean (Aristotle *E.N.* 1159b 31 and for cases of use

Gauthier–Jolif, *L'Ethique à Nicomaque* [Louvain 1959] 2.2 n. *ad loc.*).
Aristotle, who quotes it, adds as a gloss that friendship implies a
community of interest—that is, that not only one's substance and one's
effort, but one's personal involvement are at the disposal of a friend
for him to draw on. That it was so understood by the Pythagoreans
is shown by the tales of Damon and Phintias, Kleinias and Proros,
and other anecdotes, and by accounts of ready generosity. The point
of these tales is that a friend may count on his friend to the last
farthing and the last breath, not that friends must have their property
in common.

Nevertheless Timaeus does assert that Pythagoras had established
some sort of association or community to which candidates were
admitted only if they gave their property to the community and, adds
Diogenes (not necessarily on the authority of Timaeus), if they underwent the trials of a novitiate. How credible a witness is Timaeus? As
Jacoby has shown (*FGrH* 3b 530–538), his history was written during
his years at Athens. He depended largely on written sources and
research in the libraries there. We have no reason to believe that he
travelled in Sicily and Italy, consulting archives and collecting
evidence. Even if he had visited Croton to investigate the circumstances
of Pythagoras' life it is unlikely that he would have found much useful
evidence after the lapse of two centuries. There was always a dearth
of early records and any oral tradition there was, had by then been
absorbed into the legend.

Timaeus (*ca.* 356–*ca.* 260 B.C.) came to Athens some time between
317 and 312, after the death of Aristotle. He had Peripatetic connections and must have known Aristoxenus and Dicaearchus, though they
were probably of an older generation and certainly senior in the
Peripatos. In his chapters on Pythagoras he will have used their
writings but, as we have seen, there is no ground for believing that they
spoke of a Pythagorean community. If that idea arises with Timaeus,
how did he come by it? Von Fritz (68–93; cf. Jacoby *FGrH* 3b 550–552)
has argued, in the main convincingly, that Timaeus has projected into
the sixth century and the times of Pythagoras, events that occurred
only in mid-fifth century. That there then existed Pythagorean
political associations appears to be beyond doubt. Timaeus saw them
as religious-political associations founded by Pythagoras and operative
in his lifetime. Admitting that there is nothing in the tradition of such
an association, and that on historical grounds it is unlikely that any
such association in fact existed, how are we to suppose that Timaeus
came to invent it? He knew that there had been political associations of

Pythagoreans up to the middle of the fifth century. He knew of the Pythagorean *Symbola* or Precepts, and precepts imply teacher and taught. He knew of Archytas' ascendancy in Tarentum about the middle of the fourth century, and though we have no knowledge of a formal political association headed by him, it is possible that there did exist some such *hetaireiai*, though hardly with community of goods. This last notion may derive in part from the proverb we have discussed, in part from the legal status of Athenian associations such as the Academy, which did at least have a common patrimony and a legal personality (Wilamowitz, *Antigonos von Karystos* 279–280).

In his account Timaeus sought to explain both the religious and the political aspects of the association he assumed to have existed, but if we had the complete account we might find that the political aspects predominated, as they do in the summary account of Justinus (20.4) which is said to be based on Timaeus and which I translate: (discussed von Fritz, 33–67)

After this (the Battle of the Sagras) the citizens of Croton altogether abandoned pursuits of valour and the practice of military exercises. For they felt an aversion for arms after their unhappy recourse to them, and if it had not been for the philosopher Pythagoras they would have turned to a soft and self-indulgent life. Pythagoras was born at Samos, son of a rich merchant, and was educated liberally. He travelled first to Egypt, then to Babylon to study astronomy and physics, and he achieved great knowledge. On his return he went to Crete and Lacedaemon to study the then famous laws of Minos and Lycurgus. After all this study he arrived in Croton, and by his authority recalled to a frugal way of life the people of that city who had lapsed into soft living. Daily he praised virtue and told of the vices ensuing on soft and wanton living, and of the many states whose downfall had been so caused. He stirred up among the citizens such a zeal for frugality of life that it seemed incredible any of them had ever been soft or wanton. He usually instructed husbands and wives, parents and children separately . . . and succeeded in getting wives to lay aside their splendid clothes and the ornaments proper to their status and to have them consecrated to Juno in her temple, alleging that modesty and not fine attire was the true ornament of women. . . . But three hundred of the young men bound themselves by oath to a fraternal association, and lived (together with their comrades) apart from the rest of the citizens, as if they were the assembly of a secret conspiracy. This association achieved control of the state, and the other citizens determined, when they were assembled in one house, to burn down [house and] brotherhood within it. In that fire sixty members perished and the rest went into exile. At that time Pythagoras, after having spent twenty years in Croton, moved to Metapontum and died there. The veneration for him was so great that they made a temple of his home and treated him as a god.

In this passage there is first the familiar theme of *tryphe* developed in connection with the coming of Pythagoras and then, without explanation of how the transition is made, we are told of a political association of young men, of which it is not said either that it was founded by Pythagoras or that it was headed by him. It looks as if the well-worn *topos* had come from one context and the tale of political action from another and that Timaeus, in his narrative, connected them.

I conclude that, though at first sight the evidence seems to suggest a religious-political association founded by Pythagoras, on closer scrutiny we find no source earlier than Timaeus asserting the founding of such an association. It is unlikely that Timaeus had evidence foreign to our tradition, and it is easy to see how from excellent premises he might arrive at the conclusion that an association did in fact exist. We must not however finally reject his conclusion or declare it implausible until we have considered two further related details of the tradition, the *Symbola* and the alleged division of the community into *mathematici* and *acusmatici*.

If there existed a primitive division of Pythagoreans into two classes, one having access to the whole doctrine, the other to the rule or discipline only, then there was also a Pythagorean community or brotherhood. Our sources for this division are late. Porphyry (*VP* 37) tells us of a division into *mathematici* and *acusmatici*. Iamblichus (*VP* 80–87) has a more elaborate account in which he mentions first a division into Pythagoreans and Pythagorists—terms with which we are familiar from the fourth century—and then adds that "putting it another way" there were two kinds of philosophy to which corresponded two kinds of practitioners, the *mathematici* (these are the Pythagoreans) and the *acusmatici* (these are the Pythagorists). The *acusmatici*, adds Iamblichus, owe their origin to Hippasus (*DL* 8.7 and 84; Iambl. 88) who was said to have divulged Pythagorean secrets.[7]

So in Iamblichus there is a conflation of two accounts, one simply recognizing the fact of a division and two classes, the second accounting for it by a defection within the order. This defection is also explained as a real heresy respecting the fundamental doctrine of number (Iambl. *in Nicom.* 11.1; Simplic. *Phy.* 453,13d) in which it is asserted that number is the exemplar after which the physical world is made, but not the first principle or primary substance.

There were, beyond doubt, persons going by the names of Pythagorean and Pythagorist in the fourth century B.C. It is probable that any fourth-century writer explaining the division would use these terms rather than the terms *mathematici* and *acusmatici*, which suggest rather the organization of a religious community in the first centuries after Christ (cf. Joseph. 2.8.3; Philo *Opera* Cohn Wendland 6.12–13). Delatte has suggested that the information comes from Timaeus (*Vie* 169) to whom he is ready to attribute much of Iamblichus; and if we accept the attribution to him of the Justinus passage already cited (20.4) it may seem to be implied there. However, it would seem more plausible to attribute the whole notion of division to Aristoxenus. He knew of the existence in his own time of Pythagoreans—the last of whom he claimed to have known—and of Pythagorists. He repudiated the dietary regulations (especially abstinence from meat) which were practised by the Pythagorists (Wehrli, *Aristoxenus* frs. 26–29 and comment), apparently considering their vegetarianism primitive and a reproach to more enlightened Pythagoreanism. In the fragments he makes no allusion to such a division of the followers into classes, but it may be assumed from his statement that "not everything is to be communicated to all" (Wehrli fr. 43 = *D.L.* 8.15).

A division into classes within a community might be also assumed from the various references to Pythagorean "silence," (quoted ZM 2.404, n. 4), of which we must distinguish two kinds—continence in speech, and the *silentium* of an ascetic discipline mentioned by Iamblichus but not in earlier accounts. Isocrates (*Bus* 29, cf. Iambl. *VP* 94) is the first to mention continence in speech or taciturnity, saying that the Pythagoreans gained more respect by saying little than did others by saying much. This silence is rather a virtue than an ascetic practice. It is virtue commonly recognized, characterizing the "dignity" of Plato (e.g. *Rep.* 388D and by implication in references to *adoleschia*) and the magnanimous man of Aristotle (*EN* 1125a 13), its contrary vice being satirized by Theophrastus (*Char.* 3, 7). That silence characterized the Pythagorean we would expect, but a Pythagorean doctrine of silence as a virtue does not entail a division of adherents into two classes.

I conclude, therefore, that though there may have been Pythagorean political associations in the fifth century, there is no early evidence for the existence of an order or brotherhood. In the fourth century two kinds of Pythagorean may have been recognized, but the notion of a Pythagorean order or brotherhood is to be ascribed to late Hellenistic times when such ascetic communities began to be common.

This long digression has been necessary because, if there existed a Pythagorean brotherhood, the *symbola* must have been part of its rule, and the rule, in substance must have been a product of the mind of its founder. The *symbola* would then become documents of the religious beliefs and practices of Pythagoras himself. But if we reject the idea of early Pythagoreanism as a quasi-monastic order governed by a rule imposed by its founder, then the *symbola* are a collection of vetoes and precepts, homogeneous within the classes, and clearly a product of accretion in time and, probably, of editorial manipulation. This is not to deny their connection with Pythagoras, and in particular not to suggest that, because they are superstitious, they cannot be connected with him. We cannot doubt that their general character, and the original impulse to observe such precepts and vetoes, comes from Pythagoras. We shall hesitate to ascribe to him, without other evidence or probable grounds, any one precept or class of precepts.

The general character of the *symbola* is such as to suggest scruple in the performance of religious duty, and scruple of a formal kind, concerned rather with clean hands than with a pure heart. They suggest the carrying-over of this religious scruple into the practices of daily life; putting on the right shoe first, washing the left foot first, because hostile forces lurk in wait for the man who does not observe the proper forms. In forbidding certain foods, especially flesh, fish, and beans, they suggest, not a pantheistic respect for all life—a much later notion—but a respect for those forms of life in which soul may be embodied. They imply an ascesis in the sense that persons accepting any such body of precepts and vetoes necessarily accept the regulation of their life by formal scruple. That is, they accept certain limitations on their actions, and the performance of certain duties. These commands and prohibitions are such that they will impinge on their acts all day and every day. Whether to this ascesis there corresponded a positive purpose we do not know. Primitive superstitions usually promise freedom from harm rather than positive goods. This is the attitude which the *symbola* suggest—the attitude of a time where such practices were common (as they remained common throughout antiquity and, in a measure, remain common today). If the Pythagoreans were a loosely organized political *hetaireia* in the first half of the fifth century, and in the second half, after the *débâcle*, were refugees and exiles, it is likely that the negative aspect of the *symbola* was for them the important one. For Pythagoras himself, when he chose to conform to such practices, the positive aspect of his ascesis, enabling him to achieve insight into the nature of things, was probably more important than the negative one. The ascesis practised not only by Pythagoreans, Neopythagoreans, Neoplatonists, but also by many others professing the philosophical life always had the positive purpose of achieving insight. Our tradition tells us that Pythagoras was the first to institute and practise such an ascesis. This can be more readily credited if the ascesis is found to be allied, as it is in the tradition, to a doctrine of the soul.[8]

NOTES

[1]The essential material is collected by Diels (*Vors.* 1.462–466). C. Hoelk discusses the tradition in the spirit of Rohde's analysis of the sources of Iamblichus (*Kleine Schriften* 2 102–172), an analysis I have sought to show is in error, *TAPA* 90 (1959), 185–194. F. Boehm classifies them according to subject, cites their occurrences in the literature, and gives parallel instances for each precept or veto from Greek or other cultures. His study was an important step towards an understanding of the *symbola* as a cultural phenomenon which was only incidentally Pythagorean. Delatte (*Vie* 186–189; *Études* 271–286) discusses them. Nilsson (703–708) reviews the evidence and discusses their religious significance. Guthrie (182–195) emphasizes their primitive, magical character.

[2]For concordances see Boehm; Delatte, *Vie* in apparatus and notes; my article *TAPA* 94 (1963) 185–198 for a table of concordances showing relative frequencies.

[3]Burkert (150–159) in his account of the subsequent tradition of the *symbola* sees Aristotle as central to it. He suggests (159) that *acusmata* is Aristotle's term, but this is true only of the passages in Iamblichus. Plato (*Ep.* 2.314A) suggests that *symbola* is the technical term of which *acusma* is only explanatory. In Iamblichus Aristotle is not mentioned by name, and though, as Burkert says, he is probably the principal source, it is also probable that he is not the proximate one and that the term *acusma* originates with Porphyry and Iamblichus (*supra* 135). *Symbola* occurs twice in the fragments (*Fr. Sel.* 135). Burkert, with Hoelk, would attribute Porphyry *V.P.* 42 to "Androcydes" but see *supra* 23.

The date of Anaximander of Miletus is uncertain. Burkert (150, n.2) wishes to date him nearer 400 than 360 B.C. because he is mentioned together with Stesimbrotus in Xen. *Mem.* 3.6. Stesimbrotus (*RE* 2 reihe 6.2463–2467; *FGrH* 2.107) was a contemporary of Cimon who lived until after the death of Pericles' son Xanthippus 430 B.C. What he has in common with Anaximander of Miletus is the allegorical method of interpreting Homer. If Xenophon is correct in saying that Anaximander too was paid by Niceratus, the son of Nicias, who died in 404 B.C. under the oligarchs, then Anaximander must be dated to the earliest part of Artaxerxes Memnon's reign.

The "Androcydes" tradition has substance only if Porphyry *V.P.* 42, and therewith the most important group of *symbola*, is attributed to him as it is by Hoelk (50). This "Androcydes" is a nebulous figure, as Burkert (151 n.9)

concedes. He is first quoted, and on Pythagorean *symbola*, in the first century
B.C. (*Rh. Gr.* 3.193), and again by Athenaeus (10.452), also by Iamblichus
(*VP* 145). He is quoted twice in the *Paroemiographi Graeci*, once (*Mantissa* 2.81)
as saying that the four mathematical sciences are to be used as a propaedeutic
to philosophy because they accustom one to think in terms of abstract, divine
forms rather than matter. This is in the spirit of Porphyry (*V.P.* 47–50) and
apparently also of Moderatus of Gades whom he quotes. This suggests that
"Androcydes" belongs to the beginnings of Neopythagoreanism, in the first
century B.C. Whoever he was, he may have borrowed the name of the Androcydes
of Athenaeus (6.258 B), but need not have done so.

⁴It would be incumbent on us to attempt an inquiry into Orphic beliefs and
practice if it could be maintained that Pythagoreanism was a strict observance,
a sect, or an offshoot of an earlier dissenting religious movement, "Orphism,"
and if we had any real, exact knowledge of that movement. But whereas earlier
generations of scholars were ready to describe it in some detail now, as Dodds
(*The Greeks and the Irrational* 147–148) observes, there is a tendency to question
all information relating to the early period, a tendency that has found its most
effective expression in I. M. Linforth though, as Nilsson (680 n.1) remarks,
"es geht nicht an, den Orphizismus als eine scharf umrissene Grösse zu
behandeln." Much of the confusion apparent in the discussion arises from the
assumption of more or less precise analogies between Orphism and religious
movements of our own era, in particular, Protestantism.

Nilsson (678–699, esp. 678 n.1) has a cautious and conservative discussion with
references to the principal publications since his own "Early Orphism" where he
reviews earlier discussion and gives a full bibliography. Nilsson insists throughout
his discussion that Orphism cannot be considered in isolation from other kindred
religious tendencies of the archaic period, and (696) that it represents no such
radical departure from earlier religious beliefs and earlier theogonies as was once
imagined. (A few points of difference from Nilsson's views will become apparent
in the course of this discussion.)

On the crucial question of catharsis L. Moulinier (*Le pur et l'impur dans la
pensée des Grecques d'Homère à Aristote* [Paris 1952]) argues (in partial difference
from Nilsson 21) that the ritual purity demanded from earliest times was a form
of cleanliness, and that only later did it involve the notion of a taint on the *soul*.

⁵Porphyry's account which I have translated (*V.P.* 18–20) differs from that
of Iamblichus in that it omits the initial miracle, has Pythagoras first address
the senate of Croton and not the schools, and exhibits other differences chief of
which is that it omits the speeches. Porphyry (*V.P.* 21–22) has a second account,
in appearance complementary but in tenor contradictory, differing in all respects.
Here Pythagoras is the missionary sage, whereas for Dicaearchus he is the exponent of the active life.

⁶Wilamowitz, *Antigonos von Karystos* 268, notes a division within the Academy
between elder and younger members, only the former being full members and
exercising governing function, but this is not a "brotherhood" such as we find

in the Essene Manual of Discipline or the monks and auditors of the Manichee. There appears to have been no marked ascetic tendency in Greece before Socrates and the Cynics. It was then exhibited by persons like Diodorus of Aspendos, or wandering beggar philosophers like Bion and Teles who, however, were not religious and did not belong to communities.

[7]Delatte, *Vie* 43–44 and 246–249, has assembled the various references. He attempts rather arbitrarily to impose an order on the existing confusion, much of which is novellistic, the product of the imagination of romancing biographers.

[8]*Fr.Sel.* 135 prints together with the *symbola* a passage from Porphyry (*V.P.* 41) in which it is said: "Some of his sayings were of a mystical character and symbolic. Aristotle records many of them, as e.g. The sea is a tear of Chronos, the Great Bear the hands of Rhea," etc. These are clearly not *symbola* in the same sense as "do not step over a yoke," and we will conclude from Aristotle's statement no more than that that such dicta were included in the collection of *symbola*.

IO

TRANSMIGRATION

ARISTOTLE attributes a doctrine of the soul to the Pythagoreans only in the *De Anima*, where they are mentioned among those believing the soul to be the cause of motion, and are grouped together with the Atomists. Democritus is first cited as holding that soul consists in spherical particles, "like the motes we see in a sunbeam falling through a window" (*De An.* 404a 2–4). These particles are breathed in and maintain life as long as respiration continues. "Pythagorean doctrine" Aristotle continues (404a 16–20), "appears to be very similar. For some of them assert that soul is the motes in the air, others that it is what moves these motes. They observe that these are in constant motion, even in a complete windstill." This is treated by Zeller (ZN 1.560; ZM 2.554, n. 2) and by Burkert (65) as a piece of primitive superstition, like the early dictum that "everything is full of souls." But these Pythagoreans are mentioned in the course of a discussion of the doctrines of Democritus and Anaxagoras, and it can hardly be accidental that their theory is cited in almost the same words that were used immediately before of Democritus. Aristotle refers to "some"[1] Pythagoreans, and within this minority further distinguishes a group which considers the soul to be not the motes themselves but the force moving these motes. These latter, as Cherniss (291, n. 6) remarks, must be very late. All these considerations suggest the possibility that the Pythagoreans to whom reference is made may be contemporaries or near contemporaries who have accommodated their number theories to atomism and a version of the breath-soul.

Nowhere else does Aristotle ascribe a theory of the soul to Pythagoreans,[2] but both in the treatises and the monograph he is keenly aware of their doctrine of transmigration which, however, has for him no philosophical content.[3] He states his objection thus (*De An.* 407b 12–26):

This view [Plato's] and most other views concerning the soul are mistaken in that they situate the soul in and conjoin it with the body without first explaining for what reason, or what the state of the body should be. Yet such an explanation is clearly necessary. It is because of partnership with one another that there is agent and patient, mover and moved, reactions that do not occur between things taken at random. But most theorists attempt to explain only what sort of thing the soul is, without going on to give an explanation of the body that is to receive it; as if it were possible for any soul to enter into and be invested in any body, after the manner of Pythagorean accounts! Every body has its specific form [soul]. To say that any soul can enter any body is like saying that carpentry can be embodied in flutes. A craft must have for its use the tools proper to it, and so also a soul a body.

Here Aristotle is not objecting to the body/soul analysis, though he himself would qualify it, but he is arguing that in such a partnership the soul can fulfil its role as agent and mover only if endowed with the proper and appropriate body, its role in respect of the body being that of a craftsman towards his tools. The partnership cannot be a random one, as is suggested by Pythagorean accounts of transmigration.⁴

Aristotle returns to the same problem in a later context (414a 18–28), to point out that the body is not an entelechy of the soul but the soul of the body. Earlier thinkers were wrong in fitting it into any body, for the body must be of a certain kind and have certain qualitative characteristics (and so presumably you cannot have a human soul in an animal species). Failure to recognize this is a defect he finds in the theories of many of his predecessors. The Pythagoreans are barely glanced at (414a 24–25) in a phrase that recalls the earlier reference (407b 20). Only in these two places is a reference made (in the treatises) to Pythagorean transmigration doctrine. The reference need imply no more than that for them any soul could enter any body in succeeding transmigrations, though it seems probable that it implies also migration through plant and animal species.

In the fragments of his monograph Aristotle refers only once to transmigration. Myllias of Croton (Iambl. *VP* 143; Aelian *VH* 4.17 = *Fr. Sel.* 131, 132) is told by Pythagoras that he in a previous incarnation was Midas, son of Gordius, of Phrygia, and that he must perform certain rites at Midas' tomb.⁵ The fragments, though they tell us much of Pythagoras' divine or semi-divine status and of his powers, tell us nothing further of transmigration. We cannot infer from them whether the notion of transmigration was Orphic or of Pythagorean origin, nor is there any hint whether its origin is to be sought in Ionia or in Magna Graecia, and we must look elsewhere for an answer to the many questions that arise. Was it simply a doctrine of immortality? Did it teach migration of human soul from one mortal body to another? Or did the human soul migrate also through plant and animal bodies? Was its migration an ordered cycle? Where did the cycle end? Was the migration interrupted by sojourns in a world of the dead? If so, did the soul there undergo a judgment, and rewards and punishments for deeds in its previous life on earth?

Most of the evidence is both vague and late. In many cases we must draw inferences from casual hints. This meagre evidence has given rise to every variety of reconstruction: it would seem wise therefore to restrict ourselves to what is necessary for our purposes. Reconstruction in detail of the doctrine and its history, if it were possible, would be interesting and illuminating. But central to any reconstruction would be the fact, which few would now deny, that Pythagoras accepted and taught a doctrine of soul and body in which soul was the senior partner, a soul that persisted after death, was subject to judgment (with its ethical implications), and migrated through other bodies. Let us consider briefly the evidence in our tradition for these beliefs, as being a necessary background for a consideration of Aristotle's account.

Pythagoras was an Ionian, a native of Samos, who migrated to Magna Graecia only in mature years. Were there current in Ionia beliefs in immortality and transmigration such as he is reputed to have held, or must we assume that he began to adhere to those beliefs only on encountering the Orphics in Magna Graecia? There is a curious tale in Herodotus (4.95) in which Zalmoxis (whom we know to have been a Thracian divinity) is said to have been a slave of Pythagoras, "one of the most considerable of Greek philosophers." On being freed and returning to his own people Zalmoxis taught, and by a trick procured belief in, a doctrine that they would not die but only move on to a better place. Herodotus learned this story from Greek inhabitants of the Hellespont and the Black Sea. The important aspect of the story is that Zalmoxis is said to have learned his doctrine from a Greek. We may infer from this that the name of Pythagoras was connected in the public mind with a belief in immortality. There is, however, no suggestion of transmigration in the tale, and Zalmoxis tells his Thracian compatriots that they will escape death, rather than that their souls will survive the dissolution of the body. So the story is evidence only for some connection between Pythagoras and beliefs in survival.[6]

When Pythagoras left Samos for Magna Graecia he was a man of mature years and of a wide range of intellectual interests. Whatever the meaning of Heraclitus' *polymathia* (22B 129) may be, and however derogatory its sense, it must imply intellectual curiosity, wide inquiry, and reading. It is clear from the authority he acquired in the world into which he migrated that there he found scope for his gifts and an audience for his teachings. In many respects it must have been very different from Ionia, then the centre of the Greek world politically, intellectually, and artistically. Whereas the Ionians were in contact with Eastern nations from whom they accepted cultural stimulus, in Magna Graecia the Greeks were in contact, often hostile, with the lesser cultures of Southern Italy, Etruria, Sicily, to whom they owed commercial wealth rather than ideas. But it was a world of wider horizons and greater possibilities, a world in social and political ferment. Its cults were Greek and if there was any religious emphasis characteristic of the area it was on the Apollo of Delphi, the promoter of colonization and, in predominantly agricultural states, on the cult of the agrarian divinities, Demeter and Persephone. It was a world that Xenophanes found Greek enough and congenial enough, though he occasionally protested against its crudities, but it exhibited trends in religion of which he was ignorant or which he chose to ignore.

Somewhere between the time of Homer and the time of Aeschylus a shift occurred in the manner in which the human person was conceived—a gradual shift towards moral responsibility and towards the notion of soul as the dominant partner in the body/soul complex. These trends found expression in the cult of Dionysus, in the mysteries, and among "Orphics."[7] They had little or no influence on state cults. Indeed the state cults succeeded in either absorbing and disciplining them or in relegating them to the margins of religious life. But at the middle of the sixth century they were still in a phase of expansion. The characteristics of this movement we must infer from our tradition. We have no contemporary sources and no information from archaeological finds. We are even unable to link Pythagoras and the Pythagoreans of Croton to the one fixed point of the chronology of the period, the destruction of Sybaris by Croton in 510 B.C. And if our knowledge of Pythagoras is small our knowledge of the Orphics is negligible. We know nothing of their numbers, the extent of their activities, the beliefs they propagated. We can be certain that there were professed Orphics, leading an Orphic life, only in the next century. It is important to concede the extent of our ignorance, as determining the area in which some knowledge is possible. As ancient maps show the coastal areas in some detail, and then a vast, unknown interior, so in our inquiry, especially as we are basing it on Aristotle's testimony, we must recognize that there is a larger area of which we can only say "hic sunt leones."

Pythagoras may have brought with him from Ionia a doctrine of transmigration. Even if he did it is probable that he found some such belief current in Magna Graecia. A generation later it was accepted and professed by the Emmenidae, the ruling family of Acragas.[8] A generation later Empedocles of Acragas was teaching it. Aristotle says that the Pythagoreans believed in it, and his testimony must refer to the fifth century. So we may assume wide diffusion. We also know that Pythagoras taught it, for Xenophanes (21B 7) poked fun at him for believing that the soul of a man could migrate to a dog. Any further information as to the doctrine must be derived from the fragments.[9]

I have suggested (*infra* 147) that the *symbola* cannot be taken to be peculiarly Pythagorean, much less to be the beliefs and practices of Pythagoras himself; and this for the reason, amply documented by Boehm, that they are superstitious beliefs or practices for which there are early and numerous parallels, often in Greece itself. But this need not imply that they cannot, in general characteristics and positive implications, shed light on Pythagorean beliefs. Many of them doubtless reflect primitive fear and scruple. But a *hetaireia*, or any group professing common purposes and common beliefs, which would collect such *symbola* and erect them into a sort of rule governing their behaviour has some more positive purpose. The aim cannot have been confined to ritual purity and freedom from the hostile influences of the unseen world. If they considered the soul to be more important than the body in this life, and believed it to survive into succeeding lives, then their concern must have been, or have become, the soul's purity. If they believed further that the soul was subject to judgment and to rewards and punishments—a notion current at the latest in the early fifth century, as we learn from Pindar—then the general purpose of their scruple must be a moral one. The moral corollaries of the *symbola* that we find already in Aristotle are some confirmation of this.

These general considerations would lead us to suspect that the *symbola* must have a moral import. The dietary vetoes, forbidding the eating of meats and fishes, need be little more than the taboos prevailing in primitive cultures. The fact that specific foods were forbidden in the mysteries, and that there was much variety in the foods so specified, would lead us to believe that the vetoes there had no wider significance. But the Pythagorean vetoes are, *pace* Aristoxenus (Wehrli, *Aristoxenos* 25), more general. Empedocles, who also teaches transmigration, is explicit concerning his reason for abstention (31B 137): "A father takes up his son, whose shape has changed, and sacrifices him while he makes his prayer, the fool!" And he is just as explicit regarding abstention from beans (31B 141). The Pythagoreans had the same, or a similar, belief in transmigration, and the same vetoes. There can be no doubt that their motives for abstention were the same as those of Empedocles, belief in transmigration.

Why do we hear nothing of numbers in connection with these teachings about the soul? If we possessed the monograph *On the Pythagoreans* in its entirety we would be better informed as to this and other aspects of Pythagorean doctrine.[10] But it is possible that the monograph established no connection, and that, in fact, there was none, between numbers and the soul. The ascetic discipline may merely prepare the soul for penetration of the secrets of the physical world. This is the role of the mathematical disciplines in Porphyry (*V.P.* 47). The notion that a numerically-determined universe is known by a numerically-determined soul is Platonic. Nothing suggests that for early Pythagoreanism the soul was a number, nor is there any reason that their "music of the spheres" should imply a doctrine of the soul as number, perceiving music as number.

Let us then turn from the consideration of the *symbola* as a reflection, debased in the passage of time, of an ascesis instituted by Pythagoras, to a consideration of the legend; and first let us consider the status that it accords to Pythagoras. "Pythagoras used to teach that he was of higher than mortal origin" (Aelian *VH* 4.17 = *Fr. Sel.* 131).[11] "Aristotle says that Pythagoras was hailed by the people of Croton as Hyperborean Apollo" (Aelian *VH* 2.26 = *Fr. Sel.* 130). "He is said to have been an awesome person, and it was the opinion of his disciples that he was Apollo, come from the Hyperboreans" (*D.L.* 8.11 = *Fr. Sel.* 131). "One of the *acusmata* was 'Who are you, Pythagoras?' For they say he is the Hyperborean Apollo" (Iambl. *VP* 30 = *Fr. Sel.* 131). Iamblichus, after his usual fashion, elaborates on the theme and adds (*VP* 31 = *Fr. Sel.* 132) "Aristotle tells us in his book on Pythagorean philosophy that the Pythagoreans preserved among their secret doctrines a division of this sort—there are three kinds of rational creature; gods, men, and such as Pythagoras."[12]

In these passages Pythagoras is said to be Apollo because Apollo is the god of purifications, and probably also because he is the lawgiver. He is also called "Hyperborean Apollo" because the Apollo of Delphi comes from a land in the distant north where he is perfectly worshipped. Pythagoras, though he may have claimed divine status during his life, will have been recognized as an epiphany of Apollo only after his death. For it was only then that you could be revealed to have been one of the Olympian dieties.

As for Iamblichus' rationalization, it can hardly be a direct quotation from Aristotle in the form in which it is given. Aristotle is unlikely to have talked of the "secret doctrines" that are dear to the heart of Iamblichus. Nor does the division of the species "rational creature" into gods, men, and an intermediate class sound either Aristotelian or primitive. In the foregoing passage Iamblichus has in mind *daimon* status. Pythagoras is "a good *daimon*, kindly disposed to mankind," or "one of the *daimones* that inhabit the moon." That Pythagoras was said by his early followers to have been a sort of *Agathos Daimon* or an astral divinity is improbable. That they should have claimed that he was a *daimon* is likely enough; but the subdivisions of the species "rational creature" cannot be early. In the Symposium (202E). Agathon remarks, "All the *daimonic* is between a god and a mortal"; that is, the class of *daimones* lies between that of gods and that of men. This apparently current and generally acceptable definition is then interpreted by Plato to provide a peg on which to hang his notion of Eros, and to leave room for the *daimonios anêr*.

The Greek notion of *theos* and *daimon* is puzzling to us. We are accustomed to think in monotheistic terms and to conceive the gulf between divinity and humanity as an impassable one. The Greeks however could conceive of degrees of divinity, from our humanity, in which they recognized the capacity of achieving divine status, through the class of heroes to actual godhead, as in the case of Heracles. In the early period, as Nilsson has pointed out (216–222), the real difference in meaning between *Theos* and *daimon* was that *daimon* was a wider term including all divine beings and including them anonymously, without reference to cult, but as a manifestation of the invisible and mysterious powers and forces that were present and at work in their world. In this sense the followers of Pythagoras will have recognized him as both *theos* and *daimon*.[13]

It seems probable that Pythagoras himself laid claim to divine status. And the claim is not so monstrous as it might appear to us. A similar claim is made by Empedocles in the proem of the *Katharmoi* (31B 112):

O my friends, you who inhabit the great city on the heights, by Acragas' yellow stream, you who attend upon excellent crafts and offer a revered harbour to the stranger, you who have no part nor parcel in evil, I greet you and send you good news. As an immortal god and no longer as mortal I walk among men and am honoured by them.

Empedocles' claim is not in itself remarkable. Both before and after him men claimed to have achieved godhead, or declared it their aim *homoiousthai theô*. It is surprising that he should announce it to his fellow citizens as good news and a cause for their rejoicing. If it had been unthinkable that a man should become a god, or if Empedocles' fellow-citizens of Acragas would have indignantly dismissed such a claim, Empedocles would not have addressed them in the way he does. He assumes them to be aware that there is a way in which men can become gods and that he is engaged in that way.

For Empedocles the soul is a *daimon* exiled from the gods and condemned to thirty thousand seasons of wandering before it can return (B 115; Iambl. *De An.* 275w; Festugière, *La révélation* 3.209 n. 4). During its wanderings it is buffeted from one element to another (B 115) and it migrates through differing forms of life (B 117). But it need not migrate aimlessly nor without hope. If a man keeps himself free from pollution, has care of his soul, in time he can become seer, poet, healer, prince, and finally "spring up" as does a plant after long winter, like "a god most rich in honours" (B 146) to 'share the hearth and the table of the immortals (B 147; cf. Rohde 381).

Not only for divine status but also for miraculous powers we find parallels in Empedocles. He claims the ability to make winds cease (we are told how he did it, by catching them in leathern bags) to bring the dead back to life, and to cure all manner of sicknesses. That in an age which readily lent credence to miracles, he performed acts that were commonly considered miraculous there can be no doubt, for thousands followed him in his peregrinations (B 112), and believed that in the end he did not die but was translated.

If such an aura of the miraculous could surround Empedocles in the middle of the fifth century, a like aura could surround Pythagoras in the sixth. To him were attributed an even greater variety of miraculous powers. Some miracles merely attest his divinity. He is addressed by a river—or two rivers—with "Hail Pythagoras!" He exhibits a golden thigh. Abaris, sent on a mission by Apollo from the Hyperboreans, recognizes in him the living Apollo and gives him obedience.[14] He has the gift of bilocation and of prophetic foresight. He has power over animals. He strokes the head of an eagle, need not fear poisonous snakes, tames a bear, and, according to Iamblichus (*VP* 61) whispers in the ear of a bull to keep him out of a field of beans. These latter tales may imply transmigration. Pythagoras may be able to speak to the souls inhabiting animals. He calls down the eagle and speaks to the bear. But power over animals is a trait of godhead.

What are we to make of the miracles that characterize our tradition? Throughout antiquity, and in all the Christian centuries up to modern times, it was never questioned that the miraculous occurred, nor that the "laws of nature" could be and sometimes were suspended by divine intervention. If Pythagoras was a person in whom miraculous powers were credible it was only natural that such powers should be ascribed to him, as they are indeed ascribed in our tradition. It would be more surprising if his legend did not comprise miraculous events. Such events we are disposed to accept in a religious context; but a thinker must by definition be rational. So for thinkers tainted with miracle or miracle-workers of some intellectual pretensions we have invented of recent years the class of "Greek shamans."

This term, applying as it does to a heterogeneous group, serves to conceal the problem it is designed to solve. If a thinker has curious notions in other areas, as had Leibniz, or if a legend collects around his name, as in the case of some Fathers of the Church, he need not be banished from the precincts of philosophy. We can either define it more generously or else concede that shamanism is a legitimate area of its activity. But before we adopt the latter course we should perhaps ask ourselves what we mean by "shamanism" when we use the term in the context of Greek thought.

Shamanism is an important institution in northern cultures. Its features are known to us because it is still extant in Siberia, and to some extent also in the Canadian north. It is a phenomenon unknown to Indogermanic cultures.[15] In 1935 Karl Meuli advanced an interesting and carefully documented theory suggesting that northern shamanism had influenced the Scythians and the Getae, who in turn had influenced the Greeks with whom they came in contact during the Greek colonization of the Pontus; and that the institution of shamanism was in that period adopted by the Greeks in a modified form, or at least that instances of shamanism were exhibited in such persons as Aristeas, Abaris, and Hermotimus. This theory is accepted by Dodds (140–150) with some modification. "From all this," he writes (142), "it seems reasonable to conclude that the opening of the Black Sea to Greek trade and colonization in the seventh century, which introduced the Greeks for the first time to a culture based on shamanism, at any rate enriched with some remarkable new traits the traditional Greek picture of the Man of God, the *theios anêr*." The final qualifying clause is to be understood in the light of Dodds' definition of the shaman (140) as "a psychically unstable person who has received a call to the religious life." Nilsson (616–619) concedes the "Verwandtschaft der besprochenen Erscheinungen—des Hinaustretens der Seele aus dem Körper—mit dem Schamanentum." He does not say how he regards the phenomena to be related. Burkert (123–142) regards the theory as offering analogies. "Vielmehr kann der ethnologische Vergleich gerade auf griechische Gegebenheiten aufmerksam machen, die im Fortschritt der Geistesentwicklung verdunkelt wurden" (124). So Meuli's theory has come to be understood, not as explaining the origins of a Greek phenomenon, but as suggesting similarities between the known phenomenon of northern shamanism and a group of persons appearing in the archaic age of Greece, who are referred to collectively as "Greek shamans." Let us consider the theory in this minimum form (for the thesis of any direct derivation can hardly be maintained) that the "Greek shamans" share important and characteristic features with northern shamanism, and can best be understood as a parallel cultural phenomenon.

We may concede parallels, but we must observe the much more important differences. Shamanism is a central feature of the cultures in which it flourishes. In Greece we have no evidence for any such institution. There is no word for "shaman"[16] and no record of the practices characteristic of shamanism. Precedents for practices sometimes said to be shamanistic and usually connected with divination, healing, and purification or with knowledge of present, past, and future can be found in the epos or in Hesiod, before the seventh century when shamanism is said to be introduced. Nothing suggests the existence of such an institution among neighbouring peoples such as the Latins, the Etruscans, the peoples of Asia Minor. If, as Nilsson (618) suggests, it was a product of the Cimmerian incursions, it should have left traces in Asia Minor, and in Greece itself we should hear of the existence of such abnormal persons having a religious vocation, with an important, quasi-priestly function. But in fact only the persons who are supposed to be explained by "Greek shamanism" serve as evidence suggesting that such an institution existed.

Let us assume however that you could have shamans without shamanism. Do the "Greek shamans" perform shaman functions? Central to the institution in arctic cultures is the soul-journey. In a state of "mental dissociation" (Dodds 140) or trance, often artificially induced, the shaman undertakes a soul-journey. He does on behalf of his community, which believes in the institution and enjoins his journey on him. His function is performed when he returns from the journey, conveys the message he is expected to convey and emerges from trance. We are justified in looking for more or less exact correspondences to this central function in the Greek "shamans" if the term is to have any precise content. In fact, such of them as do undertake soul-journeys, do so on their own account and for unspecified purposes. Hermotimus (Apollon. *Mirab.* 3) is "absent" for long periods of time, and finally his body is burned during one of these. Bolton (132–134) has made it probable that Aristeas journeys in person, not in soul. Abaris is said to journey in person (carrying or riding on the arrow of Apollo), or as a raven. He is sent on his mission not by any community but by Apollo, and for the god's own purposes—collecting gifts for his Hyperborean temple (Iambl. *VP* 91). The *ecstasis* of Epimenides is a late development of his legend (*Vors.* 1.29 = Suidas *s.v.*). Neither Pythagoras nor Empedocles go on soul journeys (bilocation is not a soul journey). So, that which should be their most important common characteristic—the trance soul-journey undertaken on behalf of the community or its members—does not occur among the Greek "shamans."

The group so designated is a very mixed bag, having in common chiefly the fact that they appear anomalous to us. Cornford (*Princ. Sap.* 94–106) makes much of the fact that they used the medium of verse. So did the writers of the pseudo-Hesiodea, of the Orphica, almost everyone who had anything to say in the archaic age. So did Parmenides, but he (though he records a soul journey) is for some reason not supposed to have been a "shaman." Some of them are purifiers and magical healers, but neither Aristeas nor Hermotimus appear to have these functions, of which there are plentiful instances in the epos, before the coming of shamanism. Some of them—as Epimenides and Aristeas —are historical persons; others—as Abaris and Hermotimus—appear to be insubstantial apart from their legend. All of them have an aura of the magical and the miraculous, but so do many of the Heroes. Miracles and magic are part of the morphology of such legends and attach as much to the legend as to the person. If we treat as "Greek shamans" those commonly comprised in that class, there seems no reason why we should not include others of the archaic age (if we knew more of the Milesians and Heraclitus we might well find cause or pretext for including them) nor why we should limit our class to persons of that period.

That the aura of miracle and supernatural occurrence could attach to events other than those occurring in a context of religion or philosophy is shown by the legend of the Battle of the Sagra. Before that battle, the Locrians sent to Sparta for help. The Spartans' hands were full, but they solemnly sent the Dioscuri, in a ship, with envoys and crew. The Dioscuri disembarked at Locri, fought on the side of the Locrians—on white horses, in scarlet cloaks—and were instrumental in defeating the greatly superior forces of Croton. That they were in fact present at the battle was proven when one of the Crotoniate wounded was sent by an oracle to the temple of the Dioscuri in Sparta, was healed there and then miraculously returned to his home. (Dunbabin, *The Western Greeks* 358; Strabo 261; cf. *FGrH* 115 F 392).

A position as extreme as that of the proponents of Greek "shamans" is taken up by Burnet (*Greek Philosophy* 4). "There can be no philosophy where there is no rational science. . . . Now rational science is the creation of the Greeks, and we know when it began. We do not count as philosophy anything anterior to that." On this principle, as on the shaman theory, most of the thinkers of the sixth and of the fifth century are not philosophers, although we observe in them the peculiarly Greek phenomenon of rational thought in its first beginnings. But if our requirements are less stringent and we look for an effort towards clarity in presenting general problems, and an effort towards coherence in devising answers, then boundaries cannot be so clearly defined and the beginnings of philosophy need not *stricto sensu* be "philosophical." We can acknowledge that their inspired guesses, what Plato (*Ep.* 7.341D) called "sudden light," lead directly towards philosophy; for the disciplines of science exist not to produce theories but to test them.

The position we take, or the assumptions we make, as to the beginnings of philosophy are of particular importance for Pythagoras. He was an Ionian, a generation younger than Anaximander, a native of Samos in the time of Polycrates when Anacreon and Ibycus were his guests, when Eupalinus surveyed the tunnel and Rhoecus built the great temple. He was, by the testimony of Heraclitus, a man of intellectual curiosity. According to Herodotus he left behind him a reputation as *sophistes*. It is hard to imagine him, at that time and in that milieu, as a "shaman." We need not therefore deny that he had curious and unusual ideas in matters of religion. So had Aeschylus. So in his way had Pindar. It would be easy to paint a very "irrational" picture of their world. It may be true that Pythagoras deviates more radically from the norm, but it seems desirable, before fitting him into any preconceived categories, to attempt to understand the character of his thought and the impact he made on his times, on the basis of the evidence we possess.

NOTES

[1] By τίνες he need not refer to more than one person, as he does *Pol.* 1290b 5. He refers to "certain Pythagoreans" *De Caelo* 300a 17 and *De Sensu* 445a 16.

[2] The existence of a Pythagorean doctrine of "the soul as harmony" is often asserted (most recently by Guthrie, 308–317; for a summary of discussions R. S. Bluck, *Plato's Phaedo* [London 1955] 197–198). The doctrine, or some modification of it, is said to be expounded in the *Phaedo*, and the Simmias and Cebes of that dialogue are said to be Pythagoreans, a notion that has been refuted by G. M. A. Grube (Appx. 1). (Xenophon, to whom they are known (*Mem.* 1.2.48), treats them as disciples of Socrates.) It is further asserted by Guthrie (307) that "the word *harmonia* is sufficient guarantee of its (Pythagorean) authorship," a contention against which I have argued above (128) and which is not borne out by Kranz's *Wortindex* (*Vors.* vol. 3). On this basis—that *harmonia* is a Pythagorean key-word and that Socrates' interlocutors in the dialogue are Pythagoreans—we are told that "the soul as harmonia" is a Pythagorean doctrine. Let us consider the arguments of the *Phaedo*, the principal basis of the assertion.

There the theme of *harmonia* is introduced (85E) to suggest that the soul is *not* immortal, just as is the parallel theme of the old weaver and his cloak. Cebes regards both as "comparisons" (εἰκόνες—87B). Nothing in the context suggests that these "comparisons" were not inventions of Plato.

Let us, however, make the improbable assumption that the Pythagoreans had some such doctrine as is here described, and that Simmias realizes (with shock) that it entails the mortality of the soul. He then must be said to use what, for a Pythagorean, is the doctrine's fatal flaw, against what we believe to be a fundamental Pythagorean tenet, immortality of the soul. Take as an analogy, he says, the lyre. The lyre with its strings is a perishable instrument for the non-sensible, non-material, divine *harmonia* or attunement that is produced when it is properly tuned. If the chords are snapped and the instrument broken does that attunement continue to exist? Is it immortal, while the instrument is mortal?

The analogy, Simmias continues, is a good one. We think of our souls as a blending (κρᾶσις) and ἁρμονία of the qualitative opposites that are held together in a state of tension by the soul. If Simmias is here expounding Pythagorean doctrine then, according to that doctrine, the soul would be a sort of tension that maintains as a more or less permanent state the proportionate mixture of bodily opposites. It is this sense of the ambiguous word *harmonia* that we find in Heraclitus and Empedocles—a fitting-together that has no necessary connection with music. The attunement to which Phaedo refers is only that present in the strings when the lyre is tuned, and not any mathematical ratio, much less any music produced by the attuned lyre.

As variations on the theory that health was a balance between the physical opposites had been current since Alcmaeon's *isonomia* we cannot take any such doctrine of the soul, even as extended by the attunement notion, to be peculiarly Pythagorean. Plato (88D) suggests that it was a current doctrine, and Socrates (92B–C) points out obvious difficulties in the musical extension. Burnet (295–296) ingeniously attempts to suggest that Plato has reference to a Pythagorean adaptation made probably by Philolaus at the end of the fifth century, but Cherniss (323, n. 124) has shown his suggestion to be untenable. (This is also excluded by the Menon fragment (44 A–27).

The notion of the soul as *harmonia* is, in some form, older than the *Phaedo*, and it continues to be current after the *Phaedo*. Aristotle again argues against it in the *Eudemus* (*Fr. Sel.* 16–23) and Gigon (Düring and Owen, *Aristotle and Plato in the Mid-Fifth Century* [Goteborg 1960] 26–29) suggests that "some special reason must have caused Aristotle to raise afresh the much-discussed problem of ἁρμονία" and that it is probably discussed in another dialectical context. For Aristotle as for Plato such a notion excludes the immortality of the soul. The two principal arguments Aristotle uses against it (*Fr. Sel.* 20) are: (1) that there is an opposite to *harmonia*, namely its lack, but no opposite to soul, and (2) that to the proper attunement of the body the opposite is lack of attunement, and lack of attunement of the body is sickness, enfeeblement, or ugliness. To these defects answer health, strength, beauty as the *harmonia* of the body and not of the soul. Here Aristotle clearly refers to the primary thesis of the *Phaedo*, that the soul is a *harmonia* of physical qualities, rather than to the lyre analogy. The thesis is referred to as that of the *Phaedo*, and not as Pythagorean.

Aristotle returns to the subject in the *De Anima*. There is another theory current concerning the soul, he says, that recommends itself to many persons as much as any of those mentioned and that has been subjected to previous critical examination (*De An.* 407b 27–30; for text W. Theiler, *Aristoteles über die Seele ad loc.*). Aristotle proceeds to offer five summary arguments against any such theory. As to the general character of the discussion we may note: (1) that the theory is not attributed to the Pythagoreans; (2) that Aristotle elsewhere attributes to the Pythagoreans other notions of the soul and its immortality having no relation to *harmonia* (134); (3) that the soul as *harmonia*, here as in the *Phaedo*, excludes immortality; (4) that the *harmonia* to which Aristotle refers is the *harmonia* of opposites. He does not have reference to musical *harmonia*, even in the sense of the proper attunement of a musical instrument.

There are three principal versions in which we hear of the soul as *harmonia* or attunement—the versions of Plato, of Aristotle, and of Plotinus. The first is that expounded by Simmias in the *Phaedo* (85E–86D), in which the lyre with its strings and its attunement are a parallel for body and soul.

Aristotle in his turn presents it as a popular belief, saying (*De An.* 407b 27–408a 1) that "it recommends itself to many persons as much as any of those mentioned." The theory to which he alludes is precisely that of the *Phaedo*. Some of the arguments he uses against it are those of the *Phaedo*; some are those that he himself evolved in his own dialogue on the soul, the *Eudemus* (*Fr. Sel.* 19–22). (Philoponus *In Arist. De An.* 141 Hayduck = Ross, *Fr. Sel.* 19–20 systematizes the arguments of Plato and Aristotle.)

Finally Plotinus (*Enn.* 4.7.8) discusses the theory again, explicitly attributing it to the Pythagoreans. "Is it distinct from body but as it were an attunement of body? A view of this kind was held by the Pythagoreans. They thought the soul to be analogous to the attunement of the strings (of a lyre). For as on the tension of the strings there supervenes a condition that is called attunement, similarly our body comes to be by a mixture of unlike elements and the specific mixture produces life and soul, which latter is the condition supervening on the mixture." Against this theory he uses some of the arguments of Aristotle, and some arguments that Aristotle could not use, as that the soul is a substance, and that we would have to imagine another soul prior to this soul and analogous to the musician who tunes the instrument. Plotinus attributes this doctrine to the Pythagoreans but cites no authority.

Much of the confusion apparent in discussions of "the soul as harmony" arises from the ambiguity of the term. Aristotle notes (*De An.* 408a 5–9) two meanings, the first being the synthesis of the parts of a physical magnitude, the second, and derivative, being the ratios of those parts. As he uses both σύνδεσις and μεμιγμένων it would appear that in this passage he is not making the distinction between σύνθεσις and μίξις made in the *De Gen.* 328a 6–15, but is merely thinking of a physical entity having components such that they are in permanent ratios, and do not permit of the intrusion of other similar entities into their structure.

These two senses of *harmonia* are not the primary sense (see *supra* 128) nor are they the musical *harmonia* that may be the attunement of an instrument, or the attunement to one another of the notes produced by an attuned instrument, or the numerical ratios determining that attunement (but never in our sense "harmony"). For the Greek the musical connotations of the word do not immediately leap to mind.

[3]J. S. Pearce, *Collected Papers* 1.88–90, using the example of the Pythagorean tradition and the golden thigh, argues that the historian must not disregard or arbitrarily reinterpret the facts of which he cannot make sense. "We have no right at all to say that supernal powers had not put a physical mask upon him as extraordinary as was his personality." For the life of St. Francis the *Fioretti* are of more significance than are local archives.

[4]I use the vague and general term "transmigration" to cover the varieties of the doctrine as professed by the Orphics, Pythagoras, Pindar, Empedocles. The term "metempsychosis" has only pretensions to correctness, and "metensomatosis" is a Plotinian word that has even less status in English than "metempsychosis." It has been argued by W. Rathmann whose stringent criticism of the Pythagoras tradition, both ancient and modern, has been most salutary, that in this passage the Pythagoreans are not said to hold a doctrine of transmigration; but Kranz has pointed out (*Vors.* 1.504.7–9 *see also* 3.659), with reference also to his own book, *Empedokles* (78), that ἐνδύεσθαι "to put on as a garment" clearly implies transmigration. Rathmann has pointed out (10) that apart from the passages in the *De Anima* (with which we should perhaps associate *An. post.* 94b 33 where souls in Tartarus are said to be terrified by

thunderbolts, and Aelian *VH* 4.17 = *Vors*. 1.463–464 where earthquakes are said to be an assembling of the dead) there is no reference to transmigration before the first century B.C. Rathmann further argues (59–93), convincingly, that Pythagoras accepted and spread Orphic doctrines of immortality and transmigration, rather than himself initiating them. His contention is attacked (but to my mind not refuted) by A. Krüger, 37–41. H. S. Long, in a good discussion of the whole problem written under the shadow of I. M. Linforth argues that Pythagoras "introduced metempsychosis to the Greek world" (28) and that there is no early evidence for an Orphic doctrine (92). It is difficult to see how priority could ever be determined without further evidence. It seems more in accord with the evidence, and more reasonable, to assert, as does Nilsson (694–695), that the ground was prepared for such doctrines by popular belief, but that the Orphics taught transmigration "beträchtlich früher" (701).

⁵The statement of Clement of Alexandria (*Strom.* 6.6.53 = *Fr. Sel.* 133) that according to Aristotle all men have an accompanying *daimon* during the time of their *ensomatosis*, to whatever it may refer, cannot allude to a Pythagorean transmigration doctrine.

⁶Reinhardt, *Parmenides* 192–197, has sought to demonstrate an Orphic strain in Heraclitus. Guthrie (476–482) seems to incline to a similar position. Diels, on the other hand, points out (*Arch. Ges. Phil.* 2.92) that Heraclitus influenced the Orphic poems. The centres of diffusion of Orphism seem to have been Magna Graecia and Attica, and the date of incipient organized activity cannot be much earlier than the beginning of the sixth century. Orphism in Ionia before 532 B.C. seems improbable.

Shamanism has also been suggested as a possible source for Ionic religious beliefs and practices concerning the soul. The hypothesis of "Greek Shamans" has recently, and convincingly, been questioned by J. D. P. Bolton (124–141). Pythagoras as a shaman is discussed further, *supra* 159.

⁷O. Kern, has a collection of the testimonia and fragments. Diels (*Vors.* 1.1–27) has a collection of "altbezeugte" fragments, to which, however, exception has been taken. *KR* 37–48 discusses summarily and not conclusively. Reference was made above to Nilsson's discussion. G. Hermann, *Orphica* (Leipzig 1805) in his preface makes the sagacious remark: "Si mea sponte eligendus mihi fuisset scriptor in quo edendo operam meam collocarem, in quemcumque alium facilius quam in Orpheum incidissem."

It is perhaps impossible to distinguish Orphic teachings and Pythagorean teaching in the Platonic dialogues, but the following general lines of distinction may be made.

When Plato (*Gorg.* 524B, *Phaedo* 64c) defines death as the departure of the soul from the body he is offering a definition such as would be acceptable to all Greeks, with the possible exception of a few radical thinkers. From Homer onwards death occurs when the soul (*psyche*) leaves the body. The soul is not considered in this event to have achieved immortality or anything more than a bat-like survival for a time undefined and under terms such that its survival cannot be called life. In this definition the relation existing between soul and body is not further specified. But when Plato uses the metaphor of prison (*Gorg.* 525A, *Phaedo* 62B) we assume that the prisoner-soul can escape from the prison-body, and therefore that soul can exist apart from body. This is the point at which Orphic and Pythagorean notions diverge.

The Orphics, Plato suggests in one of his curious etymologizings (*Crat.* 400c), call the body σῶμα because it keeps (σώζειν) the soul as a prison keeps its inmate until that inmate has served his sentence or paid his penalty. Here clearly the soul has had a previous, and can look towards a subsequent, existence. It exists independently of the body, existed prior to that body, and will survive it. It is subject to penalties and, at least in its release from the body, to rewards.

In this same passage (*Crat.* 400B) Plato tells us that "some say that the body is the tomb of the soul, the soul being entombed in its present (earthly) existence" and already in the *Gorgias* (493A) this equation of σῶμα/σῆμα, body/tomb was cited as an inference from the verses of Euripides saying that perhaps our life is a sort of death, and to die and be dead is to live. Diels (*Vors.* 1 B 3 n.) has pointed out that the σῶμα/σῆμα doctrine is explicitly declared not to be Orphic; and Dodds (*Gorgias* pp. 297–298) has plausibly suggested that the Sicilian or Italian who uses the equation is a Pythagorean.

The Orphics, therefore, hold the body to be a prison of the soul, while the Pythagoreans, in all probability, thought of it as a tomb. They have in common the notions that the soul is prior to the body, and, rather than the body, is the true person; and that our life is an interlude during which we are either imprisoned and so kept from the freedom of "true" life, or are paying penalties for actions done in an earlier existence. The Pythagorean notion has perhaps greater implications of ascetic rigour, the life of death in the body being valued only as a preparation for true life. But the two conceptions of life and of death are very similar. Their real differences become apparent only when we consider rewards and penalties, and the judgment of souls.

Both Orphics and Pythagoreans sought ritual purity and practised purifications. Of the Pythagorean practices and vetoes we have some record in the *symbola*, and we may assume that the Orphics followed similar practices to avoid pollution as they did in abstaining from flesh. Indeed Plato would extend this abstention to all men of the earlier generations. "In those times our ancestors lived the life called Orphic, enjoying inanimate but refraining from animate food" (*Laws* 782c).

The evidence of Plato is alas ambiguous, especially if, with the Neoplatonists and most modern scholars, we are to interpret the eschatological myths and the myth of the *Phaedrus* as of Orphic inspiration. Let us here concede the common ground and consider points in which Plato discriminates, rejecting Orphic tents:

1. In the *Republic* (363A ff.) Plato deals scathingly with the Orphic picture of the future life. Musaeus and Orpheus, he says, offer a queer sort of reward to the just (not, we note, to the initiate), saying that they have the joys of the symposium in eternity, whereas the unjust must wallow forever in mud. But he goes on to explain how the rewards of the just are made available to the rich by ceremonies of purification administered, if not by Orphics, at least according

to Orphic prescription. It may be, as Dodds suggests (222), that Plato is attacking all unlicensed catharsis, but if the practitioners are not Orphic, the *teletei* are said to be Orphic. For Plato the ascesis continues through future existences and is not formal but spiritual. We may assume that Pythagorean ascesis showed the same tendency.

2. In examining the eschatological myth of the *Gorgias* Dodds in his edition of that work (372–376), concludes that its elements are *not* Orphic, and may be Pythagorean. In particular he suggests that the notion of a sort of purgatory is probably Pythagorean because the penalty is a return to earth. He further suggests that the notion of Hades, certainly used by the Orphics, was excluded for the Pythagoreans by their astronomy—a thesis that finds some confirmation in Aristotle (*De An.* 410b 29; *Meteorol.* 345a 14) but may not be early teaching.

In conclusion, the evidence we have is late, conflicting, vague. If one must hazard a guess I would suggest that both Orphics and Pythagoreans distinguished, in the human person, a better and enduring part, the soul, and an inferior vehicle, the body. For both the soul was susceptible of purification from pollutions incident on its incarnation, and was capable of further incarnations. Purification for Orphics and Pythagoreans was a form of ascesis from the beginning in which chiefly the avoidance of animate foods was practised. At the end of its life on earth the soul was subject to judgment, and underwent rewards and punishments.

Peculiar to the Orphics and not shared by the Pythagoreans, except perhaps partially and passively, was a literature consisting largely in a theogony and cosmogony in part diverging from, and apparently independent of, current myth, a literature that by Plato's time was committed to a "multitude of books" none of which are ever said to be Pythagorean.

The Pythagoreans early emphasized, more than did the Orphics, an ascetic rule, and their ascesis took on aspects of intellectual discipline, although they also emphasized ethical behaviour; for them, judgment was passed on the soul on the basis of moral conduct. So the two ways of life, in origin similar though probably never the same, become the one a means of ritual purity, the other an ascesis of intellectual character.

[8]The passages in Pindar (*Ol.* 2.56–78; fr. 127 Bowra) have been emphasized in all treatments, since that of Rohde, of the problem of transmigration. Long (29–44) reviews the discussion and discusses the passages. His conclusion (44) that "Pythagorean metempsychosis seems to have been revised in the interests of morality by some group in Sicily" is part of his general tendency to eliminate the Orphics as a source and substitute Pythagoras. It seems much more reasonable to suggest, as does Nilsson (695), that the origin of the doctrine was earlier and a natural product of the evolution of the notion of personality.

Long reasonably suggests (84–85) that as time goes on the doctrine of transmigration is always given more ethical emphasis. However, his contention (22–25) that transmigration as depicted by Herodotus (2.123)—simple passage from one body to another in an ordered series during a cycle of birth—may be attributed to Pythagoras, is in contradiction to his previous suggestion and is unconvincing. The simple migration described by Herodotus has no ethical implication, and is a form of the doctrine not otherwise encountered in Greece. Herodotus misinterpreted his Egyptian evidence, and must also have misinterpreted what he was told in Greece.

⁹Heraclides Ponticus (Wehrli, Fr. 89 and comment p. 90; see Rohde 599–601; Delatte, *Vie* 154–159) is often cited as evidence that Pythagoras himself recollected his previous incarnations, and Myllias (*Fr. Sel.* 131) may be seen as in some measure confirming this. Heraclides also suggests that these incarnations occurred cyclically, but it remains for the *Theologoumena Arithmetica* (52) to specify the length of the cycle—216 years, or 6^3. We cannot be certain that all this was more than a *jeu d'esprit* on the part of Heraclides. Certainly Dicaearchus (Wehrli fr. 36) used the theme to make sport of Pythagoras.

Heraclides may have had as his point of departure a misunderstanding of Empedocles 31 B 129, where Empedocles does not imply recollection of ten or twenty previous incarnations but only recollection covering such a time. Despite the fact that Timaeus believes Empedocles to refer to Pythagoras here, and that this is generally agreed upon (see Guthrie 161, n.1), the reference seems to allow room for doubt. It is uncertain what persons or race are meant by κείνοισιν (line 1) and it is tempting to suggest that the same persons are meant as in 31 B 128. 1. B 129 would then be part of a description of a golden age, and might refer to some early seer or sage (Orpheus?). The description better fits a poet than someone like Pythagoras, for it ascribes the gift of insight into the hidden past. Calchas (*Il.* 1.69–70) is said to have known past, present, and future. Hesiod (*Theog.* 32) lays claim to similar knowledge in almost the same words, and this is the knowledge that the Muses themselves possess (*Theog.* 34–39) when they rejoice the heart of their father Zeus on Olympus, singing of past, present, and future. Of these three divisions of time the past is the most important for the poet-seer. It is the past to which Empedocles refers.

However, both Pindar and Empedocles (B 115) speak of a cycle of births to be completed by the soul. The allied notion of a great year was already current (Guthrie 282), and Plato later elaborates on the theme. So we will readily believe that for Pythagoras and the early Pythagoreans the soul cycle ended in some determinate time. In the case of Pythagoras (and of Empedocles) it ended with divine status achieved while yet on earth.

For other important references to Pythagoras' previous incarnations see Wehrli, *Dikaiarchos* fr. 36; *Clearchus* fr. 10 and Pfeiffer, *Callimachus* fr. 191, 56–62 and note.

¹⁰The characteristics of *On the Pythagoreans* are discussed in my article *Phoenix* 17 (1963) 251–265. The fact that Alexander of Aphrodisias (75.17 = *Fr. Sel.* 137) and Simplicius (392.18 = *Fr. Sel.* 142) quote from the second part, which is probably a critique of Pythagorean doctrines, suggests that this part may have been theoretical and the first part largely legend and *symbola*. Most of our references in the fragments are references to legend and *symbola* because these do not find a place in the treatises, whereas much of the critical treatment will have found a place also there.

[11]Here the ἐδίδασκε, suggesting that the claim was habitually made by Pythagoras as part of his doctrine, is likely to be the phraseology of Aelian. The statement that he was of higher than mortal origin is immediately followed by proofs, which indicates that the claim will have been made by followers, who would cite proofs. For miracles, A. D. Nock, 254.

[12]For the Hyperboreans: D. L. Page, *Sappho and Alcaeus* (Oxford 1955) 244–252, esp. 252 on the Delphic tradition; Nilsson 548–550, who however is more concerned with Delos; J. D. P. Bolton 195–197 and *passim*. Like Page, Bolton regards the Hyperboreans as a folk-memory; see Dodds 161–162, where references are cited. For the three classes cf. Scholia *Iliad* E.1.340 where it is said that "in addition to gods and men the Pythagoreans assumed a third category, that of the king or wise man." Pythagoras himself is said to have been the object of a hero cult after his death (Arist. *Rhet.* 1398b 16).

[13]The notion of *daimon* is discussed by Nilsson (216–222) with references to the literature. There is an ample bibliography in M. Detienne, *La notion de daïmôn dans le pythagorisme ancien* (Paris 1963). Detienne, on inadequate grounds, dismisses R. Heinze, and his discussion of demonology. In establishing his own thesis Detienne uses the evidence uncritically. He makes no attempt to ascertain the semantic spectrum or the historical development of the word. He argues that the word *daimon* passes from religious to philosophical connotations apparently with Pythagoras himself. But the "philosophy" he ascribes to Pythagoras is shamanism. Dodds (39–45) does not pretend to be discussing more than aspects of the notion.

[14]Abaris: see Wehrli, *Herakleides Pontikos* frs. 73–75. In his comment Wehrli remarks that "besondere Phantastik" must have characterized the *Abaris* and cites (86) the principal discussions. Rohde (327–328) holds that "the bringing together of Abaris and Pythagoras is a late invention. It is impossible to say whether it could have occurred or did occur as early as the Aristotelian work" (*On the Pythagoreans*). On the basis of frs. 74–75 an elaborate theory has been constructed of a Katabasis of Pythagoras. Wehrli's plausible textural conjecture in fr. 75 would, as he remarks (86), remove the principal support for the theory. Dodds (141) regards Abaris as a shaman. He does not attempt to determine what our picture of Abaris owes to Heraclides, nor whether the mention of Abaris in the fragments (*Fr. Sel.* 131–132) derives from Heraclides. It is difficult to see how this could be determined, but where Heraclides has been at work we should be cautious. He was a native of the Pontus. If there was an institution similar to shamanism among the Scythians he is likely to have heard of it. He shows himself interested in Abaris, Aristeas, Hermotimus, and in miraculous tales. He is notoriously inventive.

[15]Cornford, *Principium Sapientiae* 88–98 attempts to suggest that shamanism existed among Indogermanic and other peoples, but instances only distant parallels.

[16]W. Burkert, "ΓΟΗΣ Zum griechischen Schamanismus" (*Rh. Mus.* 105 [1962] 36–55) in an interesting article discusses the word γοής as a term signifying the Greek shaman, and connects it etymologically with γόος as lamentation for

the dead. He concedes (45) that "there is no direct proof for developed shamanistic practice in our tradition" and his search for a term is an indication of how tenuous the shaman structure is. γοής seems much more likely to correspond to the "Trickster."

What H. Dörrie, *Hermes* 83 (1955) remarks of Neoplatonism is also true of the early period. "For the Pythagorean the life of the philosopher does not consist merely in the accumulation of knowledge, but must be accompanied by a clearly defined way of life."

II

CONCLUSION

IN the preceding chapters we have discussed Aristotle's account of
the Pythagorean tradition. Let us now consider how he presents
the evidence he collected, and what judgments are implicit in the
manner of its presentation. In his account he deals with three principal
themes—the Pythagoras legend, Pythagorean practice, and Pythagorean doctrine. Each is treated in a different way, and the manner
of treatment implies a differing critical evaluation.

Concerning Pythagoras himself Aristotle found current and recorded
in his monograph but excluded from the treatises a heroic legend which,
if it ever recorded political activity, anecdotes of the life, or sayings
such as were attributed to the Seven Sages, had by the fourth century
so transmuted them that the human person and thinker was no longer
recognizable in the legendary account. Aristotle records the data of the
legend, making no attempt to justify or to explain. The only judgment
he passes is a tacit one; he excludes the legend from consideration in
the treatises. Whatever it may mean, for him it cannot be relevant to
the history of thought.

Concerning the Pythagoreans the most characteristic document he
was able to discover was a collection of *Symbola* regulating Pythagorean
conduct. These *Symbola* he may himself have classified, but more probably he simply incorporated in his monograph an existing classification,
together with certain "correspondences" such as "the Pleiades are the
lyre of the Muses." These also he relegated to the monograph as allied
to the legend rather than to the thought.

What he found reported as Pythagorean theory posed a curious and
difficult problem for him. He could not simply brush it aside. It was
held to be of great importance by all the persons having most authority
within the Academy. They considered (and Aristotle agrees) that
Pythagorean number theory was not merely a formative influence but
the real foundation of their own theories of the constitution of the
cosmos and of the derivation of physical body. These theories, both in

their simpler Pythagorean form and in their later Academic elaborations, Aristotle considered an aberration, and an aberration that it was one of the chief aims of the treatises to combat. Aristotle will have been at great pains to ascertain precisely what those theories were, both for the purpose of understanding them himself and in order to argue against them effectively with colleagues to whom they were familiar. He gives us a clear, coherent, and in general consistent account, sometimes indicating that "certain" Pythagoreans differed from the views propounded in the central doctrines.

In his account Aristotle does not mention any earlier Pythagorean by name, unless Hippasus was for him a Pythagorean. And of Hippasus he tells us only that his first principle was fire. Nothing more. Of later fifth-century Pythagoreans he alludes to Philolaus and mentions Eurytus. Otherwise he always speaks of "the Pythagoreans." This practice has contributed in no small measure to the myth of a "society" or "brotherhood" but we have seen reason to believe that it is simply a locution of Aristotle's to express his *non liquet*. He could feel no certainty that the divine person of the legend, the worker of miracles, the man of the golden thigh, was also the thinker. He knew of no other Pythagorean to whom the thought could be ascribed. A collective name served his polemical purpose just as well, and the manner of transmission of the doctrines made a collective name more plausible. We have seen reason to believe that the doctrines he ascribes to "the Pythagoreans" may in substance be imputed to Pythagoras himself.

We may judge Aristotle's account, both in the monograph and in the treatises, to be fair and objective. We cannot deny that it is a partial one, leaving many of our questions unanswered, and that it is fundamentally unsympathetic or hostile. It is understandable that Aristotle should balk at the miraculous and at heroic stature. It is surprising that he should fail to grasp the possibilities inherent in theories that greatly excited his nearest colleagues. But his account, however negative, enables us to discern through the mists of time a person. On the basis of that account and of what little earlier testimony we possess let us now attempt a profile of Pythagoras and a sketch of early Pythagoreanism. Dispensing with such cautionary locutions as "it may well be," "it seems probable," "in all likelihood"—locutions that are used to lend to a hypothesis an air of truth to which it should not pretend. What follows is simply a "probable account."

During the eighth and seventh centuries the influences of their eastern neighbours on the Greeks of Asia Minor was marked. Orientalizing influences in art are observable not only in Ionia but as far afield

as Etruria. Greek penetration eastward, however, and the colonization
of the Black Sea area began as early as the eighth century, and by the
seventh "it is Greece which is in general the giver."[1] By the beginning
of the sixth century the culture of Ionia was a confident and expanding
one. If in its early years Sappho (96, 98 LP) still looked to Sardis as a
Paris of her day, a city fabled for wealth and fashion, nevertheless
her own poems are sufficient testimony to the culture of her native
Lesbos. The first half of the century was a period of material prosperity
and of a flowering of culture, a period that, in the field of thought, saw
Thales and Anaximander. But about the middle of the century, with
the Persian conquest of Lydia and the capture of Sardis, the great age
of Ionia began to come to an end. One by one the Greek cities lost
their liberties and their markets. Migrations to the north and west
began. The Greeks began to count as epoch-making the year "when
the Mede came."

Pythagoras was about twenty-five years of age when Sardis fell.
His native Samos was spared foreign domination and reached a
modus vivendi with the Persians, under the tyranny enjoying such
power and prosperity as it had not known before. "I have dwelt at
some length on the affairs of Samos" says Herodotus (3.60), "because
they built three of the greatest public works constructed by any Greek
state." All three of these were built in the lifetime of Pythagoras. The
first was a tunnel nearly a mile long, cut through a hill in order to
bring water to the island's chief city—a feat that testifies to the skill
of its engineers. The second was the improvement of the harbour by
the construction of great sea-walls, still in part extant. The third was
the rebuilding of the temple of Hera, the largest of all Greek temples,
begun by Polycrates and still unfinished at the time of his downfall.

Only in times of great prosperity, when the crafts flourished, could
public works of such magnitude have been undertaken. We have further
testimony to the prosperity of the island in the sixth century in archeo-
logical finds there, and in particular in a continuous series of marble
gravestones.[2] We know that the island was famous for its craftsmen,
especially for its workers in bronze and in the precious metals (*Hdt.*
1.51; 3.41). Polycrates further enriched it by expanding the semi-
piratical rule of the seas into a virtual blockade of Aegean commerce.
He showed his concern for its cultural life by attracting to it Democedes
of Croton, the greatest physician of his day (*Hdt.* 3.125; 3.131) and
two of the greatest contemporary poets, Anacreon (*Hdt.* 3.121) and
Ibycus (Suid. *s.v.*). In the second half of the sixth century Samos was,
briefly, the principal power of Ionia and centre of its culture. And in

this Samos Pythagoras passed his mature years. Even if he never visited Miletus—and it is more than likely that he did, as it was only a few sailing hours away—he will have had occasion to familiarize himself with the thought of the Milesians and to read, among others, Anaximander's book. We assume that Thales and Anaximander had some knowledge of Babylonian mathematics. We must make the same assumption for Pythagoras. However we may conceive of him, he cannot have remained untouched by the intellectual trends of his times. If he had been born and brought up as a peasant in Aetolia it might be suggested that his thought, or religious teaching, exhibited primitive traits of an earlier epoch. It is not credible that in the Samos of the Ionian enlightenment a superstitious and obscurantist Pythagoras (who was nevertheless the "polymath" of Heraclitus) should teach a doctrine compounded of primitive and in part non-Greek notions and yet should achieve the authority he did. Like other thinkers the cast of whose thought was religious, he may have reacted against the temper and the intellectual trends of his times. So did Plotinus, St. Augustine, Pascal. But that reaction is as much the product of social and intellectual environment as is the conformity of other contemporaries.

The years of his intellectual formation and of his early maturity Pythagoras passed in Ionia. Heraclitus, Herodotus, Ion of Chios testify that he achieved a reputation there. In respect of what doctrines did he achieve this reputation? That his teachings had something to do with the soul we know from Herodotus' curious tale of Zalmoxis. That it had a mathematical colouring or was "number-oriented" we infer from contemporary trends, observable especially in Anaximander, and from the fact that the ancient tradition with one voice attributes to him such tendencies. But though we may confidently attribute to him some doctrine of the soul and of *physis* as number, the details of those doctrines are obscure.

If we ask what doctrines of the soul were current in the Ionia of the sixth century, and from what origins and elements they derive, we find that there are no positive answers to these questions. Hints are given us in the epic and the lyric poets, in myth and legend, in what we know of cult and burial practice. These hints are often of debatable interpretation. In no case do they satisfactorily explain what seems to us a revolution in the manner of conceiving the human person. In the myth and the epic there is a great gulf fixed between immortals, the race of the ever-living gods, and mortals, creatures of a day.[3] This gulf, to all appearances unbridgeable, we find bridged in the epic in two curious ways. The first of these is translation, on which the whole person, body and soul, escapes death and achieves immortal life. Heracles is rapt to Olympus, Menelaus to the Isles of the Blest. The second is the hero cult, a cult performed at the tombs of persons supposed to have a continuing existence localized there. These heroes are thought of as having once been mortals. By the sixth century founders of cities or exceptional athletes are accorded heroic status and become objects of public cult. But few are accorded such privilege. For the rest of mankind a shadowy existence in Hades awaits their souls after death.

It is true that the mystery cults promise some amelioration in life after death—a "better lot" in Hades. But this "better lot" never is said to compensate for loss of life in the upper world. Nor does it make life on earth an episode in the soul's history. These traditional beliefs remained largely unchanged for the Athenian of the fifth century, indeed for the Greek throughout antiquity. But already in the sixth century, and probably earlier, there were current beliefs which accorded the soul pride of place in the human person, conceived of as a complex of body and soul. How could there arise a notion of soul as better and more lasting than body when Greek religion continued to picture a dismal Hades in which the after-life of a shadowy soul was at best tolerable?

The gods of Olympus were patriarchally organized—gods of the family, the tribe, the cult or craft association, the polis. It was through family or tribe, cult group or polis that the Greek approached them. But as the concept of law developed, and as they began to appear before the law and to act within their states not as members of a group but as persons, the sense of individuality, in some respects already present and self-assertive in Homer's heroes, began to be accompanied, as in the epic it usually was not, by a sense of personal responsibility. The poems of Archilochus are an expression of defiant individuality, those of Alcaeus and Theognis, the expression of individuals dismayed at the loss of a social context in which they could shift responsibility to the group or class.

That men should forego the emotional satisfactions and mutual support afforded by group cult practices for the cold comfort of a rule of law was not to be expected unless they had as direct an access to their gods as they had to the law. To two of their gods they had such access. Apollo was accessible to the healer, the soothsayer, the poet, and the musician, to the sick and the polluted. Dionysus took possession of his devotees rather than awaiting their intercession. It is perhaps somewhere in the cult of these two divinities that we should look for an interest in the after-life. Both of them have an existence apart from the divine family of Olympus. Both have if not their origin at least important areas of cult outside the Greek world. The two are associated in the religion of Delphi. The ecstatic cult of Dionysus provides favourable soil for the growth of a belief that the soul which leaves the body in ecstasy may be capable of surviving the body. In the religion of Apollo the power of the god is exercised not on the physical person but on some faculty within the person that is enabled to sing, prophesy, heal.

Having suggested that the myth reveals aspirations towards immortality, that the times demanded a new evaluation of the human person, and that certain aspects of religion would have permitted of such a new evaluation, if we then attempt to show how the notion of soul as distinct from and surviving the body arose, we find ourselves in the position of having to make our bricks without straw. Let us content ourselves with a statement of fact, that by the sixth century and the time of Pythagoras a new doctrine of the dignity and fate of the soul was current. Why then was it not welcomed and generally accepted?

We know that the religion of Dionysus encountered opposition from the city-states and in the end accepted, as a compromise, a place among the cities' cults. We know that the Orphics degenerated into practitioners of minor *teletai*, on the fringes of official cult. We accept the contention that Pythagorean beliefs concerning the soul are an expression of the same aspirations. Pythagorean beliefs and teachings about the soul are usually, and properly, illustrated by pointing to parallels with the mystery religions, the religion of Dionysus, and the Orphics. These parallels enable us to understand how, in a Greek context and in the sixth century, Pythagorean notions concerning the soul could arise. But if we are to grasp the singular character of Pythagorean teaching, differences between Pythagoreanism and similar religious movements are more significant than parallels. All other beliefs somehow merged in the main stream of Greek religion. Pythagoreanism, however curious its origins, became not a religious creed but a philosophy. We ask why this was so. The testimony of Heraclitus in a measure enlightens us.

Heraclitus was a generation younger than Pythagoras and, if Pythagoras emigrated from Samos about 532 b.c., can have known him only by repute. But he came from the neighbouring city of Ephesus, where he would have occasion to hear any accounts of Pythagoras still current

Ionia in the decades following his departure. Pythagoras, he tells us (22 B 129), practised inquiry more than any other man. He took what he could use from writings in that kind, and fashioned himself from them a learning derived from many sources, a polymathy that was mistaken in method. Heraclitus calls him (B 81) a logic-chopper or misleader, and argues (B 40) that much learning does not teach a man wisdom. If it did it would have taught Hesiod and Pythagoras, Xenophanes and Hecataeus.

If we are to see the point Heraclitus is making, we must not be misled by his acrimony. He is attacking a rival system, and attacking it on two grounds. First, Pythagoras read, studied, and used as a basis for his own thought all writings available to him. By writings Heraclitus presumably meant Homer, Hesiod and the poets, Anaximander, travellers' and merchants' tales, and chronicles such as may have served Hecataeus, accounts of Babylonian astronomy and Egyptian mensuration in whatever form they may have been accessible, in short any written (or oral) source of knowledge. Secondly, Heraclitus attacks Pythagoras because he promoted such inquiry to method— a method that was mere polymathy and a willing perversion of true wisdom. To us it is a mitigating circumstance to find Pythagoras in the company of Hesiod, Xenophanes, Hecataeus but to Heraclitus it was none. Error is not covered by a great name.

Heraclitus' own method was to inquire after the truth within himself (B 101), and the truth he found was an open secret, a simple key (B 1, 2) to the only knowledge of any value. That he should have repudiated Pythagoras' method and the whole tendency of his thought is understandable. That he should have done so repeatedly and emphatically is a token of the reputation Pythagoras had acquired, and points to the fact that he was considered first and foremost a thinker. If he had been known as a "shaman" Heraclitus would not have spoken of him in the terms in which he did.

The teachings of Pythagoras concerning the soul differed from those of the Orphics, not so much in their content as in their implications for the conduct of life. If you are persuaded that your soul is more important than its bodily vehicle you will care for your soul. If you are persuaded that it survives the body, and that your conduct in life will determine its lot in other existences, then you will seek so to conduct your life as to assure for your soul the best of possible future lots. If you are persuaded that in the course of its transmigrations your soul can progress towards a final goal of divine status, then your scruple in the care of your soul will be great. For Pythagoras this divine status can only have meant what it meant for Pythagoreans, Platonists, Neopythagoreans, Neoplatonists after him. The divine faculty was the faculty of insight, of knowing, of penetrating the secrets of the universe, the hidden nature of the visible world, and the order governing it; the faculty of seeing all, hearing all, knowing all. You subject yourself to spiritual and intellectual discipline in order that, in the words of Empedocles (B 146), you may become "seer, bard, healer, leader among men here on earth; and then achieve the full stature of a god most rich in honours."

For Pythagoras the knowledge at which he aimed was a knowledge of the structure of the universe as determined by number. His cosmos,[4] like the cosmos of Anaximander, was symmetrical, the relations of its parts being expressible in number. Its first principles were the *apeiron*— the *apeiron* of Anaximander—and the *peras* implied by that *apeiron*. Under these two first principles were subsumed Odd and Even. From the interaction of these two pairs of opposites was produced the One, our Cosmos. From the One and its surrounding *apeiron* or void were generated the number-things of our physical world. We do not know whether Pythagoras explained the manner of their generation. It seems improbable that he did. We do know that he thought the "correspondences" between disparate things, produced by their common numerical components, could be perceived.

Why Pythagoras chose to leave Samos for the West we do not know. The intellectual patrimony with which he departed consisted in his theories of the nature of the cosmos and his doctrines, partly theoretical, partly of religious origin concerning the soul. In Magna Graecia he found a milieu favourable to his teachings. Croton had just suffered a great and unexpected defeat, which it could attribute only to divine intervention and the gods' displeasure. In such crises a reaction against laxity of manners and a desire for moral reform is often to be observed. What role Pythagoras played in this reform we do not know. If he had been chosen Croton's lawgiver, its Solon, some tradition of his holding that office would have been preserved. It seems more probable that he became the conscience and leading spirit among the sterner Crotoniate moralists, and that, through this, he acquired such a personal ascendancy that his party came to be known as "the Pythagoreans."

It was probably after the destruction of Sybaris, in the first flush of that success, when there seemed to be grounds for some relaxation of discipline, that opposition to the Pythagoreans manifested itself, or perhaps that factional split occurred within the party. Pythagoras either chose, or was forced, to withdraw from Croton. He found asylum in Metapontum and there he died soon after. But his party, if they ever lost their ascendancy, soon regained it and extended their area of influence to many of the city-states of Magna Graecia. They remained in power—and were known as Pythagoreans—until shortly after the middle of the fifth century when an uprising, apparently of democratic or popular origin, overthrew and scattered them. Much blood may have been shed. In the fifth century bloodshed usually accompanied stasis. Some few went into exile in mainland Greece or in the area of Rhegium. But the persecution cannot have continued for long. When Dionysus II began to extend his dominion over Magna Graecia, "Pythagorists"—in what numbers we cannot guess—took refuge in Attica. Tarentum, which was beyond his reach, became a centre for others.

Of those calling themselves Pythagoreans during Pythagoras' life and in the half-century following his death, most will have been his political partisans, sympathizers in his moral reforms. Some, in an area where the Orphics were active, will have received and followed his teachings regarding the soul. Very few can have interested themselves in, and achieved an intellectual grasp of, his physical teachings and number theory. But his authority was sufficient to ensure the preservation and transmission of his thought in its principal aspects.

Such, as we conceive it, is the story of Pythagoras. The aura that surrounded his name, the very fact that his teachings even if they were not understood were preserved and transmitted to succeeding generations, is due to the authority he commanded among his contemporaries. The phenomenon of an authority more than human, exercised not only over his own generation but over succeeding generations, an authority capable of provoking unquestioning assent to doctrines however heterogeneous and however ill understood, is a phenomenon familiar to us but one which we are loath to recognize. Even in the case of "bad" great men we are inclined to explain their authority by such terms as mass hysteria, and their persons as manifestations of megolamania. We "cut them down to size" by emphasizing their weaknesses rather than conceding their power. The once useful formula of daemonic possession no longer serves. Yet we have seen in our time whole nations, and civilized nations, subservient to these men and by them inspired, sometimes to splendid self-sacrifice and self-abnegation, sometimes to the most brutal excess.

If "bad" great men are difficult to account for, "good" great men are so inexplicable as to be incredible. How the founders of the great religions came to acquire the power and authority they in fact possessed we can only explain by suggesting that they were of another clay. The fact of the authority of some men, both good and evil, over their kind is a phenomenon that, like some phenomena of nature, is too big to be grasped; all we can do is to recognize its presence.

Pythagoras was such a man. His importance in the history of philosophy is, in part, due to his theories of physical structure as numerically expressible and to his anticipation of quantitative analysis. These notions, taken up and rendered fruitful by Plato, were an important influence on Greek speculation throughout antiquity. But yet more important was his conception, or the pattern he established, of philosophy as a way of life and an intellectual and spiritual discipline by means of which the soul progresses towards the actualization of its divine nature and towards knowledge. By its means we make ourselves like the divine.

NOTES

[1]Dunbabin, *The Greeks and their Eastern Neighbours* (London 1957) 66. For colonization, A. R. Burn, *The Lyric Age of Greece* (London 1960) 107–122. For orientalizing influences in Etruria, M. Pallottino, *The Etruscans* (London 1955) 57.

[2]G. M. A. Richter, *The Archaic Gravestones of Attica* (London 1961) 53.

[3]That immortality was a *divine* attribute and that a man must become *divine* to become immortal is suggested by the account of the sin of Tantalus preserved by Asclepiades Tragilensis (*FGrH* 12 F 30) where it is said that as Prometheus stole the fire so Tantalus attempted to steal the nectar and ambrosia for mankind. The return of Sisyphus from Hades (*Theog.* 702 ff.: Soph. *Philoc.* 448, 624–625) is a myth of the struggle for immortality. Demeter at Eleusis and Thetis for Achilles attempt the immortalization of a mortal, and their failure indicates how difficult it was conceived to be. For the hero see A. Brelich, *Gli Eroi Greci* (Rome 1958), and especially for the classification gods/heroes/mortals (8–11). See also H. Fränkel, *Wege und Formen "Ephemeros* als Kennwort für die menschliche Natur"* (23–39) for early attitudes.

It might be suggested that the abundant myths of transformations in which gods, demi-gods, and men undergo metamorphosis might suggest migration of the soul, but all these are physical changes within one life-span and are a common mythical motif. Bolton, 71 ff., suggests that the vegetarianism of the Pythagoreans derives from the Hyperboreans, the special people of Apollo. This may be so, but an ascetic rule is a secondary phenomenon and the Hyperboreans are immortal. Can a doctrine of survival arise in connection with their myth?

⁴The important notion *kosmos* is discussed by H. Diller, "Der vorphilo-sophische Gebrauch von *Kosmos* u. *Kosmein*" in *Festschrift für Bruno Snell* (Munich 1965) where he defines (59): "*kosmos* war eine Zusammenordnung zubereiteter Teile die mit Zweckbestimmung an ein Subject herangebracht wird und ihm damit erst seine aktuelle Qualification gibt." That is, the notion derives from harness, personal adornment, etc. but implies "from the first, order." He argues that for Anaximander this order is subordinate to *dike* and so subject to destruction. Diller refers to earlier discussions, including that of Reinhardt, *Parmenides* 50. Kahn discusses *cosmos* in an appendix (219–230). He concludes that *cosmos* is an arrangement or ordering of parts, but allows for a shift in emphasis in uses subsequent to Anaximander.

Popper (*Proc. Arist. Soc.* 59 [1959] 4) has said of Anaximander's theory that it was "one of the boldest, most revolutionary and most portentous ideas in the whole history of human thought."

For Pythagoras the notion of cosmos *may* have entailed macrocosm/microcosm. Epiphanius (*Dox. Gr.* 589) tells us that according to Pythagoras the heavens "are a (physical) body, sun and moon and the other stars and planets being its members, as they occur in man." Photius, *Biblio.* 249.440 Bekker also attributes this idea to Pythagoras, and Jaeger, *Nemesios von Emesa* (Berlin 1914) 135 accepts it as *early* Pythagorean. Plutarch (*de Facie* 928A-D) suggests the analogy of the human form in the heavens and Cherniss *de Facie* (Loeb 1957) *ad loc.* cites numerous instances of the analogy between bodily organs and heavenly bodies. Aristotle (*Phy.* 252b 22–28) alludes to a possibility of projecting microcosm on macrocosm—man/god, *zoon/autozoon*. This projection of man into the heavens may have been the more primitive. When first we encounter the term microcosm in Democritus (*Vors.* 68 B 34) it would appear that the heavens are being recognized in man. Probably mutual correspondences were always recognized. That Pythagoras may rather have looked to the heavens for analogies is suggested by Aristotle, *Fr. Sel.* 135, Theon of Smyrna, 3.135. Heraclitus (*Vors.* 22 B 98) has the soul using its sense of smell in Hades (*KR* 211, n. 3) or smelling Hades-like from bad living. If physical functions of man were projected into the nether world in 500 B.C. they may also have been projected into the upper world.

APPENDIXES

APPENDIX I

BIOGRAPHY AND CHRONOLOGY

I have already discussed the early, well-attested, and credible evidence regarding the life of Pythagoras and the post-Aristotelian tradition. I have given reasons for believing that the later biographical tradition, in which conflicts are the rule, is tendentious and often the fruit of invention. I shall not attempt to resolve the conflicts, allow for tendencies and then seek a compromise. In this appendix the principal data are assembled under various headings, no distinction being made between possible fact and probable fiction. Fact and fiction are both important, as depicting the Pythagorean sage, and for the history of Neo-pythagoreanism, even if not particularly relevant to the purpose pursued in this inquiry.

Place of Birth

It is probable that Pythagoras was by birth a Samian. Herodotus (4.95) does not explicitly state that he was a Samian, but says that Zalmoxis was his slave in Samos, as does Strabo (7.3.5). Isocrates (*Bus.* 28) calls him a Samian, as does Hermippus (*DL* 8.1) and Hippobotus (Clem. Al. *Strom.* 1.62 = *Vors.* 14.8). In most casual references he is called Pythagoras of Samos.

Aristoxenus, however, makes him a Tyrrhenian "from one of the islands from which the Athenians ejected the Tyrrhenians" (*D.L.* 8.1 = Wehrli, *Aristoxenus* 11a = *Vors.* 14.8) and we are told that Theopompus (*FGrH* 115 F 72) and Aristarchus concur. This Aristarchus may have been the grammarian or the astronomer or some other. (There are no grounds for Preller's emendation to Aristoteles.)[1] The tale of Tyrrhenian paternity is meant to explain, as Wehrli (comment *ad loc.*) suggests, how Pythagoras came to be in possession of religious secrets. (Wehrli cites *Hdt.* 2.51 and Plato, *Laws* 738c). This story is known to Neanthes (or Kleanthes, Porph. *VP* 1–2; cf. *FGrH* 84 F 29) who specifies Lemnos as the island referred to. But Neanthes states that Pythagoras was a Syrian from Tyre, and Porphyry, himself a Syrian from Tyre (Porph. *V. Plot.* 21), seems to lean to this version.

Aristoxenus, possibly inspired by Theopompus (*FGrH* 115 F 72), may have wished not only to explain his secret knowledge in matters of religion, but also to lead up to a story of migration to the West and contacts with Tyrrhenians/Etruscans. The notion took root. It is reflected not only in Roman writers but also in Plutarch (*qu. conv.* 727 b-c) where it is made to explain the *symbola* and religious practices.

Iamblichus (*VP* 3), never one to do things in a small way, has him a descendant of the *oikistes* of Samos, a son of Zeus.

Paternity

His father's name was Mnesarchus, as we are told by Heraclitus (*Vors.* B 129), Herodotus (4.95), Callimachus (Fr. 61) and Diogenes Laertius (8.1). Diogenes adds that Mnesarchus was a gem-engraver. This curious piece of information, if it has any foundation, may come from Duris of Samos, a Samian of the third century B.C. who wrote a treatise on the engraving of metals and mentions Pythagoras elsewhere in his annals of Samos (*FGrH* 76 F 22). However, the story has not as good authority for it as Neanthes' statement (Porph. *V.P.* 1) that he was a merchant. For Iamblichus (*V.P.* 5), and so perhaps also for Apollonius of Tyana, he was a merchant.

Diogenes Laertius has also preserved for us what appears to be another independent tradition (*D.L.* 8.1): "Some say that he was a son of Marmacus, son of Hippasus, son of Euthyphro, son of Cleonymus; and that Marmacus was an exile from Phlius resident in Samos." Pausanias (2.13.2) has a story— possibly related—of an Hippasus who was the leader of an anti-Dorian party in Phlius and fled to Samos. In his account the descent is Hippasus–Euphranor– Mnesarchus–Pythagoras. It looks as if Diogenes' source had confused the generations and corrupted the names (for Mnesarchus is correct). It is therefore probably a mistake to connect with this Marmacus the Mamercus, brother of Stesichorus, of Eudemus' *History of Geometry* (*Vors.* 14.6a), or the Mamercus said (Plut. *Numa* 8.4–10) to have been the son of Pythagoras himself.

Pythagoras is connected with Phlius also in the anecdote deriving from Heraclides Ponticus (*D.L.* 1.12 = Wehrli, *Her. Pont.* 87) that Pythagoras was the first to use the term "philosopher," in his reply to Leon, tyrant of Sicyon or Phlius, that God alone is wise. We recall that in Plato's *Phaedo* the other person of the dialogue is Echecrates, a Pythagorean of Phlius, where the dialogue is set; and that most of "the last Pythagoreans" whom Aristoxenus claims to have known (*D.L.* 8.46) are from Phlius. It would appear that there was a Phliasian legend, at least partly independent, from which these tales came.

The name of Pythagoras' mother is not mentioned in the fourth-century tradition. Apollonius of Tyana gave it, perhaps inventing it, as Pythais (Porph. *V.P.* 2) and tells of her descent from Ancaeus, the *oikistes* of Samos. This tale Iamblichus takes up (*V.P.* 4, 6) and enlarges on at length. The Delphic oracle informs Mnesarchus that his wife Parthenis is with child of Apollo. He changes her name to Pythais. The name reveals that the mother is to be connected with, and probably has no existence apart from, the tale of Apollo's paternity, which in its turn may be modelled after the story of Plato's birth (P. Lang, *De Speusippi Academici Scriptis*, [diss. Bonn 1911] fr. 27 = *D.L.* 3.2).

Of the family of Mnesarchus we learn that he had three sons, the names of the other two being Eunostos and Tyrrhenus, according to Neanthes (Porph. *V.P.* 2) and Antonius Diogenes (Porph. *V.P.* 10), but Eunomus and Tyrrhenus according to Diogenes Laertius (8.2); both are older than Pythagoras. The names are fictional and reveal that they are to be connected with the tale of Tyrrhenian paternity.

Duris of Samos (Porph. *V.P.* 3; *FGrH* 76 fr. 23 = *Vors.* 14.6 and 56.2) tells us that, in Samos, Pythagoras had a son, Arimnestus, who was exiled, instructed Democritus (in Abdera?), returned to Samos, and erected in the temple of Hera there a bronze votive offering with an inscription citing his own paternity, "son of Pythagoras." Duris is a Samian of the early third century (*CR* 12.3 [1962] 189–192), has apparently seen the inscription, and accepts the association with our Pythagoras. In form the inscription is a possible one. One is led to suspect, however, the fabrication of a Samian background for Pythagoras by local patriotism. It is connected (Porph. *V.P.* 3) (see comment *ad Vors.* 56.2) with a curious epilogue in which one Simos steals one of the seven skills (?) from the epigram (!) and so destroys the other six, all of them apparently connected with musical theory and some form of scales (Wilamowitz, *Platon* [Berlin 1920] 2.94). This tale still awaits a satisfactory explanation. It seems unlikely to be genuine in any part.

Later legend gives him a wife and numerous progeny in Magna Graecia, but all the names are suspect (*Vors.* 14.13).

Family

The tradition that Pythagoras had a wife and family of his own in Croton would not rule out the possibility of a brotherhood but would render it somewhat less probable. Timaeus, our earliest witness, (*Vors.* 14.13 = Porph. *V.P.* 4) says that "the daughter of Pythagoras as a maiden led the maidens, and as a married woman the married women," we assume in the religious festivals of Croton. He adds that after Pythagoras' death his house became a temple of Demeter, and the street in which it stood was named Museum (But cf. Iambl. *V.P.* 170). Here it is assumed that Pythagoras had a family in Croton and a home in which they lived, not apparently as part of a community.

Since the legend had then flourished for two centuries, it is probable that Pythagorean sites were shown in Magna Graecia in the time of Timaeus. The name of Pythagoras still has magic enough today to baptize remains at Samos and in Metapontum in his name. Timaeus may have seen the temple at Croton. He may have found the name of Pythagoras' daughter, or of one of his daughters, as the earliest priestess. But it would be rash to argue from what he tells us of Pythagoras' family, to a definite civil status, and all other accounts have an air of romance. The very names, except for Mnesarchus, a son named after the grandfather, have obvious derivations; Telauges, an attribute of light or Apollo, Myia, a woman busy as a fly or bee, Arignote, "known far and wide." Even the name Theano may have suggestions of divinity, but it appears to have a surer place in the legend than the rest.

Education

That Pythagoras is said to have been a pupil of Anaximander, and on occasion even of Thales, need not concern us. The biographers, and especially the writers of *Successions* beginning with Sotion (*ca.* 200 B.C.), invented a master-pupil relationship as their schemes demanded, in some cases going further and inventing a relation of *erastes-erômenos*, a malicious device that seems to have been one of Aristoxenus' innovations (Wehrli, *Aristoxenus* 52a).

Two masters are assigned to Pythagoras in the tradition, Pherecydes of Syros and Hermodamas. The reasons for associating Pherecydes and Pythagoras are suggested in Suidas (*s.v.* Pherecydes = *Vors.* 7 A 2): "It is said that Pythagoras was instructed by him, but that Pherecydes himself had no teacher. He acquired secret books of the Phoenicians and taught himself. . . . Pherecydes was the first to introduce the doctrine of metempsychosis." The fact that Pherecydes taught doctrines best explainable as foreign and esoteric, involving the soul, made him a suitable teacher to attribute to Pythagoras.

Ion of Chios (*Vors.* 36 B 4) is the first to associate the two names, without however suggesting an association in life. The whole subsequent fiction of their relation, as Raven (*KR* 51) suggests, may have its origin in this fragment. Among subsequent writers who call Pherecydes the master of Pythagoras are the following: Duris of Samos (*D.L.* 1.119–120); Andron of Ephesus (*D.L.* 1.119); Aristoxenus (*D.L.* 1.118; Wehrli, *Aristoxenos* 14); Dicaearchus (Wehrli, *Dikaiarchos* 34 = Porph. *V.P.* 56); and, of course, Porphyry and Iamblichus. Accounts differ as to the detail and chronology of the relation. Diogenes cites "certain sources" as saying that Pythagoras went to Lesbos with a letter of introduction to Pherecydes from his uncle Zoilus, and that he returned to Samos, still a young man, only after Pherecydes' death. Dicaearchus (*supra*; cf. *FGrH* 76 F 22) says that Pherecydes died before Pythagoras left Samos and Aristoxenus (*supra*) has Pythagoras bury him in Delos. Diodorus (10.2.4) says that he returned to Delos to tend and bury Pherecydes. Once the two names were associated it was only right and fitting that the pupil should bury his master. Time and place of burial could be arranged to suit the purposes and tendency of the writer. If Pythagoras is to be made a hero of the contemplative life and so need not die in the holocaust of Croton, he can be made to depart beforehand to bury Pherecydes. Diodorus' account may be inspired by a desire to shift to Pherecydes the blame for the miracle-working. The paradoxographer Apollonius (*Mirab.* 6 = *Fr. Sel.* 130) remarks: "At first Pythagoras devoted himself to mathematical studies, but subsequently he did not refrain from the miracle-mongering of Pherecydes." Heidel in *AJP* 61 (1940) 8 ff. has shown that this introductory remark need not derive from Aristotle. Frank, in an unpublished study of the fragments, suggests Theopompus as the author. It assumes that Pherecydes intervened at a later stage in Pythagoras' education and (regrettably) influenced him in such a way as to divert his attention from mathematics to miracles, and this is Theopompus' usual bias (*FGrH* 115 F 73).

In some accounts we find miracles variously attributed to the two men. Eusebius (*Praep. Ev.* 10.3.6 = *Vors.* 7.6) tells us on the authority of Porphyry

that, according to Andron of Ephesus the miracles commonly ascribed to Pythagoras were transferred to Pherecydes by Theopompus, with some changes of
name (Burkert 120–121). We could not have a clearer indication of the sovereign
indifference with which writers, from the fourth century on, invented or borrowed
biographical details to embellish their writings.

The other master assigned to Pythagoras is Hermodamas, a descendant of
Creophylus (*D.L.* 8.2), a tale that appears to originate with Apollonius of
Tyana (Porph. *V.P.* 1.15) and that is taken up also by Iamblichus (*V.P.* 11).
Creophylus is the Samian who hospitably received Homer. The purpose of the
invention is to suggest a Homeric association and a Homeric strain in education.
M. Detienne, *Latomus* (1962) 13, on the basis of Porphyry *V.P.* 1 and Iamblichus
V.P. 9, makes Pythagoras a pupil of the Homeridae of Samos, whose school
he attends. This is said to explain the (Pythagorean) origin of the allegorical
interpretation of the poets.

Voyages of Instruction

The voyages of Pythagoras were a favourite theme of the biographical
tradition. In early times philosophers and sophists, as they shared the name of
"sophist," shared also the characteristic of travelling from city to city and from
country to country. In that he remained all his life in Athens, Socrates was an
exception to the rule. His pupil Plato, however, in his first voyage to Sicily
undertook what was a voyage of instruction in the strict sense, and thereafter it
was common for philosophers to embark on a journey abroad to learn what there
was to be learned in foreign lands. They naturally imagined their predecessors
to have made similar journeys, and when it came to writing the life of Pythagoras
they credited him not only with migration from Ionia to Magna Graecia but
also with preceding voyages of instruction. They did so the more readily because,
in the Academy of Plato's later years, a lively interest in the East developed,
and the tendency arose to seek the origins of Greek religious and philosophical
doctrines there (Jaeger, *Aristotle*[2] [1948] 131–137). That this tendency was not
restricted to the Academy is shown by the fact that Isocrates (*Bus.* 28 = *Vors.*
14.4) alludes to a journey made by Pythagoras to Egypt.

In the biographies of Pythagoras this theme of the voyages of instruction and
initiation is treated in the manner and in the stages we have observed in the case
of other themes. In the fourth century and in the Peripatetic school we find the
voyages used to explain how Pythagoras came by esoteric wisdom, foreign to
Greece. Here, as in so many instances, Aristoxenus is the first to make the suggestion. He has him travel not only to Egypt but also to the East, to Zaratas, to
whom a doctrine of immortality was (falsely) ascribed. (Wehrli, *Aristoxenus*
fr. 13 and comment; Bidez-Cumont, *Les Mages Hellénisés* [Paris 1938] 28, 38 ff.)
The purpose of his journeys (that is, what they are meant to explain) was the
study of mathematics and priestly lore in Egypt and in Asia Minor and instruction in a way of life from the Magi (Porph. *V.P.* 6).

The theme of voyages continued to be developed in about this sense and with
relative sobriety until the first century of our era. Then Apollonius of Tyana,

who claimed to be a reincarnation of Pythagoras and who himself journeyed through the then known world, in his *Life* represented his great predecessor as having undertaken journeys similar to his own and for similar purposes. His account was reflected in Porphyry's *Life* and was elaborated at great length by Iamblichus, who develops and embellishes the theme after the manner of the Hellenistic writers of romances. The episode of the journey to Egypt, when the sailors recognize his godhead and sacrifice to him is more than worthy of the other Iamblichus. But when we are told of twenty-two years' priesthood in Egypt, twelve years in Babylon when he is carried there by Cambyses, a return to Samos for some years of teaching at the age of fifty-six; then another long journey through Greece and back to Samos and finally, at what age we are not told, the departure for Magna Graecia—after all this we conclude that Iamblichus is either inventing to justify an impossible chronology or else spinning a very tall tale. The voyages of study are intrinsically improbable, given the history of the period. That the account of a voyage to Egypt or the East is more convincing than the formula *ex oriente lux*, is obvious. In the centuries during which the theme was developed we can understand that it might get out of hand.

Egypt is the earliest and most favoured goal for Pythagoras' travels. "Pythagoras the Samian," says Isocrates (*Bus.* 28 = *Vors* 14.4) "visited Egypt and became a disciple of the priests there. He was the first to introduce (their) philosophy to the Greeks and he, especially and more than all others, emphasized sacrifices and cult practices in temples." Isocrates later (12, 33) practically concedes that this is invention, but if it was intended as fiction it was accepted as fact. All subsequent writers with one accord ascribe journeys to him, and all have the journeys occurring from Samos, before his departure for Magna Graecia.

A certain Antiphon[2] in a book *Concerning those excelling in Virtue* (*D.L.* 8.3; Porph. *V.P.* 7) tells how Polycrates gave Pythagoras a letter of introduction to Amasis, how he then acquired the language of Egypt, and finally penetrated the priestly secrets, including mathematical secrets, these being, Antiphon held, a priestly discipline. The Cambyses episode (*Theol. Ar.* 53) elaborated on by Iamblichus (*V.P.* 13) carries him to Babylonia, and most of the accounts, even if they do not include the intervention of Cambyses, have him visit both areas (*Strabo* XIV 1, 16, Porph. *V.P.* 6, Iambl. *V.P.* 19). Porphyry has him visit Delos on his way to Italy, there inscribing a curious verse on the tomb of Apollo. He then goes to Crete where he undergoes ritual purifications and again inscribes a verse, this time on the tomb of Zeus (Porph. *V.P.* 17). Apuleius (*Flor.* II 15) has him encounter Epimenides there, and Diogenes Laertius (8.3) has him descend with Epimenides into the Idaean cave.

As we have seen, originally the voyages of instruction are meant to explain how Pythagoras acquired the knowledge he was said to possess, and the emphasis is on scientific knowledge—mathematics, astronomy, philosophical doctrines. With Neopythagoreanism the emphasis shifts to religion, initiation, purification, secret doctrines, and the rather bald early statements begin to be more detailed and informative. There is no reference to any voyage in the fragments of

Aristotle, and there is no reason for believing that there is a historical basis for any such journeys. That they were a recognized feature of later philosophical preparation is shown by the action of Plotinus in joining the forces of Gordian to acquaint himself with the wisdom of the Magi and the Gymnosophists (Porphyry, *V. Plot.* 3; H. Dörrie, "Ammonios der Lehrer Plotins," *Hermes* 83 [1955] 442–44).

The Death of Pythagoras

Diogenes Laertius (8.39–40) gives us four accounts of the death of Pythagoras, coming from four or more sources.[3]

(1) While the Pythagoreans, numbering about 40, are meeting in the house of Milo the house is set on fire either (a) by one who was refused admission to the association (Cylon is not mentioned by name), or (b) by the citizens of Croton who feared the establishment of a (Pythagorean) tyranny. As a result Pythagoras was (a) captured on coming out (and put to death?) (here I read with Mss. καταληφθῆναι) or (b) fled, but was captured when he refused to cross a field of beans, and was put to death (sources not cited).

(2) Dicaearchus says that he escaped to the temple of the Muses in Metapontum and died there after a voluntary fast of forty days.

(3) Heraclides Lembus says that on returning from burying Pherecydes in Delos Pythagoras finds his traditional opponent, Cylon, in power, so he then withdraws to Metapontum and starves himself to death.

(4) Hermippus has him lead the people of Acragas in a war against Syracuse. In a withdrawal he finds himself with a field of beans at his back, stands fast, and is killed. His associates, to the number of thirty-five, are burned in Tarentum(!). (This unnecessary fiction alone should discredit the authority of Hermippus.)

We have two other important accounts of the death of Pythagoras. Porphyry (*V.P.* 55–57; see *FGrH* 84 F. 30), tells us, on the authority of Neanthes of Cyzicus (*ca* 300 B.C.), that Pythagoras was absent in Delos, burying Pherecydes, at the time the house of Milo was burned. However, Porphyry adds, "Dicaearchus and the more exact authors" tell us that he was present at the time of the fire, escaped, and after vainly seeking asylum in several towns, found refuge in Metapontum in a temple of the Muses and was starved to death there.

Iamblichus (*V.P.* 248–258) has an elaborate narrative of which a substantial part is based on Aristoxenus (Wehrli, *Aristoxenus* fr. 18 and comment). Aristoxenus has Pythagoras withdrawn to Metapontum in the face of Cylon's opposition and die there, the fire in the house of Milo occurring only later.

In all this confusion we may neglect such fictions as the field of beans, apparently an invention of Neanthes, the war between Acragas and Syracuse, and the visit to Pherecydes, an episode introduced here only to get Pythagoras out of the way during the fire. There remain two basic problems:

1. There were, as we know from non-Pythagorean historical sources, sanguinary uprisings against the Pythagoreans in the middle of the fifth century. In our tradition these uprisings occur at the time of Pythagoras' death or, in

the account of Aristoxenus, shortly thereafter. Pythagoras must have died about half a century before the uprisings in fact occurred. Was there another popular movement occurring in Croton just before the time of Pythagoras' death and directed against his regime? The mention of the house of Milo, the hero of the victory over Sybaris in 510 B.C. and also of six Olympic victories (Diodor. 12.9) is puzzling. Was he already dead about 500 B.C.? And had he left his house to the Pythagorean association, or had it become a public building? And what of Cylon? He is the traditional opponent of Pythagoras but all attempts to place him in an historical context are conjecture, (von Fritz 62–64; Minar 69–71). The anti-Pythagoreans of the later uprising are called Cylonians, and so Cylon himself may be a person constructed after the name of the party, all tradition of its founder having been lost.

2. Did Pythagoras perish in an uprising? Or did he withdraw in the face of opposition to Metapontum and die there?

It is difficult if not impossible to answer these questions. We have no independent historical tradition for the earlier uprising. The two principal, alternative accounts—death in the uprising or withdrawal in the face of it—are those given by Dicaearchus and Aristoxenus respectively, and are the earliest accounts we have. Dicaearchus was portraying Pythagoras as the exemplar of the active life. His hero must be a leader in the affairs of his state, and must refuse to survive *débâcle* or at least not appear to flee in the face of it. Aristoxenus was portraying the sage whose first concern was his doctrine and way of life, an apostle of freedom but also of political harmony. It was appropriate that his Pythagoras should withdraw in the face of opposition and threatened violence, just as, when confronted with the tyranny of Polycrates, he had left Samos.

Von Fritz suggests (64) that the confusion has been created by Apollonius of Tyana, who has sought to create from all the persons and events of the tradition "one great historical picture." Apollonius has probably added to the confusion, but the fundamental difference between Dicaearchus and Aristoxenus, earlier and more authoritative witnesses than Apollonius, remains. Wehrli in his comment maintains that Dicaearchus is adhering to the details of an earlier, common account which Aristoxenus alters in accordance with his tendency. As against this we may mention the Aristotelian fragment (*Fr. Sel.* 130) in which Pythagoras prophesies sedition to "the Pythagoreans" and then withdraws unnoticed to Metapontum.

It may be possible to reconcile, and to render intelligible and plausible, all this conflicting information. The task has been attempted by many scholars with great ingenuity but so far without commanding general assent. Until some consensus is reached, or some new numismatic or archaeological evidence is presented, it would seem safer to say that we do not know the circumstances of Pythagoras' death.

Writings

Some authorities, Diogenes Laertius (8.6) asserts, maintain (wrongly) that Pythagoras left behind him no writings. We have, he says, the emphatic statement of Heraclitus (*Vors.* 22 B 129) that "Pythagoras more than all other men was given to the practice of systematic inquiry and the pursuit of knowledge; he picked and chose among the writings (he used) and set up as a philosopher with what was in fact merely a mass of information organized on mistaken and misleading lines." Diogenes misunderstood the language of Heraclitus to imply that Pythagoras himself was the author of "writings." He cites a work in three parts—on education, politics, physics—and, on the authority of Heraclides Lembus (*ca* 170 B.C.), a further six works.

It has been shown that these works are pseudepigrapha of a later date (Delatte *Vie* 159–163) and the suggestion of writings might have been dismissed if Diogenes (8.8) had not gone on to cite Ion of Chios in the *Triagmoi*, (*Vors.* 36 B 2 = A. von Blumenthal, *Ion von Chios* [Stuttgart-Berlin 1939] fr. 24) as saying that Pythagoras wrote poems he ascribed to Orpheus (cf. *Vors.* 15, 17.4; *Fr. Sel.* 75); and further, on the authority of Clement of Alexandria (*Vors.* 15) that a certain Epigenes had stated that Cercops was the real author of two Orphic books ascribed to Pythagoras, and Brotinus of two others. Linforth (115) suggests that this Epigenes is the one mentioned as a member of the Socratic circle (*Apol.* 33E; *Phaedo* 59B) but Dodds (171–172) reasonably questions this identification. Linforth further (118–119) suggests that Ion attributed certain poems to Pythagoras, but that Epigenes, being familiar with the tradition that Pythagoras wrote nothing, attributed them to otherwise nebulous Pythagoreans.

It seems highly improbable that Pythagoras should have left writings of which there is no trace or record in the earlier tradition. Also, if there had not been a gap, the pseudepigrapha, which began to be written in the fourth century, would not have attempted to fill it. Ion may have been misled, as was Diogenes Laertius, by Heraclitus' turn of phrase into thinking that the writings to which Heraclitus referred were writings of Pythagoras himself.

On the other hand, he may simply have hazarded a guess as to the authorship of the Orphic writings current at his time. In the sixth and early fifth century poems were freely ascribed[4] to Orpheus, Homer, and Hesiod, usually without intention of fraud. (In some cases the authors are known to us by name.) Hipparchus exiled Onomacritus not because he had forged poems under the name of Musaeus (*Hdt.* 7.6) but because he introduced into a collection of oracles one forged by himself.

Of this Onomacritus Aristotle tells us that he put Orphic doctrines into verse, form (*Fr. Sel.* 75 = Kern, *Orph. Fr.* 27, cf. C. A. Lobeck, *Aglaophamus* 1.348). But, for Aristotle, Orphic doctrines did not imply the existence of an Orpheus "Orpheum poetam docet Aristoteles numquam fuisse et hoc Orphicum carmen Pythagorei ferunt cuiusdam fuisse Cercopis" (Cicero, *N.D.* 1.38.107). We note that it is not Aristotle but the Neopythagoreans who ascribe the authorship of an Orphic poem to Cercops (*Vors.* 15). Clement of Alexandria (*Vors.* 15) cites Epigenes for this information, but we do not know anything further of him. Neopythagorean sources cite another early Pythagorean, Brotinus (*Vors.* 17) as having written Orphic poems.

It would be tempting to suggest that the Neopythagoreans simply annexed, as early Pythagoreans, writers to whom Orphic poems were ascribed. But the fragment of Ion of Chios forbids that. Apparently he not only associated Pythagoreans and Orphics, but also believed that some Orphic poems, of which there were many in his day, were written by Pythagoreans. That he should have ascribed them to Pythagoras, as post-Homeric epic poems were attributed to Homer, need not surprise us. Apparently Aristotle did not take the suggestion seriously.

The third century B.C. was the heyday of pseudepigrapha and at that time writings ascribed to Pythagoras began to be current. It would appear that they were entirely products of the imagination. Scholars have failed in their efforts to reconstruct from them a *Hieros Logos*. It seems entirely probable that Pythagoras himself wrote nothing, and practically certain that if he did write anything no fragments or echoes of it remain.

A Portrait of Pythagoras

On the cover of his *History of Greek Philosophy* vol. 1 Guthrie reproduces a fifth-century coin of Abdera "which shows a bearded head and bears the legend" *PUTHAGORES*. He refers to C. T. Seltman, *Greek Coins* (London 1933), 143–4 and plate 28, no. 11. Both Seltman and Guthrie seem to suggest that the head is a portrait head of Pythagoras.

The coin is to be dated slightly later than 430 B.C. but still in the fifth century, as will be suggested by a monograph (in course of publication) on the coinage of Abdera by J. M. F. May. That is, the dating is about a century after Pythagoras' departure from Samos for the West. That a likeness of Pythagoras should have survived for a century in those times seems highly improbable. Equally improbable is the suggestion that a Pythagores of Abdera had a portrait of his earlier namesake invented, and that this is therefore the first imaginary portrait of Pythagoras. Miss G. M. A. Richter, *Greek Portraits IV* (Coll. Latomus 54) (Brussels 1962) 17–19, has made the more plausible suggestion that the portrait is that of the man whose name is on the coin, and that he was the mint-master of Abdera.

This coin presents a real problem. Portraits on coins are otherwise unknown before Alexander the Great. Greek portraiture in other mediums is usually said to begin only in the fourth century. It seems to me highly improbable that the coin has any connection with Pythagoras. It is perhaps worthy of note that the coin does not show the turban characterizing many later imaginary portraits.

Conclusion

That the conclusions we have reached regarding the facts of Pythagoras' life are negative need not surprise us. Our best-attested evidence, except for casual mention in the fifth century, is of fourth-century origin. At that time the facts had been committed to an oral tradition for upwards of one hundred and fifty years, and through all those years the legend, in which the facts were embodied or imbedded, had been growing. Moreover Aristoxenus, Dicaearchus, and Neanthes, when they wrote their *Bioi*, felt themselves as free to modify the legend for their own purposes as did the tragic dramatists who reshaped heroic myth. They had no sense of the historian's responsibility for the careful checking and sifting of fact, and no requirement of objectivity.

It might be objected that a modern student of the legend, with the aid of source criticism, might salvage some data as reasonably credible, and that to do so is preferable to excessive scepticism. The historian of military and political events must at times accept evidence that is probable rather than certain, to amplify or clarify one minor feature of a larger picture. But if the historian of philosophy indulges in any such probabilities he is committed to a "larger picture," in this case to an *a priori* Pythagoras, just as were Aristoxenus and Dicaearchus. If his facts are not attested by a competent witness, or are acceptable for some other adequate reason, he distorts and falsifies the picture of philosophical development. What is important is not the chronology of the events of Pythagoras' life, but the nature and the consequences of his teaching.

Chronology

Jacoby, in his discussion of the chronology of Pythagoras (*Apollodor's Chronik* 215–227), distinguishes three schemes of establishing the dates of Pythagoras' life, not reconcilable one with another.

1. Eratosthenes, misled by a Pythagoras whose name appears on the list of victors at Olympia in the 48th Olympiad (588 b.c.) gave as his date of birth 606/5 b.c. His role as an athlete gave rise to accounts of the diet he prescribed (Porph. *V.P.* 15) and stories of "the long-haired Samian" (*FGrHist* 76 F 62 and comment).

2. An Italian tradition associated him with Numa (715–672 b.c.) and so dated his birth in the late eighth century.

3. Apollodorus chose, as the year of his *akme* and of his departure from Samos, the epoch year of Polycrates' tyranny, 532 b.c. Jacoby reconstructs the chronology of Apollodorus as follows:

571/0 b.c. year of birth
554/3 b.c. pupil of Anaximander
544/3 b.c. pupil/disciple of Pherecydes
532/1 b.c. leaves Samos for Magna Graecia
499/8 b.c. to Delos to care for and bury Pherecydes
497/6 b.c. death in his 75th year

Jacoby has pointed out that Apollodorus is probably basing himself on Aristoxenus' *Life*, for we read in Porphyry (*V.P.* 9): "When he was forty years of age, Aristoxenus says, and he saw the tyranny of Polycrates becoming more oppressive, so that it did not befit a free man to abide his rule and mastery, he took his departure for Italy." Where Aristoxenus got this information (if he did not invent it) we cannot say. Jacoby refers to his Tarentine origin and to his claim to have known "the last of the Pythagoreans." The likelihood of a sound chronological tradition in Tarentum after two centuries and a great *débâcle* is remote. As to the last Pythagoreans, Diogenes Laertius (*D.L.* 8.46) tells us that four of the five were of Phlius, onetime pupils of Philolaus and Eurytus. The fifth, Aristoxenus' own master in music, Xenophilus, was a Chalcidian and so far as we know never had Pythagorean contacts. Moreover we know that there were Pythagoreans (whether Aristoxenus chose to recognize them as such or not) in Tarentum after his time. So in claiming to have known the last of the Pythagoreans he must be seeking to establish a claim that his information is that of a privileged witness.

Our conclusion must be that the dates which Apollodorus gives are guesswork based on a synchronism of *akme* and epoch year of Polycrates, (M. E. White in *JHS* [1954] 36–43), and that therefore the association of Polycrates with Pythagoras comes from a dubious source. We do not know, and we cannot discover, the dates of Pythagoras' life. Nevertheless, as Jacoby remarks, Apollodorus' dates are the most probable we have. The association with Samos is undeniable. There may be grounds for linking Pythagoras' departure from Samos with Polycrates. The introduction of Anaximander and Pherecydes may be an inference by Apollodorus from the rest of his scheme.

In the history of philosophy relative date is more important than absolute date. If we date Pythagoras much earlier than Apollodorus does, difficulties arise. It is unlikely that he lived earlier than Anaximander; and his migration to the west is more probable after the middle of the sixth century. Nor can we date him much later if we are to leave sufficient time for teaching activity in Magna Graecia. It is unfortunate that we have no synchronism with any event of those years in Magna Graecia. A connection with the destruction of Sybaris (511–510 b.c.) is not made before Apollonius of Tyana (Iambl. *V.P.* 255) whose evidence is suspect.[5]

NOTES

[1]Wehrli, *Aristoxenus* frs. 11a, b, c has corrected the "Aristarchos" of the codices in fr. 11b, but not in 11c, to "Aristoteles," following Preller's unjustified emendation. If "Aristarchus" is to be emended—and Theodoretus (11c) does not strengthen the case for it as he probably used Clement—then the Aristippus who wrote *Of Luxury in Old Times,* (Wilamowitz *Antigonos von Karystos* 48) would be a better candidate.

[2]Zeller (ZM 2. 398, n.1) remarks that this cannot be Antiphon the Sophist. Mondolfo (*ibid.*) following Nestle, would not exclude the identification. It is difficult to believe that a sophist of Antiphon's period could be the author of extracts of this character.

[3]Delatte (*Vie* 241–244) discusses, in detail, accounts of Pythagoras' death and attempts to disentangle them. See also ZM 2. 422–425 and notes. I have not attempted to discuss anecdotes of more obviously legendary character. The legend in all its aspects is discussed by I. Lévy (*Sources*; *Légende*). Lévy's studies leave considerations of historical fact on one side and sometimes overstate their thesis, especially in suggesting that Pythagoras is the prototype of Jesus. He perhaps overestimates the role played by Heraclides Ponticus, and underestimates that of Neopythagorean elaboration. Nevertheless he has contributed greatly to our understanding of the character of the legend.

[4]For the wide-spread practice of ascription see Schwartz, *Pseudo Hesiodea* (Leiden 1960) *passim*. Thesleff 18–21 lists the pseudepigrapha. He suggests (113) an Alexandrian origin and the third/second century as date. Thesleff's suggestion that the speeches in Iamblichus derive from the 4th century B.C. seems questionable. A similar suggestion was made by Rostagni in his fanciful discussion *Scritti Minori* 35–36 = *Stud. It.*[2] (1922) 2.180–199. The speeches, if they are not the invention of Iamblichus, may derive from the *topoi* of the rhetorical schools. The moral tone they reflect is not that of the fourth century B.C. Of course, this is not to deny that Dicaearchus (Wehrli, fr. 33) says that Pythagoras made speeches on arriving at Croton, but does not quote actual words.

[5]The incuse coinage of Magna Graecia, which began to be struck at about the middle of the sixth century—that is, roughly, at the time of Pythagoras' arrival there—has been connected with his coming. If this connection could be made probable it would offer a basis for our chronology independent of the Pythagoras tradition. The Duc de Luynes (*Nouvelles Annales de l'Institut Arch. de Rome* [1836] 388 ff.) was the first to suggest that the coinage was Pythagoras' invention. Without reference to de Luynes, G. F. Hill (*Historical Greek Coins* [London 1906] 22–25) made a similar suggestion. It was taken up by U. Kahrstedt. "Zur Geschichte Grossgriechenlands im 5.ten Jahrhundert," (*Hermes* 53 [1918] 180–187). It has had a recent and enthusiastic propagandist in C. J. Seltman, "The Problem of the First Italiote Coins," *Num. Chron.* 6 (1949) 1–21; *Greek Coins*[2] (London 1955) 77–79; "Pythagoras: Artist, Statesman, Philosopher," *History Today* (1956) 522–27 and 592–97.

Seltman argues that Pythagoras belonged to a family of artisans, he, like his father Mnesarchus, being a gem-engraver or, in Seltman's term, a "celator." To recommend further the notion of a family tradition, he suggests (*Num. Chron.* 19–21) that Pythagoras of Rhegium, a sculptor in bronze of the fifth century, was a grandson of Pythagoras. The only positive grounds for this suggestion is that the sculptor once signed himself *Samios*. Seltman further argues that the excuse-incuse character is meant to symbolize "the Pythagorean opposites". And so he maintains that Pythagoras himself introduced, designed and engraved the coins in question. He further maintains as a second aspect of his thesis, that the diffusion of the coins in Magna Graecia suggests the area and extent of Pythagorean influence.

Let us consider first the suggestion that Pythagoras was the inventor of incuse coinage. Diogenes Laertius' statement (8.1) that Pythagoras' father, Mnesarchus, was *daktulioglyphos* or seal-ring engraver is not necessarily made on the authority of Hermippus of Smyrna (*fl. ca* 200 B.C.) who is cited for the Samian origin. Hermippus, working in the Alexandrian Library, produced a biographical work on the philosophers. He used learned sources, but he also collected or invented scandalous anecdote. He is known to have been a detractor of Pythagoras (*Athen.* 5. 213F). Thus, if the statement that Mnesarchus was a gem-engraver is his, we must regard it with suspicion. Our other sources for that statement are *Schol. Plato Rep.* 600B (Hesychius) where we have a jumble of the most disparate items, and Apuleius (*Flor.* 2.15). These two latter sources may well derive from Hermippus. There is no other mention of gem-engraving in our tradition. Other sources make Mnesarchus a descendant of the *oikistes* of Samos, a Tyrrhenian, a merchant, a seafarer. It seems probable that there was no authoritative tradition as to his profession.

Seltman further argues that the excuse-incuse fabric is meant to symbolize "the Pythagorean opposites". Against this it may be urged:

1. Modern scholars have been intrigued by the Table of Opposites in Aristotle's *Metaphysics* (986a 22–26). In antiquity opposites were not thought to be peculiarly characteristic of the Pythagoreans. Indeed, as I have attempted to show (44–50) contrariety was an axiomatic notion for all early Greek philosophers, and for the poets before them. If Pythagoras had had to choose a hallmark for his teachings he would probably have chosen *harmonia*, or *peras/apeiron*, a pair of opposites that would not lend itself to embellishment.

2. It is difficult to see how excuse-incuse coins could serve to symbolize contrariety. If the contraries symbolized are "back" and "front" then any coin would serve to symbolize them. In the passage adduced to show that "back" and "front" were Pythagorean opposites (*de Caelo* 285a 10–15) no reference is made to contrariety, and in fact they are complementary, not conflicting opposites. I am at a loss to understand why the *incuse* character of the coins should symbolize such a contrariety as gives rise to interaction or process.

Seltman offers a third argument for connecting the coins with Pythagoras; that the coins of Croton have the Delphic tripod from about 550 B.C., and that at a somewhat later date Caulonia, a Crotoniate colony and Metapontum, an ally, have coinage connected with Apollo. He is suggesting that emphasis on the cult of Apollo coincides with the arrival of Pythagoras. We know too little of the early cults of Magna Graecia to say what role Apollo played there in the sixth century. But it would be surprising if, at that time and in a colonial area, the god of Delphi had to await the arrival of Pythagoras before his cult began to assume special significance. (Thuc. 6.3 and W. G. Forrest, "Colonization and the Rise of Delphi," *Historia* 6 [1959] 160 ff.)

There has been much discussion of the purpose of the inventor of this incuse technique. S. P. Noe, "The Coinage of Metapontum" *NNM* 32 (1927) 13–16 and 47 (1931), who rejects the theory of Pythagorean origin, suggests (as does Seltman, *History Today* 594) that it was meant to keep coinage in the Magna Graecia area. But it is difficult to see how it would accomplish this at a time when coinage had a bullion value. Sutherland, "The Incuse Coinage of South Italy," *ANS notes* 3, 1948, (quoted with approval in Seltman, "The Problem" 3–4) suggests that it was adopted to facilitate the overstriking of other coins and to make the resulting thin flan strong. But coins can be, and later were, overstruck after a simple process of hammering them flat. C. Kraay, "Caulonia and Southern Italian Problems" (*Num. Chron.* 1960) 53–81 argues against this overstriking theory. Paul Naster, "La technique des monnaies incuses de la Grande Grèce" (*Revue Belge de Numismatique* 1947) 1–17 (cited by Seltman) suggests a Samian origin because Rhoecus and Theodorus of Samos introduced a *cire perdue* method of bronze-casting that involved a core and mantle corresponding to one another as do obverse and reverse dies of an incuse coin. The fact that we have no parallels for this singular technique makes it tempting to connect it with the singular phenomenon of Pythagoreanism, arising in the same geographical area at about the same time. But unless we have strong reasons for doing so we must prefer simpler solutions. Any outstanding die-cutter or "celator" might have invented the technique. It may not be a practical one for minting on a larger scale but it certainly recommends itself by its aesthetic effect, and experimentation does not surprise us in the earliest period of coinage. It seems unlikely that Pythagoras was its inventor, that he meant it to symbolize Pythagorean opposites, and that, almost immediately on his arrival, he was able to provoke, or impose, its acceptance by the city states of Magna Graecia, some of them on hostile terms.

What do the coins tell us? It is generally agreed that the so-called "alliance coins" with Crotoniate obverse, and reverse with the symbols of an allied state (of which there are some ten), reveals a league or alliance of independent states somehow centering on Croton. These coins are struck on a thicker flan, probably after the destruction of Sybaris in 510 B.C. (C. M. Kraay, "Coinage of Sybaris after 510 B.C.," *Num. Chron.* [1958] 18). We may therefore conclude that Croton was principal partner in a political alliance lasting from about 510 B.C. until somewhere in the decade 450–440 B.C. Poseidonia, a colony of Sybaris that never came under Crotoniate influence, ceases to strike incuse coins about 500 B.C. The diffusion of these coins in the fifth century undoubtedly provides evidence for the extent of Crotoniate political influence, and some indication of its nature.

The problem is more complex in the earlier period, from the introduction of the coinage until the destruction of Sybaris. The coinage may have been introduced as late as 530 B.C. Probably in the preceding decade, 540–530, Croton suffered a great defeat at the hands of the Locrians, and its consequent enfeeblement is reflected in a gap in its Olympic victors. At the same time Sybaris, the ally and trading partner of Miletus, is at the height of its power and of its proverbial affluence. It seems improbable that Pythagoras, if he arrived at this juncture, as he is generally supposed to have done, should almost immediately have been able to make himself felt as a political influence, over all principal cities and, just as immediately, should have invented, and have provoked the acceptance by all principal states, of a coinage to express that influence and its principles.

S. P. Noe (14) suggests that the coins have their origin in Sybaris. Kraay considers Sybaris as "a likely candidate" for the state that first struck incuse coins. As Sybaris was the state most likely to have need of coinage both for its internal expenditures and for its foreign trade, especially to the north, this seems a reasonable suggestion.

Excavations, especially at Sybaris, and the discovery of further hoards will probably cast further light on the chronology and the political history of the times, as well as on the role of the coins. Meanwhile the only conclusions they would seem to justify are that Croton was not dominant in the area before the destruction of Sybaris, and that after 510 B.C. Croton was at the head of an alliance of states. We may connect this latter fact to the existence of a political party called "the Pythagoreans" in Croton. No further inference as to Pythagoras or Pythagoreanism seems justified.

APPENDIX II

IRRATIONALS AND INCOMMENSURABILITY

THE discovery of the irrational, and in particular of $\sqrt{2}$, is no longer nowadays attributed to Pythagoras himself but to some Pythagorean or Pythagoreans of the fifth century. It is often connected with the name of Hippasus (*Vors.* 18; Guthrie 320–322). Some of the historians of mathematics give an account of the discovery, based on hints in Iamblichus and Proclus, that make one of the most exciting chapters in the exciting history of mathematics. They tell how Pythagoras discovered the theorem that "in the right-angled triangles the square on the side subtending the right angle is equal to the squares on the sides containing the right angle" (Eucl. 1.47; Heath *Maths* 1.349–368). This theorem is true for the triangle having sides 3, 4, and 5 ($3^2 + 4^2 = 5^2$); the triangle which, it is alleged, first suggested the theorem to Pythagoras. However, when this theorem began to be tested for other right-angled triangles the discovery soon was made that the length of the diagonal was not always expressible as an integer. This was the case most obviously for the diagonal of the square, the length of which proved to be $\sqrt{2}$, or irrational/ἄλογος. Some historians suggest that the term *alogos* expresses the horror of the early Pythagoreans at the discovery and that it is to be translated as "unutterable," a meaning that the word has once, in Sophocles. Otherwise it means, as one would expect, without *logos* or *ratio* and so irrational.

The awful secret that the Pythagoreans discovered is said to be either that the diagonal of a square cannot be rational ($1^2 + 1^2 = 2$, and $\sqrt{2}$ is not rational) or that the square on the hypotenuse is not commensurable with the squares on the sides, or both these truths, the first deriving from the context of arithmetic and the second from that of geometry. (We are not told, however, at what date we might expect Greek arithmetic or Greek geometry to be able to formulate and prove the theorems involved.) This secret caused consternation in "the Pythagorean brotherhood" because their whole structure of theory was built on the notion of rational numbers. The dreadful secret was therefore strictly kept and all investigation of the irrational was dropped until some of them (or some one of them according to the Euclid scholium [Heath 1.3]) made it public and, as punishment meted out by the gods, perished in a shipwreck.

Iamblichus (*VP* 88.246–247 = *c.m. sc.* 25 = *Vors.* 18.4) has several versions of the tale, the secret being promulgated by Hippasus, or by an anonymous Pythagorean, or by more than one Pythagorean; that secret being irrationality, or incommensurability, or the discovery of the dodecahedron. In all cases apparently the impious crime was punished by drowning at sea.

Our authority for all these fabulations is Neopythagorean or Neoplatonist. Seven centuries or more have elapsed since the time of Pythagoras, and the authors make no real pretence to historical veracity or to critical principles. They are partisan and seek to attribute as much of the results of mathematical inquiry as they can to the Pythagoreans, where possible to Pythagoras himself. Their evidence is tendentious and must be interpreted in the context of their times. It can be used for our purposes only with extreme caution.

The most important direct source for the history of mathematics is Proclus (*In primum Eucl. Elem. comm.* 264 Friedlein = Wehrli, *Eudemos von Rhodos* fr. 133). It is conceded that Proclus' outline derives from Eudemus, but that Proclus abbreviated, added, and changed as is remarked by Wehrli in his comment. (To the authorities Wehrli cites should be added Eva Sachs 23–41, 71–75.) In particular as regards Pythagoras, Eva Sachs has shown that the account which we find in Proclus is not to be attributed in its entirety to Eudemus. The other principal source to which the historians of mathematics turn is a critical analysis of the Elements of Euclid where, even if their results are convincing—and that only a mathematician can judge—their methods often seem questionable. At all events no agreement has been reached as to time, nature, or persons involved in the great discovery. So acute a critic as O. Neugebauer (146–149) suggests that "we have no idea of the role which the traditional heroes of Greek science played" before about 400 B.C., agreeing in this with the earlier thesis of E. Frank (227–229).

The problem of commensurability is an important one not for Pythagoras himself, but for the development of Pythagorean mathematics in the fifth century and before Archytas. We would wish to know when, where, and in what context the problem arose.

1. What technical aids existed in the fifth century? What stage in its development can we assume Greek mathematics to have reached before its results began to be published?

2. We do not doubt that the Greeks had considerable mathematical knowledge before they developed a scientific method to formulate and prove what they knew. When and how did this method arise?

3. We assume that arithmetic and geometry developed independently at first. When and how did the two branches of mathematics begin to be related? Was the discovery of incommensurability the cause of their being related?

4. At what *times* can mathematical method have reached a proficiency such that it could attack problems such as incommensurability and infinite divisibility?

Only a historian of mathematics can offer a definitive answer to these problems, but in some aspects they are within the public domain.

As for technical aids, we know from Aristophanes (*Wasps* 656–657) that finger counting was practised in his time but was considered less accurate than the use of the abacus. Mabel Lang (*Hesperia* 26.3 [1957] 271–287) has studied the use

of the abacus, particularly by Herodotus in his calculations. It was a stone slab
with indentations for counters and its columns were given positional values or
had fixed positional values indicated on them. It served well enough for the
ordinary operations of practical arithmetic, but Miss Lang has shown how
easily Herodotus made mistakes in more complex operations. It would appear
to be a tool of practical use with very limited application in mathematics. It
might be suggested that it would lend itself to the very different operations of
so-called *psephoi*-arithmetic. Its field however is limited and positional values
are associated with its columns. Nothing suggests that it was ever used for such
purposes.

It is suggested that a form of arithmetic (and of geometry) called *psephoi*-
arithmetic was practised by the Pythagoreans in the fifth century (*supra* 103 ff.).
This suggestion is developed in great detail and with much ingenuity by O.
Becker (*Das Mathematische* (40–52) and K. von Fritz (*Gnomon* [1958] 82),
though not believing the practise to go back to the sixth century, would accept
it as early. Though its physical means are not described, for there is no record
of any such method, it is apparently thought of as practised on a sand table
with pebbles not as counters but as representing units. Now in the treatises of
Nicomachus of Gerasa and of Theon of Smyrna we find number theories illustrated in a similar manner, by means of unit patterns, but they use alphas to
represent the unit, alpha being "one" in alphabetical notation. This shows that
Neopythagoreans of the second century A.D. practised something like *psephoi*-
arithmetic, and their use of the alphabetical symbol may derive from an earlier
use of pebbles on a sand-table.

The method of division practised by Plato, and the *Homoia* of Speusippus,
suggest that something like sand-tables may have been in use in the Early
Academy as a teaching aid. If there were sand-tables it is possible that pebbles
were used for certain arithmetical problems, to represent the unit. An extension
of this method to geometry seems improbable. The pebbles would lend themselves
to the representation of the patterns of an aggregate of units. From this con-
vention it is a big step to thinking of the pebbles as mere points constituting the
extremities of an imaginary, straight line; and, in any case, ruler and compass
could be used on a sand-table. There is no reason to assume that, for the early
Pythagoreans, the pebbles were now arithmetical units in a visible aggregate
and now points on an imaginary line delimiting surfaces or plane figures,
especially when there was an earlier and traditional method for use in the problems of geometry.

The hypothesis of *psephoi*-arithmetic is meant to suggest how arithmetic
and geometry could have grown up together in the early Pythagorean milieu.
It is then suggested that the discovery of the irrational, or of incommensurability, induced the Pythagoreans, as Taylor says (*Commentary* 367) "to cut
geometry loose from arithmetic." But the organization of Euclid's *Elements*
suggests that the divorce was neither complete nor of long standing, and the
discovery of the irrational may just as easily have led to a closer association

between arithmetic and geometry, as it posed the identical problem for both. *Psephoi*-arithmetic illustrates for us, as it did for the Neopythagoreans, how the early Pythagoreans may have arrived at some of their number theories, especially as to odd and even, the relative positions or patterns that units can assume, square and oblong numbers, etc. But there is nothing to suggest that the method was in fact practised in the fifth century; and as a hypothesis it does not give the best or most convincing explanation of the problems.

Becker and others have borrowed this hypothesis of *psephoi*-arithmetic from Burnet (*Early Greek Philosophy*⁴ 99–107), and Burnet attempts historical justifications as they do not. He points to the method of Eurytus (Aristot. *Metaph.* 1092b 8–15) who by an arrangement of pebbles represented the form (μορφή) of man or horse. This, however, cannot be an arithmetical procedure, but suggests rather the way in which stars are used as critical points in representations of constellations such as Orion. Aristotle, however, adds "like those who dispose pebbles in the form of triangle and square." From this I would conclude that in the second half of the fourth century simple geometrical figures were represented by pebbles, perhaps for purposes of instruction. Burnet however concludes that "at this date, and *earlier*" there existed "a *genuinely primitive* method of indicating *numbers*." (My italics.)

A further argument used by Burnet for some kind of *psephoi*-arithmetic at the time of Aristotle is his mention of the gnomon (*Phys.* 203a 13. See Ross's comment *ad loc.* and Heath 1.370–372, Heath *Aristotle* 101–102), the first mention of it in this sense except for a dubious fragment of Philolaus (*Vors.* 44 B 11). For Oinopides (*Vors.* 41.13) it meant a perpendicular to a straight line, a meaning obviously suggested by its role in the sundial. Whatever the operation may be to which Aristotle alludes in the *Physics* (168, n. 14), the gnomons placed around the unit "and apart from it" do not create geometrical figures but serve to show that the odd is limited, the even unlimited. The application is arithmological. The two passages of Aristotle, however, do indicate that pebbles and gnomons were in use at his time, i.e. after the great advance in mathematical studies that occurred in the first half of the century. That these were perhaps teaching devices is suggested by [Plato] *Amat.* 132a–b, where in the school of Dionysius we observe two youths in earnest dispute about some problem arising in Oinopides or Anaxagoras. They describe circles (on the ground or on sand tables?) and represent inclinations (to the ecliptic?) by angles formed by two hands.

There is nothing in all this, however, which authorizes us to project into the early fifth century methods of the late fourth; nor to suggest that these were the primary form of Pythagorean arithmetic from which others evolved; nor to affirm that the discovery of the irrational was made early and in connection with an arithmetic of this character. (Becker 51–52 in his ingenious suggestion of how the discovery of the irrational could arise in *psephoi*-arithmetic, himself illustrates by geometrical figures.) But even if we assume that pebbles, sand-tables, gnomons, compass in some form, and plumb-line (*Theog.* 805) were in use, these seem inadequate technical aids for the development of a mathematical science. That development would probably have to await a more common use of writing materials, perhaps towards the end of the fifth century.

As to scientific method, Hippocrates of Chios is said, by Proclus on the authority of Eudemus, to have been the first mathematician to write a treatise on *Elements* (*Vors.* 42.1; Cardini 2.28–37). There is reason to believe that the principal advances made in mathematics proper, in the fifth century, were made in Ionia (Heidel *AJP*, [1940] 1–33); and that the first steps towards a Euclidean mathematics were taken there does not surprise us. But the extent of the advance which Hippocrates' *Elements* represents must be questionable when we see Archytas, a mathematician younger by at least a generation, whose skills were greater and whose field of interest wider, maintaining that arithmetic furnishes better and surer proofs than geometry (*Vors.* 47 B 4). Further we observe Theodorus of Cyrene, roughly the contemporary of Archytas, attacking the problem of irrationals not as a general problem but by dealing singly with irrationals from 3 to 17 and then stopping. (Plato *Theaet.* 147D; see Heath 3.1–5 and van der Waerden 693–700).

As we are unable to trace and observe the development of mathematical method until it appears fully-fledged in Euclid's *Elements*, and as it is known that earlier works on arithmetic, geometry, and geometrical algebra preceded the *Elements* and served as a base for them, it is natural to attempt to discover in Euclid influences, traces, and indeed, parts of the treatises of his predecessors. The historians of mathematics attempt to reconstruct Pythagorean mathematics after this manner, analysing in particular Books 7 to 10. Their reconstructions are usually ingenious and penetrating, but their initial assumptions seem to me doubtful. If they have evidence for the early use of a piece of mathematical knowledge, for instance application of areas, and if a late writer furnishes information as to method and proofs they accept the late writer's statements because *it must be so*. They themselves sometimes offer similar hypotheses, convinced that the early mathematician must have been able to formulate and prove. But this may not have been the case. They also make general assumptions that colour their subsequent treatment, as van der Waerden, who can assert (135): "The Pythagoreans engaged intensively in the mathematical sciences according to the absolutely unanimous testimony of Plato, Aristotle, and all later writers. The distinguishing mark of Pythagorean *mathemata*, by which they differ from other branches of knowledge and arts, was their logical structure, their articulation in formulae and proofs." What Plato tells us of the Pythagoreans is very little, and that little does not suggest that they pursued mathematics as a science. Aristotle has a great deal to say about them, but he does not suggest that their mathematics was a science. There is talk of their mathematics only among Neopythagoreans and writers subsequent to them. As for formal structure and proof there is nothing in our tradition to suggest that they either valued or practised them. Even Archytas, a great mathematician, does not yet possess the techniques of presenting and proving his theories.

In dealing with the Pythagoreans historical fact must be kept in mind.

About 450 B.C. there was a Pythagorean *débâcle* in Magna Graecia that led to a diaspora. Philolaus and others migrated to Greece proper, and of these, Philolaus appears to be the only one who was intellectually outstanding. If the fragments are any indication of his scientific activity he was not a mathematician. Some few Pythagoreans may have remained in Magna Graecia (Rhegium?), but there is nothing to suggest that they engaged in any philosophical or mathematical pursuits, nor indeed that they were outstanding in any way. About 400 B.C. Philolaus was able to return to Tarentum. It can be assumed that he found other Pythagoreans there, but there is no indication of philosophical or mathematical activity before Archytas.

As it seems highly unlikely that any progress in mathematics is to be attributed to the Pythagoreans between 450 and 400 B.C., their pursuit of mathematics as a science must have occurred before that time, or should be attributed to Archytas and any immediate predecessors he may have had. What we know about mathematics in the first half of the fifth century is very limited indeed. Let us, nevertheless, ask ourselves whether the problem of incommensurability (or of the irrational) could have arisen at that time. Any discussion of this problem must have, as its point of departure, *Theaet.* 147B–148D where it is stated that Theodorus (*ca.* 400 B.C.) discussed with his pupils the surds from $\sqrt{3}$ to $\sqrt{17}$ (Heath 2.288) or rather "that the sides of squares of three square feet and five square feet are not commensurable with the line of one foot." Theaetetus and his master Theodorus are geometers and discuss their problem in terms of geometry, not of arithmetic. From this passage we can conclude that $\sqrt{2}$ was already known and need not be discussed. How much earlier than about 400 B.C. was it known?

We need not consider Neoplatonist fables about Hippasus and other anonymous Pythagorean "first discoverers," unless we have every reason to believe that the discovery was made in Pythagorean circles and at an early time. We are justified in this by what we know of Neopythagorean and Neoplatonist "historical method," and because there was a Hellenistic vogue for tales of "first discoverers." So any hypothesis we construct will be at best probable. How probable is it that the Pythagoreans discovered the irrational some time between 500 and 450 B.C.? It is not impossible that they did so and concluded simply that their discovery closed one avenue of mathematical progress. They may even have been horrified and have shrunk from their inquiry, though that does not strike one as a Greek reaction. But that it should have remained an almost unspeakable nightmare for two generations, until the time of Theodorus, not even our fables assert. So there would seem to be grounds for attempting an alternative explanation.

Early Pythagorean number speculation, it is now generally held, was predominantly arithmological; that is, it was concerned with the natural numbers (and with prime, amicable, square, oblong numbers, etc.) rather than with arithmetical manipulation. Pythagoras apparently taught that from Limit/Odd and Unlimited/Even proceeded the One, and from the One, the number-things that constitute our physical universe. It is in this context that the early

Pythagoreans must have speculated about number; and Aristotle represents them as still speculating in this context up to his time. In so far as they are mathematicians their interest is centred on the Theory of Number.

Little or nothing is known of philosophical debate and controversy in the first half of the fifth century. But the principal event for the history of philosophy was the publication of Parmenides' poem in which he maintained that there is only one existent—Being or The One. Just as important as his denial of motion, change, void, and discrete quantity, was the form of argumentation he used, a method further developed by Zeno (on whom Aristotle fathers dialectic) for use against Parmenides' critics. It proved so effective that from then on the battles of philosophy were fought with the weapons of Zeno.

In defence of the Parmenidean position, Zeno argued not positively, but negatively. He accepted as his postulate what Parmenides' critics themselves posited, and proceeded to draw contradictory or impossible inferences. "If a plurality exists and existents are a plurality" then they must exist as indivisible, atomic magnitudes or else be infinitely divisible. If we accept the alternative of least bodies the problem of the existence of bodies in space arises, and the difficulties "involved in a pluralistic theory of discontinuous Being" (Cherniss 145). Our concern is with infinite divisibility. The point of Zeno's paradoxes concerning motion, as Cherniss (156) points out, is that they are directed against this second horn of the dilemma. If it is conceded that existents are infinitely divisible then it will follow that Achilles can never overtake the tortoise. Parmenides had argued that the One must be a continuum. Zeno argues that this continuum cannot be divisible because, if it were, then it would either consist of indivisible magnitudes or be infinitely divisible, and in either case absurd consequences follow.

It has been pointed out that Zeno's argument does not involve the infinitesimal (Fränkel 202). It does however involve an infinitely divisible, finite continuum, and incommensurability is a consequence of infinite divisibility. The division of a line into halves, quarters, etc. will not result in incommensurable lines; but if from the diagonal of a unit square we subtract the unit side, then from the side subtract the resultant segment, and so on the division will go on *ad infinitum* and the lines will all be irrationals.

Are we to suppose that Zeno knew of the irrational and of incommensurability? It is usually suggested (as Burnet 314, Cherniss 390) that Zeno was arguing against the Pythagoreans, and that the Pythagoreans had already discovered the irrational. But is it not more natural to suppose that the opponents of the Parmenidean doctrine would be not only Pythagoreans but all contemporary thinkers? Parmenides' uncompromising monism must have been an offence against common sense and an enormity for all of them. In fact we find Anaxagoras, Empedocles, and Melissus all trying to escape the consequences of his theories. And as Zeno's arguments do not appear to have any mathematical colouring but to be purely dialectical (I would regard as such the arguments that Fränkel discusses [220–222]), would it not be more natural to suppose that it was a mathematical application of the notion of infinite divisibility that led to the discovery of the irrational? The problems of the infinite, of infinite divisibility, and of indivisible lines plagued philosophers throughout the fourth century. Should we not rather assume that the problem of incommensurability arose for mathematicians as a consequence of the problems raised by Zeno in its special applications to geometry and arithmetic? Or in other words that the problems of mathematics in the fifth century (but not in the fourth) were special applications of more general problems arising in philosophical or physical discussions?

If we accept such an hypothesis the consequences to be drawn are far-reaching:

1. Early developments in mathematics are then seen as arising as a result of philosophical discussion rather than internal products of mathematical inquiry; mathematical method, like dialectical and logical method, as a product of the innovations of Parmenides and Zeno, evolving late rather than early.

2. The accounts of early Pythagorean mathematics would then be Neo-pythagorean myth. Up to about 450 b.c. their inquiry would take the form of speculation in number theory of a rather primitive kind. After the dispersion in 450 b.c. they resumed scientific pursuits only about 400 b.c. and must have been largely dependent on external stimuli, particularly in mathematics which had meanwhile begun to evolve as an independent discipline.

Van der Waerden, *Math. An.* 117 (1940–41) 140–161, concludes that there was no pre-Zeno crisis in Greek mathematics, but that a crisis within the discipline itself arose early in the fourth century, probably in the milieu of Theaetetus, in connection with the problem of the "irrational," and that it was solved by a resort to geometrical algebra.

The fact, however, that the problem became so acute for mathematicians that a mathematician's solution had to be found does not necessarily mean that it was not first raised and dialectically explored by non-mathematicians, and in any case we are hardly warranted in considering the sciences to be specialized and self-contained at such an early date. Plato and Aristotle did not hesitate to attack mathematical problems.

Such an hypothesis seems to me to explain the historical evolution better than the projection of mathematical discoveries and scientific method into the first half of the fifth century. It remains, however, for the mathematicians to consider whether it satisfactorily explains developments within their discipline.[1]

NOTES

[1]For further discussions of this question see K. von Fritz, "The discovery of Incommensurability by Hippasus of Metapontum"; also the lengthy discussion by Burkert, *Weisheit und Wissenschaft* 379–403, where sources and discussions are cited in detail and where a similar conclusion is reached.

SELECT BIBLIOGRAPHY

ALLAN, D. J. *Aristotelis De Caelo*. Oxford 1936.

BECKER, O. *Das Mathematische Denken der Antike*. Göttingen 1957.

—— "Die Lehre vom Geraden und Ungeraden im neunten Buch der Euklidischen Elemente" (*Quellen u. Stud. zur Gesch. der Math.* 3 [1936]) 533–553.

BERTERMANN, G. *De Iamblichi vitae Pythagoricae fontibus*. diss. Königsberg 1913.

BIDEZ, J., CUMONT, F. *Les Mages Hellénisés*. Paris 1938.

BOECKH, A. *Philolaos des Pythagoreers Lehren*. Berlin 1819.

BOEHM, F. *De Symbolis Pythagoreis*. diss. Berlin 1905.

BOLLINGER, J. *Die sogenannten Pythagoreer des Aristoteles*. diss. Zürich 1925.

BOLTON, J. D. P. *Aristeas of Proconnessus*. Oxford 1962.

BONITZ, H. *Aristotelis Metaphysica*. Bonn 1848.

—— *Index Aristotelicus*. Berlin 1870.

BORGHORST, G. *De Anatolii Fontibus*. diss. Berlin 1904.

BOYANCÉ, P. "Sur la vie pythagoricienne de Iamblichus" (*REG* 52 [1939]) 36–50.

BREITENBACH, H. *et al. Diogenis Laertii vita Platonis*. Basel 1907.

BURNET, J. *Early Greek Philosophy*[4]. London 1930.

—— *Greek Philosophy: Thales to Plato*. London 1914.

—— *Plato's Phaedo*. Oxford 1911.

BURKERT, W. *Weisheit und Wissenschaft: Studien zu Pythagoras, Philolaos, und Platon. Erlanger Beiträge X*. Nürnberg 1962.

—— "Hellenistische Pseudopythagorica" (*Philologus* 105 [1961] 16–43, 226–246).

—— "Zur griechischen Schamanismus." *Rh. Mus.* 105 [1962]. 36–55.

CAMERON, A. *The Pythagorean Background of the Theory of Recollection*. Menasha 1938.

CARCOPINO, J. *De Pythagore aux apôtres*. Paris 1956.

CARDINI, M. T. *Pitagorici: Testimonianze e Frammenti*. 2 vols. Florence 1958–1962.

CHERNISS, H. *Aristotle's Criticism of Plato and the Academy*. Baltimore 1944.

———— *Aristotle's Criticism of Presocratic Philosophy*. Baltimore 1935.

COHEN, M. R. and DRABKIN, I. E. *A Source-book of Greek Science*. New York 1948.

CORSSEN, P. "Die Schrift des Artzes Androkydes" (*Rh. Mus.* 67 [1912]) 240–263.

———— "Zum Abaris des Heraklides Pontikos" (*Rh. Mus.* 67 [1912]) 20–47.

CORNFORD, F. M. *Plato and Parmenides*. London 1939.

———— *Plato's Cosmology*. London 1937.

———— *Principium Sapientiae: The Origins of Greek Philosophical Thought*. Cambridge 1952.

———— "Mysticism and Science in the Pythagorean Tradition" (*CQ* 1922) 137–150; (1923) 1–12.

DELATTE, A. *Études sur la littérature pythagoricienne*. Paris 1915.

———— *Essai sur la politique pythagoricienne*. Liège 1922.

———— *La Vie de Pythagore de Diogène Laërce*. Brussels 1922.

———— "Faba Pythagorae Cognata" (*Serta Leodiensia*. Liège 1930) 33–57.

DIELS, H. *Elementum*. Leipzig 1899.

———— *Parmenides' Lehrgedicht*. Berlin 1897.

———— *Doxographi Graeci*. Berlin 1879.

DODDS, E. R. *The Greeks and the Irrational*. Berkeley 1951.

———— *Plato: Gorgias*. Oxford 1959.

D'OOGE, M. L., ROBBINS, F. E., and KARPINSKI, L. C. *Nichomachus: Introduction to Arithmetic*. New York 1926.

DUNBABIN, T. J. *The Western Greeks*. Oxford 1948.

———— *The Greeks and their Eastern Neighbours*. London 1957.

DÜRING, I. *Herodicus the Cratetean*. Stockholm 1941.

FESTA, N. *Iamblichus de communi mathematica scientia*. Leipzig 1891.

FESTUGIÈRE, A. J. *De l'ancienne médecine*. Paris 1948.

———— *La révélation d'Hermès Trismégiste*. 4 vols. Paris 1949–1954.

———— "Les mémoires pythagoriques cités par Alexandre Polyhistor" *REG* 58 (1945) 1–65.

FRÄNKEL, H. *Wege und Formen frühgriechischen Denkens*. Munich 1960.

———— *Dichtung und Philosophie des frühen Griechentums*. New York 1951.

FRANK, E. *Plato und die sogenannten Pythagoreer.* Halle 1923, reprinted Tübingen 1962.

FRIEDLEIN, G. *Proclus: In Euclidem Commentarius.* Leipzig 1873.

FRITZ, K. VON *Pythagorean Politics in Southern Italy.* New York 1940.

―――― "The Discovery of incommensurability by Hippasus of Metapontum," *Ann. Maths.* 46 (1945), 242–264.

―――― "Mathematiker und Akusmatiker bei den alten Pythagoreern," *Sitzber. Bay. Akad.* (Munich 1960) 11.

―――― "Pythagoras," in *RE* 24 (1963).

GERMAIN, G. *Homère et la mystique des nombres.* Paris 1954.

GIGON, O. *Der Ursprung der griechischen Philosophie.* Basel 1945.

GILBERT, O. "Aristoteles' Urteile über die pythagoreische Lehre," *Arch. Ges. Phil.* 22 (1909) 22–48, 145–165.

GOMPERZ, H. *Greek Thinkers.* London 1901–1912.

GRUBE, G. M. A. *Plato's Thought.* London 1931.

GUTHRIE, W. K. C. *A History of Greek Philosophy: I.* Cambridge 1962.

―――― *Orpheus and Greek Religion.* London 1952.

―――― "Aristotle as a Historian of Philosophy," *JHS* (1957) 35–41.

HACKFORTH, R. *Plato's Examination of Pleasure.* Cambridge 1945.

―――― *Plato's Phaedrus.* Cambridge 1952.

―――― *Plato's Phaedo.* Cambridge 1955.

HARDER, R. *Ocellus lucanus.* Berlin 1926.

HEATH, T. L. *A History of Greek Mathematics.* 2 vols. Oxford 1921.

―――― *The Thirteen Books of Euclid's Elements.* 2nd ed. 3 vols. Oxford 1926.

―――― *Aristarchus of Samos, the Ancient Copernicus.* Oxford 1913.

―――― *Mathematics in Aristotle.* Oxford 1949.

HEIBERG, I. L. *Geschichte der Mathematik und Naturwissenschaften im Altertum.* Munich 1925.

HEIDEL, W. A. "Peras and Apeiron in the Pythagorean philosophy," *Arch. Ges. Phil.* 14 (1901) 384–399.

―――― "Notes on Philolaus," *AJP* 28 (1907) 77–81.

―――― "The Pythagoreans and Greek Mathematics" *AJP* 61 (1940) 1–33.

HEINZE, R. *Xenokrates: Darstellung der Lehre und Sammlung der Fragmente.* Leipzig 1892.

HENDERSON, I. "Ancient Greek Music," in *New Oxford Dictionary of Music.* Oxford 1957.

HERMANN, O. F. *Platonis Dialogi.* Leipzig 1858–1860. vol. 4, 407–

421: Timaeus Locrus; vol. 6, 145–398: Albini Isagoge, Alcinoi Didascalicus, Olympiodori vita, Platonis Scholia.

HICKS, R. D. *Diogenes Laertius*. 2 vols. London 1942.

HÖLK, C. *De acusmatis sive symbolis pythagoreis*. diss. Kiel 1894.

HORST, P. C. VAN DER *Les Vers d'Or pythagoriciens*. diss. Leiden 1932.

JACOBY, F. *Apollodors Chronik*. Berlin 1902.

JÄGER, H. *Die Quellen des Porphyrius in seiner Pythagoras-biographie*. diss. Zürich 1919.

JAEGER, W. *Aristotle: Fundamentals of the History of his Development*. tr. R. Robinson. 2nd ed. Oxford 1948.

——— *Paideia: The ideals of Greek culture*. tr. G. Highet. 3 vols. Oxford 1939–1945.

——— *The Theology of the Early Greek Philosophers*. Oxford 1947.

JONES, W. H. S. *The Medical Writings of Anonymus Londinensis*. Cambridge 1947.

JUNGE, G. "Von Hippasos bis Philolaos: Das Irrational und die geometrischen Grundbegriffe," *Class. et Med.* 19 (1958) 41–72.

——— "Die pythagoreische Zahlenlehre," *DeutscheMath.* 5 (1940) 341–357.

KAHN, C. H. *Anaximander and the Origins of Greek Cosmogony*. New York 1960.

KAHRSTEDT, U. "Zur Geschichte Grossgriechenlands im 5ten Jahrhundert," *Hermes* 53 (1918) 180–187.

KERENYI, K. *Pythagoras und Orpheus*. Zurich 1950.

KERN, O. *Orphicorum Fragmenta*. Berlin 1922.

KIRK, G. S. *Heraclitus: The Cosmic Fragments*. Cambridge 1954.

KRANZ, W. *Empedokles*. Zurich 1949.

KUCHARSKI, P. *Étude sur la doctrine pythagoricienne de la tétrade*. Paris 1952.

KRÜGER, O. *Quaestiones Orphicae*. diss. Halle 1934.

LANG, P. *De Speusippi Academici scriptis*. diss. Bonn 1911.

LÉVY, I. *Recherches sur les sources de la légende de Pythagore*. Paris 1926.

——— *La légende de Pythagore de Grèce en Palestine*. Paris 1927.

LINFORTH, I. M. *The Arts of Orpheus*. Berkeley 1941.

LOBECK, C. A. *Aglaophamus*. Königsberg 1829.

LONG, H. S. *A study of the doctrine of metempsychosis in Greece from Pythagoras to Plato*. diss. Princeton 1948.

McDIARMID, J. B. "Theophrastus on the Presocratic causes," *Harv. Stud.* 61 (1953) 85–156.

MADDALENA, A. *I Pitagorici*. Bari 1954.

Méautis, G. *Recherches sur le pythagorisme.* Neuchâtel 1922.

Merlan, P. *From Platonism to Neoplatonism*[2]. The Hague 1960.

—— *Studies in Epicurus and Aristotle.* Wiesbaden 1960.

Meuli, K. "Scythica," *Hermes* 70 (1935) 121–176.

Mewaldt, J. *De Aristoxeni Pythagoricis Sententiis et Vita Pythagorica.* diss. Berlin 1904.

Minar, E. L., jr. *Early Pythagorean Politics.* Baltimore 1942.

Mondolfo, R. *L'infinito nel pensieri dell'antichità classica*[2]. Florence 1956. (see also Zeller-Mondolfo, *La filosofia dei Greci.*)

Morrison, J. S. "Pythagoras of Samos," *CQ* 50 (1956) 135–156.

—— "The origins of Plato's philosopher-statesman," *CQ* 52 (1958) 198–218.

Neugebauer, O. *The Exact Sciences in Antiquity*[2]. Providence 1957.

Nestle, W. See Zeller fourth entry.

Nilsson, M. P. *Geschichte der griechischen Religion: I.* 2nd ed. Munich 1955.

—— "Early Orphism and kindred religious movements." *Harv. Theol. Rev.* 28 (1935) 181–230 = *Opuscula* 2, 628–683. Lund 1952.

Nock, A. D. *Conversion.* Oxford 1933.

Owen, G. E. L. "Zeno and the Mathematicians," *Proc. Aristot. Soc.* (1958) 199–222.

Photius *Bibliotheca.* Cod. 249 (Vita Pythagorae).

Pistelli, H. *Iamblichi Protrepticus.* Leipzig 1888.

—— *Iamblichus. In Nicomachi arithmeticam introductionem.* Leipzig 1894.

Praechter, K. *Die Philosophie des Altertums*[14]. Basel:Stuttgart 1957.

Rathmann, W. *Quaestiones Pythagoreae Orphicae Empedocleae.* diss. Halle 1933.

Raven, J. E. *Pythagoreans and Eleatics.* Cambridge 1948.

Reidemeister, K. *Das exakte Denken der Griechen.* Leipzig 1949.

Reinhardt, K. *Parmenides und die Geschichte der griechischen Philosophie.* Bonn 1916.

—— *Poseidonios von Apamea.* Stuttgart 1954.

Robin, L. *Greek Thought.* London 1928.

—— *La théorie platonicienne des idées et des nombres d'après Platon.* Paris 1908.

Rohde, E. *Psyche: The Cult of Souls and Belief in Immortality among the Greeks.* London 1925.

—— "Die Quellen des Iamblichus in seiner Biographie des Pythagoras," *Rh Mus* 26 (1871) 554–576; 27 (1872) 23–61 = *Kleine Schriften* (Tübingen 1901) 2, 102–172.

Rose, V. *Aristotelis Fragmenta*. Leipzig 1886.

Ross, W. D. *Plato's Theory of Ideas*. Oxford 1951.

Rostagni, A. *Il Verbo di Pitagora*. Turin 1924.

———— "Un nuovo capitolo nella storia della retorica e della sofistica," *Scritti Minori*. Turin 1955. 1, 1–59.

Rothenbücher, A. *Das system der Pythagoreer nach den Angaben des Aristoteles*. Berlin 1867.

Sachs, Eva *Die fünf platonischen Körper*. Berlin 1917.

Saffrey, H. D. *Le peri philosophias d'Aristote et la théorie platonicienne des idées nombres*. Leiden 1955.

Samburský, S. *The Physical World of the Greeks*. London 1956.

———— *The Physical World of Late Antiquity*. London 1962.

Snell, B. *The Discovery of the Mind*. Oxford 1953.

Stenzel, J. *Zahl und Gestalt³*. Bad Homburg 1959.

Tannery, P. *Pour l'histoire de la science hellène²*. Paris 1930.

Taylor, A. E. *A Commentary on Plato's Timaeus*. Oxford 1928.

———— *Plato: Philebus and Epinomis*. London 1956.

Thesleff, H. *An Introduction to the Pythagorean Writings of the Hellenistic Period*. Abo 1961.

———— *The Pythagorean Texts of the Hellenistic Period*. Abo 1965.

Theiler, W. *Die Vorbereitung des Neuplatonismus*. Berlin 1930.

———— *Aristoteles über die Seele*. Berlin 1959.

Ueberweg-Praechter *Grundriss der Geschichte der Philosophie*. ed. K. Praechter. Vol. 1, 14th ed., Basel: Stuttgart 1957.

Vogel, C. J. de *Greek Philosophy: A Collection of Texts*. 3 vols. Leiden 1953–1959.

Wachtler, J. *De Alcmaeone Crotoniata*. Leipzig 1896.

Waerden, B. L. van der *Science Awakening*. Groningen 1954.

———— *Die Astronomie der Pythagoreer*. Amsterdam 1951.

———— "Zenon und die Grundlagenkrise der griechischen Mathematik." *Math. Ann.* 117 (1941) 141–161.

———— "Die Arithmetik der Pythagoreer." *Math. Ann.* 120 (1947–1949) 127–152; 676–700.

———— "Die Harmonielehre der Pythagoreer." *Hermes* 78 (1943) 163–199.

Wehrli, F. *Die Schule des Aristoteles*. 10 Hefte. Basel 1944–1960; With reference especially to: (1) Dikaiarchos (1944); (2) Aristoxenos (1945); (3) Herakleides Pontikos (1953); (4) Eudemos von Rhodos (1955).

Wellmann, M. "Eine pythagoreische Urkunde des 4ten Jahrhundert v. Chr." *Hermes* 54 (1919) 225–248.

WHITE, M. E.   "The Duration of the Samian Tyranny." *JHS* (1954) 36–43.

WILAMOWITZ MOELLENDORF, U. VON   *Platon²*. 2 vols. Berlin 1920.

――― *Der Glaube der Hellenen*. 2 vols. Berlin 1931–32.

――― *Antigonos von Karystos. Philol. Unters.* 4 (Berlin 1881).

WILPERT, P.   "Reste verlorener Aristotelesschriften bei Alexander von Aphrodisias," *Hermes* 75 (1940) 369–396.

――― *Zwei aristotelische Frühschriften über die Ideenlehre*. Regensburg 1949.

ZELLER, E.   *Die Philosophie der Griechen in ihrer geschichtlichen Entwicklung*. Leipzig. Vol. II, 2 (1922); II, 2 (1920); III, 1 (1923); III. 2 (1923).

――― "Ueber die ältesten Zeugnisse zur Geschichte des Pythagoras," *Kleine Schriften: I* (Berlin 1910), 458–472.

ZELLER, E. and MONDOLFO, R.   *La filosofia dei Greci nel suo sviluppo storico*. Florence. Vol. I (1932); Vol. II, 1 (1938); Vol. VI, 3 (1961).

ZELLER, E. and NESTLE, W.   *Die Philosophie der Griechen in ihrer geschichtlichen Entwicklung*. Leipzig. Vol. I, 1⁷ (1923); I, 2⁶ (1920).

INDEX

INDEX LOCORUM